RECONCILIATION, JUSTICE, AND PEACE

RECONCILIATION, JUSTICE, AND PEACE

The Second African Synod

AGBONKHIANMEGHE E. OROBATOR, EDITOR

ORBIS BOOKS

Maryknoll, New York 10545

Founded in 1970, Orbis Books endeavors to publish works that enlighten the mind, nourish the spirit, and challenge the conscience. The publishing arm of the Maryknoll Fathers and Brothers, Orbis seeks to explore the global dimensions of the Christian faith and mission, to invite dialogue with diverse cultures and religious traditions, and to serve the cause of reconciliation and peace. The books published reflect the views of their authors and do not represent the official position of the Maryknoll Society. To learn more about Maryknoll and Orbis Books, please visit our website at www.maryknollsociety.org.

Published by Orbis Books, Maryknoll, New York 10545-0302.
Manufactured in the United States of America.
Manuscript editing and typesetting by Joan Weber Laflamme.

Library of Congress Cataloging-in-Publication Data

Reconciliation, justice, and peace : the Second African Synod /
Agbonkhianmeghe E. Orobator, editor.
        p. cm.
    Includes index.
    ISBN 978-1-57075-916-1 (pbk.)
    1. African Synod (2nd : 2009 : Rome, Italy) 2. Christian sociology—
Catholic Church—Congresses. 3. Christian sociology—Africa—Congresses. 4.
Catholic Church—Africa—Congresses. I. Orobator, A. E. (Agbonkhianmeghe E.)
    BX1675.A1A34 2009z
    261.8096—dc22
                                                            2010051006

Contents

PART I
THEOLOGY OF THE CHURCH, INTERRELIGIOUS DIALOGUE, AND THE CHALLENGE OF RECONCILIATION, JUSTICE, AND PEACE

PART II
THE MISSION OF THE CHURCH IN THE PUBLIC SPHERE

PART III
ECCLESIAL LEADERSHIP AND GENDER JUSTICE
IN CHURCH AND SOCIETY

PART IV
INTEGRITY OF THE EARTH—
ECOLOGY, NATURAL RESOURCES, POVERTY,
AND THE CHURCH

PART V
THEOLOGICAL AND ETHICAL ISSUES AND HIV/AIDS

Documents of the Second African Synod
Used in This Book

(In Chronological Order)

Lineamenta—an elaborate questionnaire with discussion points for Christian communities, dioceses, episcopal conferences, and religious groups in preparation for the synod

Instrumentum Laboris—a summary of various responses to the *Lineamenta* and an outline of the agenda for the synod

"Homily of His Holiness Benedict XVI"—at the opening mass of the African Synod, October 4, 2009

Relatio ante Disceptationem—a preliminary report presented to the synod by Cardinal Peter Turkson, president of the Pontifical Council for Justice and Peace

Relatio post Disceptationem—a report presented after the deliberations of the synod that summarizes the key points of the discussion

Elenchus Finalis Propositionum—a final list of fifty-seven propositions and recommendations presented by the synod to Benedict XVI that would form the basis of the pope's post-synodal exhortation

Nuntius or *Message of the Synod*—the official message of the bishops of Africa to the people of God after the African Synod, October 23, 2009

"Courage! Get on Your Feet, Continent of Africa"—homily of His Holiness Benedict XVI at the closing mass of the African Synod, October 25, 2009

Note: Official church documents referred to in this book are available on the vatican.va website.

Acknowledgments

It all began at a lunchtime meeting with Joseph Healey, MM, and Laurenti Magesa in 2008. Once Joe planted in my head the idea of editing a book on the second African Synod, he made sure it never left me. Over several lunchtime meetings he has shown unwavering interest and support for this project.

The list of contributors does not include all the participants at our first conference on the second African Synod held in March 2010, in Nairobi, Kenya, where the ideas contained in this book were first presented and discussed during a series of "palaver" sessions. I am profoundly grateful to all the participants, the rector, Gabriel Mmassi, SJ, and the Jesuit Community and staff of Hekima College. A generous grant from an anonymous foundation subsidized the cost of organizing and hosting the conference.

I am indebted to Jim Keenan, SJ, and David Hollenbach, SJ, who have inspired me to engage in the kind of theological research and scholarship that make a difference in the world church. T. Frank Kennedy, SJ, was always generous and willing to help. I owe much gratitude to my Jesuit companions of the Eastern Africa Province of the Society of Jesus, who continue to enrich my life with their companionship.

My deep gratitude goes to my editor at Orbis Books, Susan Perry. The publication of this book is as much the fruit of her profound spirituality and inspiration as it is of her editorial expertise.

Oghomwen n'Oghomwen (Anne Arabome, SSS) and Oko (Chuks Afiawari, SJ) never lost faith in me and continued to support me even when editorial demands and other commitments got in the way of our shared vocation in Christ and our life in God—your love and your grace are enough for me!

Nollywood (Nigerian) movies typically end with the praise phrase "To God be the glory!" For all the graces that will be bestowed upon our church and our world through the medium of the second African Synod and this book, *To God be the glory!*

Introduction

The Synod as Ecclesial Conversation

AGBONKHIANMEGHE E. OROBATOR

Africa is not helpless. Our destiny is still in our hands. All she is asking for is the space to breathe and thrive. Africa is already moving; and the Church is moving with her, offering her the light of the Gospel.
— MESSAGE OF THE BISHOPS OF AFRICA TO THE PEOPLE OF GOD
AT THE CONCLUSION OF THE SECOND AFRICAN SYNOD, NO. 42

The movement from the first African Synod in 1994 to the second African Synod in 2009 traces the trajectory of a steadily maturing theology of the nature and mission of the church in Africa. The continuity between both synods reflects the vitality of theological reflection in Africa and its implication for the self-understanding of the community called church. While the earlier synod identified the nature of this community as family of God, the later synod assigned it a new mission, namely, to work toward reconciliation, justice, and peace. The full title of the second synod is "The Church in Africa in Service to Reconciliation, Justice and Peace: 'You are the salt of the earth. . . . You are the light of the world' (Mt 5:13, 14)."

A distinct nature and a coherent mission form part of the essence of the church. African Christians appreciate the poignancy of the mission of the church as embodied in the synod's theme, because this theme touches the core of Africa's contemporary socioeconomic, cultural, religious, and political predicament. On a continent synonymous with deep crises, contradictions, and strife, "Church as Family" represents an opportunity for attaining the reconciliation, justice, and peace of God's reign that hitherto have seemed to elude Africa. And on a continent infamous for its high levels of poverty, abuse of human rights, and disregard for human dignity, reconciliation, justice, and peace define clear imperatives of ecclesial renewal and social transformation.

A synod marks a pivotal event in the life of the church. In theological terms it represents a *kairos* for the church, an opportune moment to take

1

stock of its history and experience, to assess its context and challenges, and to rekindle its hopes and aspirations. As such, a synod involves a process that brings the past, present, and future realities of the church into sharper focus. More important, it is a communal event that takes the form of conversation. To speak of a synod as conversation might seem incongruent in the context of a highly stratified and hierarchical church. Yet that is the nature of a synod.

Judging by the accounts of participants and observers, the second African Synod paralleled a conversational event reminiscent of "the age-old ecclesial tradition in Africa, defended in ancient times by Saint Cyprian, Bishop of Carthage, of listening to the Holy Spirit and the Word of God" (*Instrumentum Laboris*, no. 2). According to this venerable "ecclesial tradition," participants at the synod represent all levels of affiliation, participation, and ministry in the universal church. To quote *Gaudium et Spes*, the views that they express and the discussions that they conduct form part of a wider circle of conversation that encompasses the "joys and the hopes, the griefs and the anxieties" of the people of God (no. 1). Critical to the experience and process of a synod are the virtues of dialogue and mutual listening that preclude a stifling monopoly of the conversation, the arbitrary exclusion of interlocutors, and ideological manipulation of the agenda.

It needs to be stressed that a synod serves a broader ecclesiological project: it is a way of being church that recognizes the church as a universal family with an equally global mission. During the second African Synod the dialogue partners and interlocutors of the synod were first and foremost the people of God, the church "from all countries of Africa and Madagascar and the adjacent Islands, with brother bishops and colleagues from all continents, with and under the Head of the Episcopal College, with the participation of some fraternal delegates from other Christian traditions" (*Message of the Synod*, no. 1). In this sense the event served two interrelated purposes. First, it delineated a privileged locus for raising substantial matters concerning the nature of the church and its mission. Second, it provided impetus for the conversations on the nature and mission of the church among the people of God to rise to the level of theological analysis and examination. This conversational process generated new meaning and created a fresh synthesis of theological and ethical approaches to issues that confront church and society.

On the evidence of the *Instrumentum Laboris* of the second African Synod, in addition to the virtues of dialogue and mutual listening, two prerequisites can be established for the conversational process of a synod. The first is the ability to "listen to what the Spirit is saying to the churches" (Rv 2:7), and the second is to pay attention to what the Word of God is accomplishing "among us" (Jn 1:14). Perceived in such profoundly scriptural terms, a synod typifies a pentecostal and incarnational moment in the life of the church. It possesses an invaluable potential for strengthening faith, regenerating hope, and spreading charity within and beyond the community called church.

In this age of globalization, when multiple centers of power, influence, and action intersect in the world, the synod defines for both church and society a new way of interrelating and communicating in the human community according to the approach prioritized and recommended by Vatican II, especially in *Gaudium et Spes,* its document on the church in the modern world. Rather than perceive the world in antagonistic terms such as *secularism, relativism, materialism,* and *atheism,* as was repeatedly heard at the second African Synod, the church plays a role in facilitating dialogue among these competing and complementary claims, conflicts, and institutions. The measure in which the church succeeds in undertaking this role confirms its mission as a humble yet authentic servant of reconciliation, justice, and peace. This awareness undergirded the objectives of the second African Synod.

This methodology of dialogue and "listening in conversation" has been adapted to the purposes of this book. The preparatory phase included a two-day conference in Nairobi, Kenya, in March 2010. The conference served as an occasion to explore the synodal literature and to conduct intensive discussion among the contributors and other invited participants. The contributors were required to submit their papers in advance, and these papers were distributed before the conference to all the participants.

At the conference each contributor briefly summarized the central thesis of his or her paper, and then a designated respondent presented a critical response. Each paper was then subjected to an intensive discussion by all attendees. This volume contains the papers revised and edited for publication in light of the overall discussion and conclusions of the conference. Not all the papers are published in this volume, but the final list of chapters represents the fruit of active dialogue and intensive listening among theologians and friends. It exemplifies the practice of palaver that emphasizes open conversation in community and prioritizes consensus over confrontation. The conversational ethics of dialogue and listening characteristic of the second African Synod provides the foundation and inspiration for this volume.

In the understanding of the editor and contributors, the second African Synod served primarily as a catalyst; that is, it launched a process of theological conversation. Thus the articles are not intended merely to publicize the conclusions and positions of the synod. Instead, the contributors identify multiple theological and ethical issues surfaced by the synod but expand the focus of its concerns to a variety of areas, topics, and domains. The table of contents does not begin to exhaust the list of questions and problems that engaged the minds and energies of the synod participants during their three weeks in Rome. The selection of items for analysis and reflection was guided by the interest, experience, and expertise of the contributors in light of the issues that presently shape the nature and mission of the church in Africa. They offer materials for critical reflection on the life of the church much beyond the scope envisaged or anticipated by the synod.

In this regard it is important to note that the outcome of the synod is not ossified in the ensuing official documents. Consequently, in light of the objectives expressed in the *Instrumentum Laboris*, this volume focuses on generating thought and prompting discussion aimed at shaping, guiding, and sustaining an unfolding theological narrative of the self-understanding and mission of the church in Africa. While some of the analyses and conclusions of the essays strain traditional categories, ultimately they offer fresh and innovative accounts of the church as a vehicle of reconciliation, justice, and peace on a divided, conflicted, and turbulent continent.

Pope Benedict XVI departed from synodal tradition to make public the list of final propositions of the second African Synod. Thus the pope inaugurated the post-synodal process of thought, discussion, and conversation much sooner than the publication of the post-synodal exhortation would have allowed. The situation of the church and African society gives credence to the pope's unprecedented decision. According to the *Message of the Synod,* reconciliation, justice, and peace constitute "a theme of the greatest urgency for Africa . . . a continent that is very much in dire need of these graces and virtues" (no. 1).

In his preface to *Instrumentum Laboris*, the general secretary of the Synod of Bishops, Archbishop Nikola Eterović, underlined the pressing and urgent character of the work of reconciliation on a continent "torn by many conflicts and ethnic, social and religious divisions, which oftentimes erupt into hateful and violent happenings." The mission of peace "has never been more timely in Africa, because of her conflicts, wars and violence." In the understanding of the editor and contributors to this volume, Benedict's apparent departure from tradition presents an urgent invitation to theologians and theological ethicists to examine the theme of the synod and extend its application beyond the confines of official church pronouncements.

Perhaps the most significant contribution envisaged in this book lies in the awareness that reconciliation, justice, and peace are not understood exclusively as concerns for the secular world; they impinge primarily and significantly on the nature and mission of the church. The contributors temper the strong extroverted orientation of the synod *(ad extra)* with a critical introspection and assessment of the practice of reconciliation, justice, and peace within the church *(ad intra)*. As such, this collection of essays constitutes a teaching forum of African theologians, theological ethicists, and other scholars as they deliberate and discuss issues of critical concern to the church in Africa. Several features of this book call for brief additional comments.

Some contributors were also participants at the synod in various capacities as auditors, experts, or assistants. Several others served on preparatory committees, facilitated workshops, or helped to draft texts in preparation

for the synod. In addition, since the conclusion of the synod many participants have conducted research on various issues generated by the synod. In
their capacity as synod participants, several contributors offer eyewitness
accounts not often captured in official documentation. "The mouth does
not always tell what the eyes see," says an African proverb. As is customary
at such ecclesiastical assemblies, some participants were sworn to secrecy
and confidentiality during and after the event. While they may not tell the
whole inside story of what happened at the second African Synod, all the
contributors approach the issues, questions, and problems with an acute
awareness of what they mean for the church in Africa and for African society.

In keeping with the conversational methodology alluded to above, this
book adopts an interdisciplinary approach. As a quick glance at the list of
contributors shows, not all are theologians. They come from diverse back-
grounds—political science, peace studies, social ethics, history, scripture,
spirituality, philosophy, and theology. In this context this project represents a way of doing theology in a community of dialogue partners that
evokes elements of traditional African palaver. Rather than a dialogue of
like-minded inquirers, producing a sanitized chorus of theological formulas, this methodology creates a shared intellectual space allowing theologians
to expand the horizon and frontier of their understanding of God, faith,
and the community called church.

The benefit of a wider horizon and frontier makes possible theological
analysis and reflection that sharpen understanding, generate new possibilities, and enable creative action capable of transforming church and society.
In brief, interdisciplinarity invites and empowers theologians to break new
grounds in doctrine and praxis. Whereas this approach might seem threatening to those in the church who remain conservatively committed to a
monologue and offer only a univocal answer to complex theological and
ethical issues, this collection of articles demonstrates the broad scope of
possibilities open to those who still conceive of theological investigation as
an exhilarating enterprise of faith seeking understanding.

One obvious consequence of the interdisciplinary approach of this book
shows up in divergence of interpretations of the synod and the positions
adopted by the individual contributors. The similarities among their positions are apparent, but so too are differences. Evaluating the progress and
status of the church in Africa and assessing the continent's complicity in its
predicament are tasks that defy facile and straightforward hermeneutics.
These essays read Africa and the church differently. The social location,
intellectual tradition, and disciplinary affiliation of each contributor reveal
unique perspectives and biases. Oftentimes the contrasts are striking: where
some see crises and misery, others celebrate hope and progress. This should
hardly surprise any keen observer of the continent of Africa, for such is
the contradictory and enigmatic nature of the continent—never sitting
still long enough for researchers and scholars to cast it in a definitive

historical, economic, political, and cultural mold. And when one appears more or less set, sea changes occur revealing dents and fissures. It takes a global conversation to see the broken pieces coalesce into some clearer, albeit imperfect, image of the church in Africa at the service of reconciliation, justice, and peace, and a source and a foundation for hope, creativity, and innovation.

The Organization of the Book

The five parts of this book, each focusing on a set of issues discussed at the synod, represent the theological and ethical concerns of the contributors.

Part I focuses on the theology of the church in global terms. Teresa Okure's expert analysis of the meaning and theology of the church draws on the scriptural foundations of ecclesiology to argue a point that makes for uncomfortable reading among the hierarchy—that the primary place for practicing reconciliation, justice, and peace is within the church. Its credibility as the family of God stands or falls on its ability to exemplify and practice what it teaches and demands of society, specifically in regard to the leadership roles of women in the church-family of God.

Laurenti Magesa and Festo Mkenda approach the question of dialogue in the church from two different but complementary perspectives. Magesa unmasks Christianity's historical prejudices and antagonisms toward African Religion and argues for the status of the latter as an indispensable dialogue partner if Christianity is to take root on the continent and if Africans are to become fully Christian. Mkenda draws on historical data to underscore the importance of language as a medium of interreligious dialogue. He launches a challenge to African theologians to take seriously African languages as a vehicle for theological reflection and scholarship. In either case the benefit would be immense: indigenous religious and linguistic resources offer the promise of a fresh approach to theology and Christianity in Africa and between it and the world church.

The multivalent character of the Word of God forms the basis for Paul Béré's insightful exploration of its various applications and manifestations. When correlated with the Word of God, the oral traditions of the continent of Africa offer useful pathways for understanding and practicing reconciliation in church and society. Joseph Healey's extensive exploration of Small Christian Communities (SCCs) in Eastern Africa assembles a rich collection of data, anecdotes, and examples of their pastoral relevance and social effectiveness. SCCs offer the most viable models and means for the church in Africa to become real, relevant, and local in the lives of ordinary Christians.

One of the salient features of the second African Synod is the extent to which it tries to engage secular society on a wide range of political and economic issues. This approach raises the question of how to conceive of the role or mission of the church in Africa in the public sphere. The chapters in Part II focus on this question. Elias Omondi Opongo demonstrates how injustice is a rapidly mutating reality, moving from a simple state to complex systems and networks. In this context the challenge facing the church is how to allow its approach to the problem of injustice to evolve. More than just a passive reality, the church's response needs to be an active commitment to vigilance and attentiveness to innovative means of transforming social ills in light of Christian values and principles.

Yvon Christian Elenga takes up a similar theme. The voice of the church is an essential element in society. Although the perception of the church and its relationship to other constituents of the public sphere have not always been positive, the contemporary situation offers new possibilities for engagement that focuses on social transformation. On the matter of the church's engagement with secular society and its institutions, because the synod addresses issues of continental and global concerns, it faces the temptation to remain at an abstract and theoretical level.

In their essays Anthony Egan and Odomaro Mubangizi attempt to apply the theoretical presuppositions of the synod to concrete situations. Egan uses the South African context to demonstrate how the church is not immune to historical circumstances and political development within contemporary South Africa. While the task of redefining the church's role in this context is not as simple as synodal rhetoric might suggest, the example of the Catholic Parliamentary Liaison Office in South Africa offers the church a viable model for engaging in political debates and shaping social policies. Mubangizi interprets the phenomenon of globalization as a new opportunity for the church as a global Christian community. Perceived in this light, the task of the church is not limited to justice, peace, and reconciliation. It also includes promoting sustainable development, healthcare, higher education for social transformation, and good governance.

The core issue in Part III is leadership in the church—both the conception of and practice of—and the factors that affect it. Anne Arabome leads the debate by describing instances of unjust repression of women's creative voices, energies, and potential for leadership. For her, the synod offers some correctives but falls significantly short. Only a radical conversion of the entire Christian community can guarantee renewal and wholeness for the church and the liberation of the entire human family. Ngozi Frances Uti makes the same point. Gender-based injustice is not a myth. Uti's examples come from her experience of the church in Nigeria, but they are not confined to this geographical location. She contends that the biblical principle of gender justice is a precondition for the church to fulfill its potential as "a powerful leaven of reconciliation" in Africa.

David Kaulem's contribution focuses strongly on issues of governance, democratic principles, and Catholic social teaching, using the contemporary political arrangement in Zimbabwe as an illustration. However, his witty and satirical narrative of the preparatory phases and perceptions of the synod among lay Christians qualifies it as a critical analysis of how ecclesial events and processes like the synod often bypass the critical mass of Christians. Without their participation the church's avowed desire to be a credible and effective player in the public sphere remains pious rhetoric. An effective church in the public sphere is one that recognizes, forms, and validates the leadership potential of its lay members.

Ecology now constitutes a major theme in theological and ethical literature. Part IV outlines and discusses some of the theological and ethical issues relating to ecology and natural resources. As Peter Knox demonstrates, the theological resources in this area available before, during, and after the synod remain relatively scant, but the potential for a far-reaching theological and ethical reflection in this domain appears as vast as the continent's reserve of natural and ecological resources. A credible theology for our times must preserve the vital connection between the mission of the church and concern for the environment.

In the same context Peter Kanyandago addresses the thorny issue of the curse of natural resources or the paradox of plenty, that is, the fact that African countries remain economically impoverished despite being rich in natural and mineral resources. Although fuelled by historical racial prejudices, Africa's anthropological poverty in the midst of plenty is not insurmountable. In this sphere the church plays a critical role that must include advocacy informed by accurate analysis. Nathanaël Yaovi Soédé's essay is a critical analysis of the situation of poverty and its implication for the church in Africa. Facile answers and explanations do little or no good for the church and the continent. Soédé uses two biblical characters, one from the first African Synod (the victim of bandits on the road to Jericho) and the second from the second African Synod (the blind beggar, Bartimaeus), to argue that for the continent and its church to function as a healthy "spiritual lung" for the rest of humanity, both must free themselves from a culture of blaming the West, on which they depend, and assume responsibility for their own destiny.

The dominant issue addressed in Part V is HIV/AIDS. Michael Czerny traces the evolution of the subject in the second African Synod. Particularly heartening is the centrality of this pandemic to the church's self-understanding and mission of reconciliation, justice, and peace in a context where HIV/AIDS appears to have lost its urgency as a pressing social issue. One issue that continues to weigh heavily upon ethical considerations of the challenge of HIV/AIDS is the (im)morality of condom use. This debate has its value, as Paterne-Auxence Mombé makes clear in his essay. He points out that, ultimately, the debate must shift to weightier matters of justice, empowerment, and equity in the prevention and treatment of HIV/AIDS. The church's role in effecting this shift remains critical.

The causes of Africa's predicament are routinely categorized as "foreign" ideologies, viruses, and pathologies. Paulinus I. Odozor provides evidence for making this claim. Essentially, though, Africa's destiny lies in its own hands. Odozor argues that putting the blame on foreign elements has a limited life span and that developing the continent's limitless potential is a more valuable and life-enhancing option for church and society. Corruption does not normally feature on the same list as reconciliation, justice, and peace. Gabriel Mmassi's correlation of this social scourge with the synod's theme shows how the best laid plans of the synod risk total failure unless the menace of corruption is eradicated. Only then can we talk of a reconciled, just, and peaceful church and society in Africa and elsewhere.

The synod's theme of reconciliation, justice, and peace can be construed in spiritual or political terms. Either way, a church that takes these issues seriously faces the challenge of how to balance its commitment to growth in the spiritual life with its mission of social transformation in the public sphere. Using the Zambian example, Peter J. Henriot concludes this collection of essays by identifying conditions under which the synod's outcome will not remain just pious formulas but will provide powerful incentives for transformative social and political action in Africa.

Of Women, Spiritual Lung, and Church

Notwithstanding the multidisciplinary background of contributors to this volume, the numerical preponderance of clergy-contributors reflects the constitutional imbalance of theological research and scholarship in the church in Africa and elsewhere. One lay man, three women religious, and no lay woman among twenty-one contributors is hardly representative of a reconciled, just, and peaceful church. In her chapter on the meaning of the church-family of God, Okure rightly denounces this imbalance and the underlying biases and prejudices. This situation ought to motivate theologians and religious leaders in Africa to relocate theology from ecclesiastical enclaves to the market square, or rather, to expand the locus and focus of theology to encompass the views and contributions of all Christians, especially women.

On this note the contributors call the church to the task of redefining itself, not merely as God's mouthpiece or proclaimer of reconciliation, justice, and peace (ad extra), but as a credible embodiment and authentic practitioner of these same virtues (ad intra). The old maxim *charity begins at home* is relevant here. The areas in the church that stand to benefit from the "domestic practice" of reconciliation, justice, and peace are as diverse as they are urgent. They include the mission of the laity in a clericalist and hierarchical church, the role of women in a sexist and patriarchal church, the meaning of the gospel in an ethnically divided church, the equality of all baptized Christians in a ministerially segregated church, and so forth. In this volume the women contributors unmask latent prejudices of some of the male contributors in regard to ecclesial leadership, gender justice, and human rights. As Okure, Arabome, and Uti demonstrate, grandiloquent pronouncements and lofty principles no longer suffice; a radical conversion of hearts and minds, head and members, is imperative if the church is to become effective as the salt, light, and leaven of reconciliation, justice, and peace in the world. Their message to the church is simple, loud, and clear: practice what you preach!

Pope Benedict's potent imagery of the vital role of the African church in the world church—a spiritual lung for humanity—captured the imagination of several contributors. Flattering as this epithet might be, the implications are neither immediately apparent nor unequivocally complimentary. Odozor's and Soédé's dissections of the symbolism of "spiritual lung" reveal layers of meanings, implications, and challenges for the church and for the continent. Their shared diagnosis offers substantial material for further reflection and analysis. Both of them correct the misconception that all of Africa's socioeconomic and political woes can be blamed on foreign agents, religious ideologies, and toxic spiritual waste. The West will not serve as perpetual scapegoat and pollutant of Africa's spiritual resources, contrary to what Benedict implies in his inaugural homily. Even though the pope's statement contains certain elements of reality, nevertheless it oversimplifies the very complex historical situation of the African continent. Africa is mature enough to take hold of its destiny as church and society: "Africa is not helpless. Our destiny is still in our hands." In reaching the same conclusion as the *Message of the Synod*, the essays in this volume echo the pope's rallying cry to the church and continent of Africa at the close of the second African Synod: "Courage! Get on your feet!" This command defines the task facing the church in Africa in the twenty-first century more acutely than the pontiff's summary attribution of blame to the West for poisoning the spiritual lung of Africa.

This introductory chapter emphasizes conversation as a constitutive element of the synodal experience without claiming that it is the only valid approach. Like the synod, the kind of conversation envisaged in this volume is an ongoing process. The overall intention of this volume qualifies it as a modest contribution to an ecclesial conversation en route for the future. We may see yet another African synod.

Part I

Theology of the Church, Interreligious Dialogue, and the Challenge of Reconciliation, Justice, and Peace

1

Church-Family of God

The Place of God's
Reconciliation, Justice, and Peace

TERESA OKURE

Ecclesiology, or what it means to be church, is a hotly debated and critical issue today, especially in the Roman Catholic Church.* The recent open letter of Hans Küng to Catholic bishops of the world is a case in point, whether or not one agrees with his position on the issues raised. Vatican Council II produced two fundamental documents on the church: *The Dogmatic Constitution on the Church (Lumen Gentium)* and *The Church in the Modern World (Gaudium et Spes)*. In 1994 the first African Synod adopted the family model as the best way to understand what it means to be church, especially in Africa.[1] Efforts by theologians to work out the implications of this understanding of church have generated a substantial response.[2]

The second African Synod deliberated on the theme "The Church in Service to Reconciliation, Justice and Peace: 'You are the salt of the earth. . . . You are the light of the world'" in many interventions and official documents on the mission of the Church as a reconciling agent of God's reconciliation, justice, and peace. The bulk of the official *Message of the Synod* is devoted to the "Church in Africa" (nos. 14–28). This document focuses on the different ways in which all members of the church can best serve as agents of reconciliation, justice, and peace. After thanking God, the pope, and his predecessor for calling the synod (nos. 1–3), the *Message* addresses the relationship of the Church in Africa with the world (nos. 4–6), the universal Church (nos. 9–13), and the place of faith in the entire synod proceedings (nos. 7–8). It devotes the central section (nos. 14–28) to different ecclesial sectors. The fifty-seven-point "Final Propositions," directed

---

*For purposes of clarity, *Church* with a capital C throughout this essay refers to the Roman Catholic Church, except in citations and titles; otherwise, the reference is to church in general.

13

to every category of members except the bishops themselves, indicates ways in which the *Message* is to be realized. The underlying structure of the Church as described in this document is clearly hierarchical.

The need to look afresh and courageously at the Church *itself*, the place and agent of God's reconciliation, was lacking in the interventions and official submissions of the synod and in the *Lineamenta* and *Instrumentum Laboris*. Chapter IV of the *Lineamenta,* "The Witness of the Church Reflecting the Light of Christ," includes a passionate call to the bishops to remember their duties to all and sundry (nos. 54–57). The same applies to the sections on priests, consecrated persons, and institutes of formation (nos. 58, 59, 60, respectively). There also appears to be great progress in integrating the laity into the Church (nos. 61–66). Their "mission pertains to the very nature of the Church" and "through them the Church is present to the world and the world to the Church." Yet the service of the laity in the world still attracts the designation of "secular."

The issue of the internal, structural relationships between the different bodies in the Church still remains to be courageously addressed christologically from the gospel perspective. This is crucial since the Church is first of all the living witness and place of God's reconciliation of humanity to the divine self. For obvious reasons the Church needs to give exemplary witness to God's reconciliation. At stake is not what the Church does or should do, but what the Church is or should be.

Some basic questions need to be raised. What concrete actions can we take with deep humility to promote reconciliation, justice, and peace *within* the Church of God? To what extent does the notion of "Church-Family of God" actually affect our manner of being Church in Africa? After the second African Synod, what sustainable, gospel-based ways can we adopt as Church-Family of God in Africa and beyond so that we can truly be the "salt of the earth" and "light of the world?" Why are these questions still relevant, given the innumerable books on ecclesiology in Africa and other parts of the world?[3]

To date, certain expressions make it clear that often when we refer to the Church we do not mean the people of God (of *Lumen Gentium*) or the Church-Family of God (of *Ecclesia in Africa*), but principally the hierarchy. A key area is the priest-laity relationship. *The Concise Dictionary of Theology* defines the laity as "the faithful who have been fully incorporated into the church through baptism, confirmation and communion (1 Pet 2:9–10), but who have not received holy orders and become clerics." It further adds that the "NT recognizes different offices, ministries and gifts of the Spirit as given to be exercised in harmonious collaboration for the good of the whole church (1 Cor 12:4–31; Rom 12:3–8)" but that a "later sharp distinction between clergy and laity sometimes involves an emphasis on the former as if they alone were the real church."[4] Vatican II reviewed the place and role of the laity (all non-ordained ministers, including non-clerical religious) in the Church. Still, it consolidates *dogmatically* the clergy/laity divide (*LG*, chaps. III and VI).

Does this bipolar understanding of the Church conform to the idea of Church-Family of God? Does the Church comprise members of the household of God (Eph 2:19–22) from whom every parenthood in heaven and on earth has its origin (Eph 3:15–16)?[5] Is this consonant with a church understood as the tangible evidence of God's own reconciliation of humanity to the divine Self, in particular all the baptized? If not, where does the problem lie? What resources do we have for effectively addressing *the problem of ecclesiology from within* with christological courage and that freedom which the Spirit gives? The Church must not be merely God's agent proclaiming reconciliation, justice, and peace to the world, but a body that visibly lives, incarnates, and models this divine reconciliation.

Thesis of the Essay

The question of what it means to be the Church-Family of God in service to reconciliation, justice, and peace requires critical attention. It cannot be taken for granted that our self-organization as Church needs no revision. The thesis of this study is that many of the practical problems in the Church today (governance; the exercise of authority, power, and control; the clergy-laity divide; financial and ministerial accountability; issues of women; interpersonal relationships at individual and corporate levels; relationship with other Christians and peoples of other faiths; and even the sexual abuse issue) have their roots in an incorrect understanding of what it means to be church, according to the mind of Christ. In Matthew's gospel the promise made to Peter shows that Christ, not Peter, will build Christ's church, and when this church breaks forth like light in darkness, the gates of hell will be powerless to withstand its Spirit-filled splendor (Mt 16:18).

John 1:5 makes the same point. "The light shines in the darkness; and the darkness was unable to overcome it." Light chases away darkness, which is the absence of light. Since the church (all Christ's disciples) is called to *be* light to the world and salt of the earth as agent of divine reconciliation to a humanity that is experiencing what appears to be a "crisis of faith and hope,"[6] all must anchor their understanding and actual way of being church in the gospel, if we are to adequately meet the external challenges.

This essay thus has one main concern, to highlight the need for the church, and the Roman Catholic Church in particular, to address this issue of reconciliation from within, especially in relation to its structures, using its God-given resources. It briefly reviews what it means to be church from the biblical (specifically New Testament perspective), then examines the resources available for being church according to God's gospel, and finally suggests some ways of meeting these challenges.

Scope of Church in the New Testament
and in This Essay

The word *church* can be understood at three levels: the Roman Catholic Church (of which the pope is the head); the church of Christ (embracing all believers in Christ); and the church of God, which is God's gathering together of the entire creation to the divine Self. As Benedict XVI pointed out, John Paul II saw the church at these three levels.[7] The intercessions of the Good Friday liturgy that include believers, Jews, people of other faiths, and atheists clearly acknowledge that God's church embraces all human beings because by his incarnation Christ, the New Humanity (*Adam*; 1 Cor 15:22; Eph 4:24) has united every human being to himself.[8]

The New Testament understanding of church embraces the community of believers (including the Church), humanity, and the entire creation. It is clearly articulated in 2 Corinthians 5:19, Colossians 1:20, and Ephesians 1:10. This Pauline conception finds a backing in Jesus' own statements that when lifted up and glorified, he would draw of all peoples to himself (Jn 12:32). He is destined to die "not only for the nation [Israel] but to gather together all God's scattered children" (Jn 11:52).

Derived from the Hebrew *edah* (assembly), the Greek *synagogē* and *ekklēsia* (a gathering) denote God's fulfillment of the plan to reconcile the entire creation to the divine Self, thus restoring the relationship disrupted by the prehistoric or original sin (Gn 3:16) and its repeat in the Babel incident (Gn 11:1–9). God in Jesus effected this reconciliation first in person—"the word became flesh" (Jn 1:14; Gal 4:4)—and subsequently through Jesus' passion, death, and resurrection, as pure act of grace.

Reconciliation is thus essentially God's work. God justifies us, declares us righteous, and gives us divine peace (making us whole). Humanity and the entire creation benefit from this reconciliation (Col 1:20; Rom 8:19–21). The church, God's building (1 Cor 3:9), becomes the privileged place and visible evidence of this divine reconciliation. Reconciled to God in and through Christ, believers are to mirror the reality of this reconciliation as a way of life, as the community of the reconciled. They, in turn, become God's ambassadors, persuading others to allow themselves to be reconciled to God (2 Cor 5:19—6:1). The primary mission of the Church-Family of God is to be a living witness as light to the world and salt of the earth, the locus where God's reconciliation thrives.[9]

This brief survey makes it evident that the church embraces all humanity. The focus here, however, is the Church. The rationale is that when this parent church gets on track internally, in regard to the incarnation, it will be in a better position to serve as God's agent of reconciliation for other churches and faiths.

Historical Causes of Deviations from New Testament Ecclesiology

Our faith in God's reconciling of humanity to the divine Self notwithstanding, the ecclesiology that governs our thinking, consolidated for years by the one-sided ecclesiology of Vatican Council I, is that the church is primarily the hierarchy.[10] Vatican Council I was to develop the concept of church as hierarchy and people of God. Only the first part was developed before war disrupted the council. As a result, we were saddled with, and for years have lived with, that incomplete ecclesiology of the church as a hierarchy. Almost a century later Vatican II developed the concept of the people of God (*Lumen Gentium [LG]*, no. 2). Meanwhile, we had constructed our theologies, canon law, ecclesiology, and even church buildings in the hierarchical model, radically identifying church with clergy.

This awareness impels us to seek richer, more gospel-based ways of being church-family of God today. The church's hierarchy has already taken some bold steps to strip itself of the trappings of the empire by dropping the pope's triple crown and the practice of his being carried to a papal audience. It needs to be emphasized that hierarchy and leadership are not synonymous; Jesus clearly provided for leadership in his church (Jn 21:15–19), different from that of the kings of the Gentiles.

Resources for Being Church and Agent of Reconciliation

Two major resources help us come to grips with the church as the locus of God's reconciliation: first, the encyclical letter *Novo Millennio Ineunte*[11] of John Paul II, and second, the scripture, particularly the New Testament. In *Novo Millennio Ineunte* John Paul II observed that for the past two thousand years the church, like Peter and his companions, had fished all night, catching nothing (Lk 5:1–11). At the dawn of the third millennium we are to listen to Jesus standing on the shore, asking us to admit the fruitlessness of our toils and to obey him as he directs us to cast our nets into the deep *(duc in altum)* for the real catch. The pope's position echoes the injunction given to religious congregations by Vatican II to return to the charism of their founders in their search for authentic renewal.[12]

Unlike the pre-jubilee document *Tertio Millennio Adveniente (The Coming of the Third Millennium)*, *Novo Millennio Ineunte* has no time frame. Rather, it challenges each person and the church as a body to take a sober and critical look at all we have been doing over the past two thousand years, admit what we did wrong, and from this admission, like Peter, allow Jesus to direct us to do it correctly. Remarkably, John Paul II addressed this call to all members of the Church, calling them "dear brothers and sisters," not "dear sons and daughters," as in his first encyclical *Redemptor Hominis*.

If this papal insight and call are taken seriously, no sector or aspect of the Church's life should be left unexamined.

Besides church structure we need to review the traditions received from the fathers of the Church and interpreted as willed by God. Our theological and canonical presuppositions and biblical hermeneutics stand to be reviewed against the backdrop of the sociocultural, religious, and political contexts from which they emerged. Reviewing these cherished traditions need not necessarily mean discarding them. Fishing remained a constant in Peter's call. What changed was the type and manner of fishing. The outcome for him personally was the grace to grow from received human traditions to the complete truth to which God's Spirit leads us (Jn 16:13). His experience in the house of Cornelius (Acts 10) confirms this. We should not be afraid to tackle these traditions or attempt to clutch at them (see Mk 7:1–13) at the expense of Jesus, God's gospel (Rom 1:1–2, 16). Ignatius of Antioch saw Jesus as the yardstick for whatever the church does. By courageously undertaking this task, the church will be like a wise scribe who brings out of his or her treasure house both the new and the old (Mt 13:52).

Scripture and a New Pentecost

Scripture as a resource for reevaluating what it means to be church cannot be overemphasized. Jesus, not Peter, owns and builds the Church; Christ is both its foundation (1 Cor 3:11) and cornerstone (Eph 2:20). An ecclesiastical tendency toward the end of the first century already sees the apostles and prophets as the foundation, with Christ as the cornerstone, probably to emphasize that Jewish and Gentile Christians are bound together in and by him. All practices and structures in church and scripture stand to be validated by the reality of Jesus, God-Word incarnate, in whom we see, hear, and touch the God who sent him in the flesh for our sake (Jn 1:14; 1 Jn 1:1–4; Heb 4:15.16).

The synod used the imagery of a New Pentecost to describe what the Spirit is doing today in the church in Africa in relation to reconciliation, justice, and peace. It occurred in some interventions and formed a leitmotif in the reports before and after the interventions and deliberations at the synod. It also formed the basis of Proposition 2. At Pentecost, the birth of the church on mission,[13] God's Spirit propelled simultaneously to one place the disciples in the upper room and the dwellers in Jerusalem "from every nation under heaven" (symbolic of all humanity). The 120 disciples, including many women, received the Holy Spirit as tongues of fire, since they were to be the speakers;[14] the Jerusalem dwellers received the gift of hearing the disciples speak in their own language. On this neutral ground both groups spoke and heard, respectively, of God's mighty deeds.

Peter interpreted the event as the fulfillment of the promised outpouring of God's Spirit on all "flesh," the outpouring of God's transforming love that levels all ranks and eliminates all barriers.[15] As a result, both speakers and believing hearers formed a new community, the *ekklēsia* of God. In that new community no member was ever in want, even if the members had to struggle with the inbred temptation to ethnicism in the case of the neglect of the Greek-speaking widows (Acts 6). By crossing their sociocultural and racial barriers they became the church of Christ. The imagery of a new Pentecost invites us, in turn, to demolish all human barriers within the church, especially, sexism, classism, and racism/ethnicism (decried by the synod as a virus), which Jesus had programmatically demolished by his death on the cross. God poured the Holy Spirit on all classes of peoples without discrimination: sons and daughters, old men and women, even male and female slaves.

The reception of the Holy Spirit had personal and communal consequences. As evidence of their new birth and bonding together in Christ, believers saw themselves as a new creation (2 Cor 5:17), called to abandon their old discriminatory ways of living and to embrace one another with Christ's love as blood brothers and sisters, irrespective of whether they were Jew or Gentile, old or young, slave or free (Gal 3:25–28), barbarian or Scythian (Col 3:11). For Paul, even knowledge of Christ according to the flesh (in other words, before his resurrection) is immaterial. What matters is faith in Jesus that expresses itself in love (Gal 6:15).

On the personal level baptism gives a Christian a new status and dignity as a child and heir of God and coheir with Christ (Rom 8:14–17; Gal 4:4–6); it makes one a member of God's own household and an integral part of Christ's body. Since the baptized have put on Christ and are incorporated in Christ as branches of the vine, they share equally in Christ's dignity and status as God's firstborn (Heb 12:23). Every believer enters under the same conditions—gratis—as a totally free and unmerited gift from God who makes no distinctions among persons when distributing God's free gift of sonship and daughtership. Vatican Council II recognized this when it said, "The followers of Christ are called by God, not because of their works, but according to his own purpose and grace. They are justified in the Lord Jesus, because in the Baptism of faith they truly become sons of God and sharers in the divine nature" (*LG*, no. 40). The absolute gratuitousness of this divine gift and the equality in dignity and status it confers cannot be overemphasized.

The imagery of church as God's family and household has its roots in scripture in the incarnation, by which Christ united himself inseparably with our humanity (Eph 2:11–22; 3:15–21). In Christ, believers are in substance God's children with equal rights and dignity (Jn 1:12–13).[16] Jesus' discourse with Nicodemus (Jn 3:1–21) elaborates on this, while 1 John 1:9 actually says that God's "seed" *(sperma)* is in the believer. No member of a family remains an infant for life. No child assumes the right to "rule" and "govern" others, to treat them as "subjects" or to exercise "paternal care" over them (see *LG*, III). Members of a loving family do not stratify themselves into ranks. It is therefore anti-christological to reduce some of God's children to the permanent status of lay/laity (which connotes inexperience and lack of maturity), since every member of this family has his or her dignity directly from God by "a divine choice" and not from the hierarchy, as *Lumen Gentium* rightly observes (no. 32).

The imageries of the vine (Jn 15:1–17) and the body (1 Cor 12:12–30) register the same truth. No single part of the body constitutes the body. Jesus promised to be with us "always till the end of time" (Mt 28:20) and even "when two or three are gathered" in his name (Mt 18:20). Consciousness of his ever-abiding presence will powerfully spur us on to be stewards of a great mystery: Christ among us in his brothers and sisters.

Consequences of the New Testament Understanding of Church

To become effective and credible witnesses of God's reconciliation, justice, and peace, the Roman Catholic Church and other churches urgently need to address the laity-clergy divide, the issue of women and ranks in the church, and the use of language that tends to subvert the gospel, for example by dissociating the "sacred" from the "secular."

The Laity-Clergy Divide

The issue of clergy and laity needs to be revisited in light of the dignity and status of each person that has been conferred by God. To be courageously rejected are diverse actions that tend to socialize some Christians into believing that as laity they are nobodies (*nkana owo* in my language, Ibibio, literally "empty person") or that they are merely helpers in their church-family (the church's official teaching to the contrary notwithstanding). It is not for the clergy to decide whether or not they want or need co-workers; all are God's co-workers. Besides, the term *laity* is not a category in the New Testament. If anything, Jesus and the early Christians were viewed as laypeople in their context (see Acts 4:13). The *Lineamenta*, drawing from other church documents, rightly upholds that God has given laypeople their own unique role to play.

Women and the Church

One needs to tread softly but with gospel radicalism and boldness when dealing with the issue of women in the church. Doubtless the church recognizes the invaluable role women play in maintaining the church (*Message of the Bishops* 25; Proposition 47). However, their exclusion on the sole basis of their God-given gender from participating in ministerial offices or being called to the ministerial priesthood belies the truth of their full incorporation into Christ. It decrees a priori that although the call to the priesthood is from God, God can never call women to this vocation. Thus, Jesus can use the voice of a man who is incorporated into him by virtue of baptism to say "this is my body," but not the voice of a woman, even though she is also equally incorporated into him, to say "this is my body."[17] Ironically the church, woman/mother, is the primary sacrament; she ordains priests and bishops and elects the pope.

The issue of women in the church is a justice issue (with justice understood as truth in relationship) on two counts: justice to God, who re-creates and declares all justified without any personal merit or considerations based on gender; and justice to women, who, like men, are baptized into Christ and thereby entitled to full and inalienable membership in him. Both men and women need to be involved in reviewing the Thomistic-Aristotelian anthropology used in elaborating what constitutes matter and form in the sacraments in the light of the gospel and the mystery of the incarnation. Failure to do so means obstructing God's reconciliation, justice, and peace for both men and women and the continued wasting of women's talents that God gives freely for building up the church. When anyone is in Christ, that person, male or female, is a new creation (2 Cor 5:17).

Rank within the Church

The hierarchical church operates with ranks (*LG*, III). On the other hand, the early Christians emphasized *functions* in the church: some were called as apostles, prophets, evangelists, pastors, and so forth. These gifts of the Holy Spirit, given freely and at will and not based on gender or race, were not used for personal aggrandizement but for building up the body of Christ so that the entire body would attain the fullness of Christ's own maturity (Eph 4:4–3, 16). The current emphasis on rank in the church and the privileging of the clergy are legacies of the Roman imperial order initiated by Constantine and consolidated by Theodosius. As church, we need to liberate ourselves from preoccupation with rank. The attribution of rank and its consequences in the daily life of the church-family of God should be a core concern of all. To what extent does rank promote awareness that as a eucharistic church *(Ecclesia de Eucharistia)* all are intrinsically called to be full sharers of Christ's priesthood—not just ministerially, but by daily breaking the bread of their lives so that others may eat and have life in its fullness?

We need to address how the language we use can camouflage the fact that certain practices that we cherish are actually subverting the gospel and its values. The use of terms such as *priest/sacred* and *laity/secular* for God's children reinforces class/rank distinctions. God has sanctified, chosen, and set apart *all* the baptized and has stamped and sealed them with the Holy Spirit as God's children. Timothy Radclife observes that the "stiff clericalism and authoritarianism" that developed as a result of the Tridentine reforms and helped the church to survive Protestantism at that time "do not help the Church now to thrive and be a sign of God's friendship for humanity." He adds, "we need a new culture of authority from the Vatican to the parish council, which lifts people up into the mystery of loving equality, which is the life of the Trinity."[18] This "mystery of loving equality, which is the life of the Trinity," is that into which all are baptized. What is said here of priests' authoritarian use of power applies equally and in some respects even more so to episcopal use of power (as some bishops noted at the synod). It applies equally in religious congregations and even in lay associations, where some parish council members and leaders of pious societies act as if they are the church. A leadership model from the top, good or bad, seeps down to the bottom.

Wither This Reflection?

As church we need to reexamine whether our current way of being church, in terms of interpersonal relationships, organizational structures, and use of language, actually mirrors what we claim to be, the church-family of God. Outdated empire values "re-baptized" as gospel need to be courageously and fearlessly discarded, no matter how alluring and advantageous they may seem. The key resource for doing this is Jesus. Through him and in him God's act of reconciliation binds all the reconciled to the divine Self, at the cost of the divine Self ("making peace with his body on the cross"). To be the church-family of God in service to reconciliation, justice, and peace impels all to be God's building and tilling (1 Cor 3:9; Eph 2:10), the visible, tangible witnesses of this divine reconciliation, by relating to one another as divine siblings.

Effecting this task inevitably requires structural changes. We must seek concrete ways of promoting the reality and vocation of the priesthood of all baptized into Christ—prophet, priest, and king. It might require reintroducing the diversity of aforementioned ministries in the New Testament, which are currently invested only in the clergy. This should be a task of the twenty-first century for a church that desires to be light of the world and salt of the earth, serving God's gratuitous reconciliation and justification of all humanity to the divine Self. By being light and salt in this way, the church-family of God will truly be in service to reconciliation within itself and then in its ambassadorial appeal to a world in dire need of God's reconciliation.

Pope Benedict XVI repeatedly said at the synod that reconciliation, justice, and peace should not be politicized. Their roots lie in the human heart. If Christians commit themselves to be as Christ to others, we will make unimaginable progress toward becoming a church that is always in service to reconciliation. At every stage and in every aspect of the church's life Christ will be all in all (Col 3:11), giving to the world through believers a peace (wholeness) that our polarized and wartorn world can never give itself.

May God's Holy Spirit who constantly renews the church, who empowered our ancestors in the faith to break age-old barriers and become living witnesses and ministers of God's good news, continue to guide us today as we face the new challenge of being church in this third millennium. May we, with humility, discarding whatever obstructs God's reconciliation, justice, and peace for all, courageously launch into the deep to make the catch of the century. *Duc in altum* (Put out into the deep).

Notes

[1] Special Assembly for Africa of the Synod of Bishops, "The Church in Africa and Her Evangelizing Mission: 'You shall be my witnesses from Jerusalem to Judea and to the ends of the earth' (Acts 1:8)" (Rome, 1994).

[2] See, for example, A. E. Orobator, *The Church as Family: African Ecclesiology in Its Social Context* (Nairobi: Paulines Publications, 2000), and the Pan African Association of Catholic Exegetes (PACE), which has systematically devoted its biennial congresses since 1994 to studying biblical themes from the perspective of the Church-Family of God. The Catholic Institute of West Africa devotes an annual Theology Week entirely to exploring the concept from the biblical and other theological perspectives. Many students have also written theses on this.

[3] The *International Journal for the Study of the Christian Church (IJSCC)* 8, no. 4 (2008) was entirely devoted 8, no. 4 (2008) to ecclesiology in Africa. See also Teresa Okure, "The Church in the World: A Dialogue in Ecclesiology," in *Theology as Conversation: Towards a Relational Theology*, ed. J. Haers and P. de Mey, 393–437 (Leuven: Leuven University Press, 2003), 393–437.

[4] Gerald O'Collins and Edward G. Farrugia, eds., *The Concise Dictionary of Theology*, rev. exp. ed. (London: T & T Clark, 2000). The reference is to "Denzinger and Hunemann 3050–75, ND 814–40"—pre–Second Vatican Council documents.

[5] The Greek word rendered "father" and "fatherhood" in many translations of these verses "denotes any social group which owes its existence and unity to a common ancestor" (NJB, note h to Ephesians 3:15).

[6] Homily of His Holiness Benedict XVI, Homily at the Opening Mass of the Synod, *Synod Bulletin,* 03.

[7] John Paul II to the Bishop Friends of the Focolare Movement, "The Ecumenical Way Is the Church's Way," *L'Osservatore Romano* (January 17, 2001), 6.

[8] See *Redemptor Hominis,* no. 13.1; *Lumen Gentium* II.16; and *Gaudim et Spes* 22.

[9] Peter Cardinal Turkson gave a good exposé of *light* and *salt* from the biblical perspective in the *Relatio ante* and *post Disceptationem* of the synod.

[10] *LG*, III, is entitled "The Church Is Hierarchical." Though this is not the same as saying that the church is a hierarchy, understood as clergy, in practice it does attract this understanding.

[11] John Paul II, *Novo Millennio Ineunte* (Vatican City: Libreria Editrice Vaticana, 2001).

[12] See, in particular, *Perfectae Caritatis* (October 28, 1965), no. 2, and *Renovationis Causam* (January 6, 1969).

[13] The fathers of the church rightly hold that Jesus gave birth to the church on the cross, nourishing us with his body and blood, even as a woman gives birth to a

child and nourishes it with the milk from her body. The ancient hymn "Pie Pelicane" depicts this very well when it says, "Lord Jesus, Good Pelican, wash me clean with your blood, one drop of which can free the entire world of all its sins."

[14] All the disciples received the Holy Spirit, not only the apostles, with our Lady at the center, as paintings of Pentecost and the third glorious mystery socialize us to believe.

[15] See further, Teresa Okure, ed., *To Cast Fire upon the Earth: Bible and Mission Collaborating in Today's Multi-Cultural Global Context* (Pietermaritzburg: Cluster Publications, 2000).

[16] The Greek words *tekna* and *gennaō*, used only for biological begetting, register this fact.

[17] Jesus himself views it differently; for instance, he told Paul, who was persecuting men, women, and children, "I am Jesus and you are persecuting me" (Acts 9:5).

[18] Timothy Radclife, "Towards a Humble Church," *The Tablet* (January 2, 2010), 4.

2

On Speaking Terms

African Religion and Christianity in Dialogue

Laurenti Magesa

Interreligious relations in Africa were an important concern of the 2009 Second Special Assembly for Africa of the Synod of Bishops. The important documents surrounding the assembly—the *Lineamenta*, *Instrumentum Laboris*, *Propositions of the Synod*, and *Message of the Bishops of Africa to the People of God*—aspects of which will form the content of the pope's *Apostolic Exhortation*, mention this issue.[1] In the *Message*, for instance, the bishops explicitly note that besides ecumenical collaboration with other Christian churches "we also look forward to more dialogue and cooperation with Muslims, the adherents of African Traditional Religion (ATR) and people of other faiths" (no. 38).

My interest here concerns what the bishops call "African Traditional Religion." In my opinion this appellation is anachronistic and inaccurate as a designation of what Africans themselves refer to simply as "our religion," "our faith," "our belief," or "our way of life." As well, most scholars today refer to the African belief system as African Religion, meaning the sum total of its adherents' beliefs, creeds, codes of behavior, and rituals. These are elements that make up any religion. The qualifier *traditional* with reference to African Religion is therefore redundant and serves no useful purpose in the designation. Further, as dimensions or expressions of African Religion, the terms *African spirituality* or *African religiosity* may be used interchangeably with it.[2]

Historical Precedents

The African Synod's interest in relating with African Religion indicates a breakthrough in the history of Christianity on a level such as a synod. It is

---

I wish to acknowledge the assistance of Professor Joseph Bracken, SJ, who read this essay and made useful suggestions.

true that missionary work in sub-Saharan Africa since the nineteenth century[3] reveals some precedents in taking African Religion seriously. Records show that a number of individual Christian missionaries did voice the desire for some form of dialogue with African Religion.

In the Catholic Church, for example, there were people like Francis Libermann of the Holy Ghost Fathers and Daniel Comboni of the Verona Fathers. As founders of missionary groups working in Africa, both advised their members to learn from the culture and habits of the African people. "The regeneration of Africa by means of Africa itself seems to me the only possible way to Christianize the continent," Comboni maintained.[4] Libermann, despite a touch of condescension typical of his time, was of a similar mind. He warned his members against imposing European ways of doing things on Africa. "Become Negroes with Negroes," he insisted. "Adapt yourselves to them as servants have to adapt themselves to their masters, their customs, taste, and manners . . . [so as to] transform them slowly but gradually into a people of God."[5] In expressing these sentiments, both men were forerunners of the thinking of the second African Synod. They were encouraging not "radical discontinuity" but a dialogue of life between Christianity and African Religion.[6]

Nevertheless, this insight rarely enjoyed official church authorization. Libermann and Comboni represented rare personal foresight, and more often than not their members observed it in the breach. A certain fundamentalist reading of biblical tradition controlled European missionary perception of evangelization. It dismissed almost entirely African Religion, its "customs, taste, and manners," and wanted it extinct.

The belief that visionaries like Libermann and Comboni espoused was to reemerge with some clarity and official sanction at the Second Vatican Council (1962–65). Admittedly, the council did not refer explicitly to dialogue with African Religion. Yet, given the Catholic Church's perception of other religions since the Protestant Reformation, the council's endorsement of dialogue with other religions was revolutionary. It slightly opened the door for consideration of African Religion as a dialogue partner. Indeed, just three years after the end of the council in 1968, the Secretariat for Non-Christians held a meeting in Rome precisely on this subject. Its conclusions were published in a significant booklet called *Meeting the African Religions*.[7] In the same year, in Eastern Africa, a pastoral institute was established at Gaba in Uganda to train pastoral agents in processes of serious inculturation.[8] The effort, however, eventually fizzled out.

One of the briefest documents of Vatican II is *Nostra Aetate*, the *Declaration on the Relationship of the Church to Non-Christian Religions*. Here, the recommendation for interreligious dialogue is elevated to almost a mandate. *Nostra Aetate* recognizes that non-Christian religions contain important dimensions of divine revelation and truth to which the church must be receptive. The church must appreciate the values found in other religions because their presence is evidence of the common inherent desire in all human beings to search for the divine. In the words of the document, the church calls on all faithful, through dialogue and collaboration "with followers of other religions," to "acknowledge, preserve and promote the spiritual and moral goods found among these men, as well as the values in their society and culture" (no. 2).

Despite this admission, the council failed to make a clear and direct connection between the need for dialogue and the demands of justice. This link appears only implicitly in the concluding paragraph of *Nostra Aetate*, where the council rejects any form of discrimination against people, even on the basis of their religious beliefs. It describes discrimination as "foreign to the mind of Christ" and urges all Catholics to respect people of different religions. Christians must do all they can to be at peace with everyone, irrespective of religious differences, so as to be true witnesses of God's love for all humanity. "A man's relationship with God the Father," the document teaches, "and his relationship with his brother men are so linked together that Scripture says: 'He who does not love does not know God'" (no. 5).

In what way does the perception of the second African Synod differ from that of Vatican II? Perhaps a better way of stating the issue is to inquire what elements in the synod push the insights of the Vatican II on dialogue to their ultimate conclusion.

The second African Synod makes the link between dialogue and justice more explicit than did the council. First of all, the synod makes the duty of the church to serve justice, peace, and reconciliation its overall theme. One reading of the theme would suggest that African Religion as an expression of the *being* of the African person requires justice in treatment. This is a critical issue that may be clarified by a brief survey into the historical attitudes of Christianity toward African Religion.

A Deplorable Interpretation of Biblical Tradition

Prior to Vatican II the dominant perception of African Religion was shaped by an extreme fundamentalist interpretation of the Bible, one that relied purely on a literal understanding of the biblical text rather than its spirit. On the basis of this reading, one finds in most biblical books neither tolerance nor encouragement for interreligious relations, but rather prejudice and exclusion.

Read literally, the Hebrew Bible (the Old Testament) is very explicit in its condemnation of any belief that appears to contradict the Shema, the central creed of the Jewish faith. The declaration, *Shema Yisrael Adonai Eloheinu Adonai Echad* ("Hear, O Israel: the Lord is our God, the Lord is One" [Dt 6:4, The African Bible]) is exclusive in its interpretation as found in the traditions of the Hebrew Bible.

Regulations on Israel's behavior toward peoples of other faiths are spelled out based on this principle. Deuteronomy 7 is an example. Apart from prohibitions against any kind of social contact with people of other cultures and religions, including intermarriage and all forms of political alliance—no treaties of peace with Gentiles, but on the contrary, "you shall doom them. Make no covenant with them and show them no mercy"—there must be absolutely no religious communication with them. The divine mandate is clear; it requires that Israel "tear down their altars, smash their sacred pillars, chop down their sacred poles, and destroy their idols by fire." No leniency is allowed "lest you be ensnared into serving their gods" (Dt 7:5, 16ff.). The so-called historical books of the Hebrew Bible carry more or less the same message.[9]

This theology, driven by perceptions of religious purity and fear of contamination, advances the principle of eradication of the religiously different other, without compunction or remorse, as a basic religious duty. There are concrete rewards and blessings accompanying obedience to this duty and severe punishment for disobedience. These are expressed in the form of personal and national health, wealth, and numerous offspring, on the one hand, and various forms of disaster, including conquest by hostile tribes, exile, and slavery, on the other.

Though more subtle and without any suggestion of physical violence, the Christian Bible (the New Testament) does not completely abandon the principle of hostility toward other religions. The African feminist scholar Musa Dube has illustrated this in her critical study on the customary interpretation of Matthew 15:21–28 as an interplay between "empire and mission."[10] She observes this within the text itself and in its historical application. It is easy to extend Dube's argument to the predominant understanding of the Great Commission (Mt 28:19–20; Mk 16:15–18; and in a slightly different format, Acts 1:8): "Go . . . and make disciples of all nations." As in the Hebrew Bible, a promise is attached to this command. In the Gospel of Mark it consists of salvation for those who comply with the message preached and condemnation for those who don't (16:16). The proclaimers and believers are further promised unfailing security against physical harm (see Mk 16:18; Lk 10:19) but also (beneficial) suffering in the line of duty (Mk 13:9–10; Lk 12:11).

The question Dube poses is pertinent to the Great Commission's historical application: Is there room for dialogue in the process of proclaiming the gospel of Jesus Christ? Is it absolutely impossible to consider the contribution of other faiths, beliefs, and religions to Christianity? Vatican II and the second African Synod bring a different answer to the question.

An Alternative Hermeneutic

The Book of Acts in the New Testament seeks to provide a basis for this response. Acts describes how in general the early disciples of Christ prevaricated concerning their relationship with non-Jews, called Gentiles, preferring

Jewish-Christian expressions of faith in Christ to any other (Acts 10—11). Paul, though by his own admission an orthodox Jew, thoroughly trained in the Torah under the best teachers, miraculously transcended this myopic view of the faith (see Acts 9:1–19). He became the main protagonist of the "inculturation" of the gospel for non-Jews. He is the premier example in the entire New Testament of a fierce critic of Christian chauvinism, exclusivism, and cultural imposition in the name of faith (Acts 15ff.).

Paul, more than most of his contemporaries, appreciated much better the deeper meaning of divine revelation. He refutes what fundamentalist interpreters throughout the ages have assumed to be the sense of Israel's "election." Paul recognized that Israel's election is much wider than divine favor restricted to the people of Israel. The message of divine election, as Paul understood it, is that God is not only the God of Israel, but of all nations. Israel's election is paradigmatically symbolic; it is not for her alone but, through her, for the whole world.

This fine print of revelation had to be impressed upon Peter by a miraculous vision in order to expand his narrow perception of Israel's election as exclusive. The baptism of Cornelius the Gentile and his household's reception of the Spirit of God constrained Peter to recognize the writing on the wall: "In truth, I see that God shows no partiality. Rather, in every nation whoever fears him and acts uprightly is acceptable to him" (Acts 10:34–35). As Paul changed from persecutor to believer in Christ after a dramatic conversion moment, so Peter's experience in Joppa at Cornelius's house made him receptive to universal divine election. It is not difficult to imagine how shocking this change must have been to the Jewish Christians of his day. Actually, its implications for Africa have not been quite palatable to many Western Christians.

In subsequent ages the significance of the conversions of Peter and Paul escaped most mainstream Christian evangelizers. Soon after the apostolic period the tendency to impose certain Greek and Roman cultural and imperial expressions and forms of belief in Christ as normative and universal became habitual. Still, the approach oftentimes caused resistance, as numerous heresies[11] and schisms that arose testify. These were sometimes so strong that they had to be suppressed by convenient alliances between church authorities and political powers, as was the case with Emperor Constantine against Arianism at the Council of Nicea in the fourth century.

With European imperial hegemony over most of the world by the end of the fifteenth century, imposition of European forms of Christian expressions became widespread. The advice of one Acosta to missionaries in South America in the sixteenth century typifies a practice that became commonplace in Africa as well, one reminiscent of the superficial reading of the biblical texts already discussed. "While it is not permitted to constrain barbarian subjects to baptism and the Christian faith," Acosta decrees, "it is licit and desirable to suppress their idolatrous cults even by force." Acosta explained that in practice this meant "to destroy their altars and their temples, and to banish their devilish superstition—things which, all of them are not only an obstacle to the grace of the Gospels, but contrary to the natural law as well."[12]

The African experience of this form of christianization began in earnest toward the end of the nineteenth century. Since then there have been very few cases where the altars of the African gods have not literally or figuratively been torn down, their sacred pillars and poles smashed, and their sacred images destroyed by fire, to paraphrase Acosta. Psychological coercion has also formed part of the process and has worked even more effectively than physical coercion. F. Eboussi Boulaga describes the psychological violence done to Africa as consisting in the show of the superiority of the Christian faith over African Religion through a fivefold form of discourse, which he characterizes as "derision," "refutation," "demonstration," "orthodoxy," and "conformity."

These forms of discourse are not dialogical but domineering, dictatorial, and alienating. According to Boulaga, the "language of derision" implies that African gods are no gods, and those paying adherence to them are backward; they ought to be ashamed of themselves. The "language of refutation" is meant to demonstrate that African beliefs are infantile, a sign of utter lack of intelligence. The "language of demonstration" sets out to prove the superiority of Christian beliefs in their dogmatic expression. This calls forth the "language of orthodoxy," demanding adherence to a uniform formulation of the faith as the only possible one. Obviously, orthodoxy evokes the "language of conformity," the unquestioning loyalty to dogmatic expressions as the ultimate end of the search for God.[13]

Confession of Sin and Asking for Forgiveness

The damaging implications of this method of evangelization are easy to see, as Paul pointed out to Peter (Gal 2:11–14). The historical facts that took place to this effect are too well known to repeat here, even if until recently the church did not quite own up to them. In modern times, however, Pope Pius XII in his 1943 encyclical letter *Mystici Corporis (The Mystical Body of Christ)* sensed the problem and declared that "no one may be forced to accept the Catholic faith against his will." If this should happen, he said, "we cannot do otherwise . . . than disavow such an action" (no. 104).

Yet, as was the case in the time of Comboni and Libermann, these and similar injunctions have often fallen on deaf ears in pastoral practice. Rather than follow the deep scriptural understanding of universal divine revelation that Paul and Peter represent, it is the destruction model of the Acostas that has largely prevailed.

Theologically and morally it is clear today that this method of evangelization is patently wrong. In the 1990s Pope John Paul II openly lamented and repudiated it, characterizing it variously as faulty, erroneous, unjust, and even sinful. In his Apostolic Letter of 1994, *Tertio Millennio Adveniente (On the Threshold of the Third Millennium)*, the pope proposed that the church examine her conscience for such historical wrongs, repent, and seek forgiveness. His gesture of asking for forgiveness formed one of the most striking features of his pontificate. It was an unexpected step; never before had a pope so openly admitted fault and guilt for wrongful approaches in the process of the proclamation of the gospel.

Of particular significance for us in Africa was the pope's recognition of moral failure for attitudes of "acquiescence . . . given . . . to intolerance and even the use of violence in the service of truth" (no. 35). Although, according to the pope, this must be judged in the proper historical and cultural contexts that may have encouraged an overriding sense that "authentic witness to the truth could include suppressing the opinions of others or at least paying no attention to them," the failure remains. The "mitigating factors" notwithstanding, Pope John Paul II maintains that it cannot be possible to "exonerate the Church from the obligation to express profound regret" for these attitudes. The proclamation of the gospel is done authentically only when the principle that "the truth cannot impose itself except by virtue of its own truth, as it wins over the mind with both gentleness and power" is respected (no. 35).

In *Tertio Millennio Adveniente* John Paul II overlooks one thing. He attributes the errors in evangelization methods to the sinfulness of "her [the church's] sons and daughters" (no. 33), as if to exonerate the church itself or the "church as such" from the injustice committed in this regard. But one must argue that if these "sinful sons and daughters" are the very ones that constitute the church, there is no escaping the conclusion that it is the "church as such" that needs to repent, ask for forgiveness, and be reconciled with itself and other religions.[14] Besides, intolerance was often not only the erroneous view of a few members of the church; in several clear cases it was official church policy. One example will suffice. By the papal bull *Dum Diversas* of 1452, Pope Nicholas V granted King Afonso V of Portugal "full and free faculty to capture and subjugate Saracens and pagans, and other unbelievers and enemies of Christ" wherever they were to be found. "By apostolic authority" Pope Nicholas permitted King Afonso to "seize" their "moveable or immovable" goods, to "invade and conquer" their lands, and to "reduce to slavery their inhabitants."[15] Elsewhere in this volume Peter Kanyandago mentions similar papal bulls to the same effect.

Pope John Paul II openly disavowed this kind of attitude and rejected any form of violence as a tool of evangelization. In 1994 he sent a memorandum to all the cardinals, calling them to an examination of conscience on this matter on behalf of the whole church. He recommended that "the Church, on its own initiative, should look again at the dark aspects of its own history, judging it in the light of the principles of the Gospel."[16] The pope referred to this review as a process of "purification of memory," of remembering the past so as to heal the present and change the future.[17]

There was, however, an omission in Pope John Paul's *mea culpa* that must be pointed out. Although the need for purification and healing of historical memory features strongly in his apology to Africa concerning the slave trade, racial discrimination, and cultural alienation, it is lacking in areas that concern missionary violence against African Religion. We understand today how damaging the spiritual marginalization by missionaries of African values was to African identity. A more comprehensive apology must include this aspect. More important, it must form any process of the church's attitudinal change in new approaches to evangelization. For, in spite of what has been said since Vatican II and recently emphasized by the two synods for Africa, positive consideration of African religious values is not yet the governing factor for evangelization on this continent.

Considering all this, it is obvious that the call by the second African Synod for justice, reconciliation, and peace does not apply only in the political and economic arenas, but also in the cultural and religious spheres. "The church in Africa in service to reconciliation, justice and peace" must recall the historical dark aspects of its practical evangelizing mission in Africa. In the interests of the healing of memory, the church must interpret her history under the criterion of divine universal salvation, often overlooked by literal and superficial readings of scripture. Progress in this, as James Carroll says referring to a similar context, "requires fundamental changes in the way history has been written, theology has been taught, and Scripture has been interpreted."[18]

In the *Lineamenta* (nos. 24–26), *Instrumentum Laboris* (III, nos. 1–3), *Propositions* (no. 33), *Message* (no. 38), and other documents, the second African Synod appeals to the church to be continually attentive to justice and human dignity in her relations with other religions. Arguably, the appeal could have used more clarity, detail, and emphasis. Yet what is said is enough to infer that the synod also intended to underline just and peaceful relationships between Christianity and African Religion. This can only happen when both traditions respect each other enough to engage in a genuine and mature encounter. This implies conversation based on the principle of give-and-take in terms of each one's lived values and their common search and goal for God, the universal God who is beyond any single tradition's absolute comprehension.

On Speaking Terms: Toward Justice and Reconciliation

So, what does the future hold? An ongoing task for the second African Synod lies in the area of interreligious dialogue in Africa. It may be summarized in one major requirement: instead of the previous campaign by the churches to annihilate African Religion as the purpose and goal of Christian mission, the future lies in genuine conversation between Christianity and African Religion, to discover and uncover as much as possible God's presence in each. Unqualified antagonism against African Religion not only breeds in some Africans deep-seated resentment against Christianity for demonizing their cultural identity (and, by implication, their humanity), but also does not help Christianity to pay attention to, learn from, and so enrich itself from divine values found in African Religion.

With regard to reconciliation, justice, and peace, what can Christianity learn from African religious processes? Paul Béré and Gabriel Mmassi discuss these issues in their respective contributions to this volume. The values of communion and participation so valued in African communities can serve as principles upon which reconciliation, justice, and peace can be built. Peter Knox, in *AIDS, Ancestors, and Salvation*, begins to show how African ancestral beliefs survive and how respecting their religious role can provide viable approaches to the scourge of the HIV/AIDS pandemic in Africa.[19]

Christian opposition to African Religion is often a child of stereotyping, whereby complex African spiritual perceptions and longings are compared to Christian rational dogmatic formulations. But such stereotypes often pay scant attention to questions that lie at the heart of the African person's life. Thus, overall hostility violates the integrity of the Africans' humanity and alienates them from themselves. The estrangement expresses itself in two ways. On the one hand, there is the phenomenon of double religious consciousness or spiritual schizophrenia among the majority of African Christians, who are unable to integrate Christian dogmatic demands into their African spirituality. On the other, there is the mushrooming of breakaway sects, churches, and movements generally clustered under African Initiated, Pentecostal, and Prosperity Gospel churches. Paradoxically, both phenomena show that Africans do not in principle reject faith in Christ, only certain expressions of it foreign to their experience of God. They object to a form of Christianity that alienates them from themselves, from their African identity, and from their spirituality, all in the name of faith in Christ.

The only necessity for the future is "the dialogical imperative."[20] Is it not time, as David Lochhead proposes, that the church discard the historical "ideologies" of "isolation," "hostility," "competition," and even "partnership"[21] vis-à-vis African Religion in favor of a better, more Christlike approach of genuine discernment? "For whoever is not against us is for us," said Jesus (Mk 9:40; also Lk 9:50). Is it not possible to embrace the approach of sincere communication or dialogue with African Religion? The relationship of dialogue stands at a different level from mindless derision and refutation. It calls above all for mutuality and respect. Only in the light of mutual respect can justice be done to African Religion and its adherents. Only in this light can Christian spirituality grow by learning from the divine presence in African Religion. Only from this angle can the recommendations made in Propositions 11, 13, 33, and in 38 of the *Message* concerning an informed openness in encountering African Religion avoid being an exercise in animosity and conflict but instead lead to peace, reconciliation, and true inculturation.

Proposition 11 makes it explicit that interreligious dialogue is a sociological and theological necessity. Sociologically, "peace in Africa and other parts of the world is very much determined by the relations among religions," it points out. "Therefore, promoting the value of dialogue is important so that believers work together in associations dedicated to peace and justice, in a spirit of mutual trust and support and families be taught the values of listening patiently and fearlessly respecting one another."

Theologically, according to the same proposition, "dialogue with other religions, especially Islam and African Traditional Religion, is an integral part of the proclamation of the Gospel and the Church's pastoral activity on behalf of reconciliation and peace." Accordingly, the prayer of the synod assembly was "that religious intolerance and violence be minimized and eliminated through interreligious dialogue." Thus the synod brings dialogue with African Religion for the sake of peace to the forefront of its goals by stressing the role of the dialogical encounter in fostering true justice, reconciliation, and peace—and authentic evangelization. The minimization and eventual elimination of intolerance and violence facilitated by this approach lead toward putting an end to these pathologies. This is a step toward building God's kingdom, toward which Christians are mandated to struggle.

For Christianity and African Religion to grow together into dialogue or, at the very least, to be on speaking terms is evidently what the synod expects. The process should lead to reciprocal understanding, benefiting each of these faiths as they learn and appreciate God's creative wonders in each other. At any rate the good news of Jesus will become clearer in Africa when seen in the context of African Religion. African persons, freely assuming belief in Christ in this new situation, will not feel estranged from God's presence in their own culture.

Belief in a loving God is perhaps the common ground on which dialogue between Christianity and African Religion can take place. This dialogue will not be primarily for the sake of "converting" or baptizing adherents of African Religion. Rather, it will aim at trying to open up to them as clearly as possible the love of God for humanity manifested in Jesus Christ and thereby *persuading* African religionists to accept Christ as the perfect way to this love. This is all that is required of Christian evangelizers. As a method of proclamation of the gospel, "the call to dialogue, to open, trusting and loving relationships with the neighbor, is clear and unambiguous. Dialogue needs no justification outside itself."[22] Decisive for Christian discipleship though it may be, genuine Christian proclamation cannot take place in the absence of dialogue or truth that leads to truth. This insight from Vatican II and Pope John Paul II, carried forth and completed by the second African Synod, is critical in Christianity–African Religion relations.

Conclusion

A most significant theme that joined the first and second African Synods is their interest in interreligious relations. If the first assembly addressed the church's responsibility in evangelization, the second considered the elements of reconciliation, justice, and peace as constituent parts of this responsibility. Both assemblies had a twofold message for the African church. First, effective evangelization cannot take place without contact and understanding with the local faiths and religions of the people. Second, true justice, reconciliation, and peace on the larger social plane will not materialize without peace among religions. In both respects dialogue is the essential component for awareness and appreciation of one another. If witnessing to the gospel is the primary task of the church, and acting as salt and light through justice for the sake of peace is the preferred method, neither can succeed without the art of seriously speaking together. This must go beyond mere exchanges of bodies of knowledge to become a process of mutuality and friendship. Dialogue between Christianity and African Religion cannot be dispensed with inauthentic evangelization.

Notes

[1] These documents appear in a variety of sources. Whenever I refer to them in this chapter, I will simply indicate within the text the paragraph in the proper document where the particular reference appears.

[2] Questions keep arising about whether African Religion is one or many, and whether it is a world religion, and who are its dialogue representatives. Yet they have already been addressed exhaustively in scholarship in favor of its parity with other world religions with their internal diversity in unity. For instance, see Laurenti Magesa, *African Religion: The Moral Traditions of Abundant Life* (Maryknoll, NY: Orbis Books, 1997), 1–34.

[3] Historically, there are three phases of evangelization of Africa. The first is dated from the first to the sixth century. The second coincides with the slave trade, from the fourteenth to the eighteenth century. The third and current arrived with Western colonialism in Africa toward the end of the nineteenth century. Within this third phase, I note a sub-phase, which I characterize as the phase of the renaissance of the values of African Religion, or *inculturation,* for short.

[4] Quoted in John Baur, *2000 Years of Christianity in Africa: An African Church History* (Nairobi: Paulines Publications Africa, 2009), 172.

[5] Quoted in ibid., 137.

[6] I am indebted to Paulinus I. Odozor for this insight in a verbal reaction to the ideas expressed in this essay.

[7] *Meeting the African Religions* (Rome: Libreria Editrice Ancora, 1969). This meeting was obviously motivated by Pope Paul VI's 1967 "Message to the Countries of Africa," *Africae Terrarum*, in which he said, among other things, "*The Church views with great respect the moral and religious values of the African tradition, not only because of their meaning, but also because the Church sees them as*

providential, as the basis for spreading the Gospel message and beginning the establishment of the new society in Christ" (quoted in Teresa Okure et al., eds., *32 Articles Evaluating Inculturation of Christianity in Africa* [Eldoret: AMECEA Gaba Publications, 1990], 19. Italics in the original).

⁸ See Richard Gribble, *Vincent McCauley: Bishop of the Poor, Apostle of East Africa* (Notre Dame, IN: Ave Maria Press, 2008), 280–88.

⁹ For the ironical, subversive meaning of these books against Israel's misguided religious and political chauvinism, see Daniel Berrigan, *The Kings and Their Gods: The Pathology of Power* (Grand Rapids, MI: William B. Eerdmans, 2008).

¹⁰ Musa W. Dube, *Postcolonial Feminist Interpretation of the Bible* (St. Louis, MO: Chalice Press, 2000), 127–95.

¹¹ Technically, a heretic is a person who holds a view divergent from the conventional. At times, heretics were prepared to defend their position at the expense of their lives. In their camp, they are the religious equivalent of the Christian martyrs.

¹² Quoted in F. Eboussi Boulaga, *Christianity without Fetishes: An African Critique and Recapture of Christianity* (Maryknoll, NY: Orbis Books, 1984), 43–44.

¹³ See ibid., 30–56.

¹⁴ In a slightly different context, that of the Holocaust, James Carroll discusses this point in *Toward a New Catholic Church* (Boston: Houghton Mifflin, 2002), 31–33.

¹⁵ See Tissa Balasuriya, "A Missing Dimension in Papal Encyclical," *SEDOS Bulletin* 41, no. 9/10 (September-October 2009): 240.

¹⁶ Quoted in Luigi Accattoli, *When a Pope Asks Forgiveness: The Mea Culpa's of John Paul II* (New York: Alba House, 1998), 174.

¹⁷ See ibid., xxi.

¹⁸ Carroll, *Toward a New Catholic Church*, 32.

¹⁹ Peter Knox, *AIDS, Ancestors, and Salvation: Local Beliefs in Christian Ministry to the Sick* (Nairobi: Paulines Publications Africa, 2008), esp. 90–108.

²⁰ See David Lochhead, *The Dialogical Imperative: A Christian Reflection on Interfaith Encounter* (Maryknoll, NY: Orbis Books, 1988).

²¹ See ibid, 5–26. Other scholars have studied these attitudes in terms of the notions of exclusivism, inclusivism, and pluralism including, among many others, Paul Knitter, *Introducing Theologies of Religions* (Maryknoll, NY: Orbis Books, 2002); Eugene Hillman, *Many Paths: A Catholic Approach to Religious Pluralism* (Maryknoll, NY: Orbis Books, 1989); and Hans Küng, *Theology for the Third Millennium: An Ecumenical View* (New York: Anchor Books, 1990).

²² Lochhead, *The Dialogical Imperative*, 81.

3

Language, Politics, and Religious Dialogue

The Case of Kiswahili in Eastern Africa

FESTO MKENDA

Writing in 1911 about the religions of primitive races, the missionary Le Roy narrated an incident at Bagamoyo, coastal Tanzania, where a European gentleman hired a caravan of Wanyamwezi to accompany him inland for an ivory-searching expedition.[1] As they started off, the head of the caravan prayed: "God be propitious to us!" The gentleman reacted: "God! . . . We don't need *Him*. My money and my gun are God enough for *me*!" The response of "these simple folk" to the alien indifference to God was stunning: they "looked at one another, laid down their burdens, and began to withdraw." When Le Roy pleaded with them on the gentleman's behalf, they became even more adamant: "No," they protested, "this white man is bad; didn't you hear him insult God? With him, only misfortune could happen to us." The so-called primitives never relented.[2]

The religious attitude of these Wanyamwezi is akin to what Benedict XVI called for in his inaugural homily at the beginning of the Second Special Assembly for Africa of the Synod of Bishops. The pope said, "There is absolutely no doubt that the so-called 'First' World has exported up to now and continues to export its spiritual toxic waste that contaminates the peoples of other continents, in particular those of Africa." This statement is as rich as it is challenging. Considering that most first-world spiritual export goes in Christian packaging, the statement dares Africans, like the Wanyamwezi, to assess and if necessary reject versions of Christianity from the West. It confirms a growing realization in the universal church that a truly African church, built on the best of African traditions and on the gospel, is not merely expedient but actually necessary. Pope John Paul II had already urged Africans to stop looking beyond Africa for "the so-called 'freedom of the modern way of life'" and, instead, to look inside themselves, to the riches of

37

their own traditions and to the faith which the church celebrates.[3] Such trust almost implies an era marked by African Christianity.

Arguably, dialogue will be a defining aspect of African Christianity. This is obvious in nearly every report from the second African Synod. In fact, it is already evident in the synodal theme, "The Church in Africa in Service of Reconciliation, Justice and Peace," and in the accompanying scripture verse, "You are the salt of the earth. . . . You are the light of the world" (Mt 5:13–14). In a way, where there is hatred, injustice, and violence, the virtues of reconciliation, justice, and peace can only be established through dialogue. Moreover, in an intrinsically multireligious context such as Africa, the church has to be an equal partner in dialogue with others, and dialogue itself is indispensible. Even if an entirely Christian Africa were the goal, its active pursuit could not merit the church's limited resources. The African church will have to become "salt" that flavors and preserves an earth larger than itself, and "light" that illuminates a world vaster than itself.

In accordance with this synodal position, human beings can live together in community irrespective of their different creeds. Properly understood, faith does not uproot people from their communities but establishes them there as "salt" and "light" in the form of reconciled lives lived in justice and peace. Such faith does not advance facile tolerance but promotes vibrant communities in which life is genuinely shared.

Community implies shared meaning mediated by verbal communication and by other symbols imbued with cultural significance. In this sense a community owns its "language," its culture. It also follows that the choice of a language for whatever purpose is unavoidably political, as it may mark the boundaries of inclusion and exclusion. From this viewpoint I argue that the choice of a theological medium cannot be determined solely by a desire for doctrinal rectitude. In the context of dialogue the medium has to avoid turning the local church into a religious ghetto with a language exclusively its own. Failure in this matter will obstruct dialogue and even limit the platform for witness. Indeed Bishop Augustine Shao of Zanzibar reported at the synod that the language we use to describe those we are meant to be in dialogue with can impede the very dialogue we desire.[4]

An overview of the Eastern African Kiswahili language and context highlights this region's historical facility for dialogue and religious harmony. It is such localized exposure, I argue, that can preserve the region from foreign spiritual toxic waste, especially in its contemporary form of religious hatred and violence. More practically, the last part of this essay focuses on the pastoral significance of Kiswahili within its context. While remaining with the theme of language and dialogue, this part responds to recent scholarship that sees "problems" in the use of Kiswahili in theology, especially because of its historical association with Islam. Contrary to such views, I present Kiswahili within its context as an opportunity for the kind of dialogue envisioned by the second African Synod.

The Kiswahili Multireligious Heritage

Current global awareness of religious plurality and its popular perception as a problem can be directly linked to growing multiculturalism in Europe and America. The "climate of increased cultural and religious pluralism" noted by John Paul II in 2001 relates more to the West than to the East and the South.[5] That the church's concern coincides with a clamor for multiculturalism in Western secular societies lends credence to this observation. Today, there are more Muslims, Hindus, Buddhists, and atheists in the West than at any time in recent history. The West is thus confronted with different ways of perceiving reality that question, if not threaten, parochial ways that had been presumed synonymous with Christianity. It is this new Western context that explains the urgency of dialogue and dictates the form it must take there. However, where communities have been nothing but multicultural and multireligious, Western approaches to dialogue will be found wanting.

The Eastern African Kiswahili context is one example where communities have been multireligious for ages. The Eastern African coast has for centuries served as a doorway to external influence, especially from Persia and Oman. This influence became increasingly significant following the ninth century, when trade and Islam pushed more foreigners to settle in the region. Omani Arabs, who by the nineteenth century constituted the majority of immigrants, did not replace the languages of their hosts in Eastern Africa. Although they preserved the Qur'an in Arabic, they carried out commercial transactions in "the language of the coastal people," which is what *swahili* denotes. Accordingly, the role of Kiswahili as a socioeconomic language precedes its role as a religious medium and remains the major reason for its tenacious spread.

For its part, Kiswahili was enriched, not replaced, by the Arabic language. To date, the language remains entirely indigenous African in structure, with 65 percent of its stems belonging to the Bantu family of languages. Only about 20 percent of its words originate in Arabic. The remaining 15 percent can be traced to such diverse origins as Hindi, German, Portuguese, and English, in ascending order. Most of the Arabic roots are of some religious background, reflecting the fact that the Muslim faith is the most obvious Arabic patrimony in Eastern Africa. Recent borrowings from European languages tend to be more scientific than religious, suggesting that there is more scientific than religious interpenetration between Eastern Africa and the West, or that the West has nothing religiously novel to offer.

Thus, viewed before the nineteenth century, Kiswahili etymology proves an encounter between at least two religious traditions: Islam and indigenous African religion. It can even be argued that the African religions had the upper hand in this encounter, since they provided the bedrock on which

Islam was laid and contributed most of the vocabulary in which it was expressed. For, although Arabic remained the language of formal worship, few Muslims native to Eastern Africa became fluent in that language, just as did few Christian converts became fluent in Latin in later years. A significant piece of evidence for Africanized Islam in Eastern Africa remains its believers' ignorance of Arabic.[6] The imams who delivered their sermons in Kiswahili used religious terminology of a purely African background. Even where the terminology was originally Arabic, it had to be thoroughly *swahilized* before use. Despite the strictures against Qur'anic translation as discussed by Lamin Sanneh,[7] scholars have not failed to acknowledge the high standard of the meanings of the holy book rendered into Kiswahili. Imtiyaz Yusuf, for example, has analyzed "how the translation of the Qur'ân into a non-Arabic medium has led East African Muslims to adopt alien religious terminology without compromising the fundamentals of Islam"— a process he says made different religious world views "conceptually compatible."[8]

Such compatibility was facilitated by several factors. First, most early Arab migrants to East Africa were traders, not proselytizers. As such, they never wished for mass conversions, which could have entailed holding fellow Muslims in slavery. For local residents on the coast, becoming a Muslim came to symbolize status and security. Beyond the coast, however, only a few Muslim communities developed around trading centers like Tabora and Ujiji in the interior of Tanzania. Those from other parts who did not immediately face a similar social threat did not rush en masse to become Muslims.

In later years, as trade continued to take Kiswahili to the interior of East and Central Africa, Islam remained largely a coastal phenomenon. This also meant that the original Kiswahili-speaking community at the coast, now almost entirely Muslim, was losing its grip on this fast-spreading language. By the twentieth century the percentage in the total population that used Kiswahili had significantly shrunk. Scattered colonial records indicate that between 1913 and 1921, Muslims in Tanganyika (mainland Tanzania) numbered just above 7 percent of a total population of over four million, and that figure includes "a considerable number who merely observe certain rites and whose connection with Islam is quite superficial."[9] If Kiswahili was a *lingua franca* in the sense of a widely spread and commonly used second language, as the same records suggest, then the majority of its users must have been non-Muslims.

The context in which Kiswahili evolved before the mid-nineteenth century can thus be viewed as thoroughly multireligious. Kiswahili was never at any point wholly Islamic. Neither was it purely traditional African within the period under discussion. The language served the two religious traditions concurrently and thus sustained a broad community of meaning.

In the mid-nineteenth century Christianity was a newcomer in this community, as earlier European contacts made little or no religious impact; for example, the sixteenth-century Portuguese, with their emblematic Fort Jesus on coastal Kenya, left hardly a convert. Available evidence suggests that Christian missionaries landed in an environment that was relatively free of religious competition, animosity, or suspicion. Zanzibar, for example, which was by this time a largely Muslim society, was a missionary springboard. Most missionaries did their language training in Zanzibar before going to the interior. Indeed, it was the Muslim Sayyid Said—then ruler of the East African islands with suzerain authority over the coastal strip—who granted Rev. Ludwig Krapf permission to preach Christianity. The *sayyid* furnished the pioneering missionary with a letter addressed to all the governors of the coast, instructing them "to be kind to Dr. Krapf, who wishes to convert the world to God."[10] Again in the 1860s, Bishop Edward Steere expressed his wish to translate the Bible into Kiswahili. The bishop received much help in Zanzibar, not least from one Sheikh Abd al Aziz, who translated parts of the Arabic Psalter into "the best and purest Swahili."[11]

Such religious collaboration was not limited to Islam. Local authorities in the interior were just as welcoming to the Christian message. In 1878 Chief Mandara of Moshi on the slopes of Mt. Kilimanjaro had a letter written for him in Arabic, requesting a book and inviting members of the Church Missionary Society (CMS) at Frere Town near Mombasa to come to his territory and teach the children there. A copy of the Bible in Arabic was promptly sent to him.[12] Later in 1890 the French Holy Ghost Missionaries also sought to evangelize Kilimanjaro. On reaching the mountain, one of their immediate observations was the extent to which coastal Swahili culture, including Islam, was already established in the region. Yet it was Pfumba of Kilema, a local Chagga chief, who was their host. Through an indigenous ritual Pfumba granted the missionaries permission to stay and evangelize among his people. He said the Chagga knew God, but since they did not know well what God had said, the missionaries could stay and teach. To solemnize the deal, the chief and the missionaries became blood brothers through a ceremony presided over by an indigenous religious elder.[13]

These interreligious encounters were made possible by Kiswahili, either directly or indirectly through translations. The open-minded missionary did not have to stay long in the region to realize that Kiswahili was the obvious linguistic option for missionary work. After a brief visit to the CMS missions in Mombasa in the 1870s, Bishop Rayston of Mauritius wrote:

> Might I suggest here how very important it would be for the various societies who have agents in this part, to direct them to confer with those of other Missions as to translation, &c., in the Suaheli language? From all I can learn, there is no reason why the slightly differing dialectic shades of north and south should not be merged into one tongue, to be "fixed," as has often been the case, by Christian literature. This Suaheli seems so easy, so effective, and so widespread, that it might be an organ of speech to the very heart of the continent.[14]

It is sufficiently clear, therefore, that Christian missionaries studied Kiswahili not because they wanted to spread it, but because it was already known in the regions they wished to evangelize. However, the very nature of their work further promoted Kiswahili. Having had their language training in Zanzibar and their missions in the interior, they unwittingly popularized Kiunguja, the Zanzibari dialect of Kiswahili, later to be declared the standard written form. And besides running schools that instructed in Kiswahili, the missionaries translated the scriptures and prayer books as well as producing the first Kiswahili dictionaries and newspapers. This contribution is hugely significant. As they joined the already existing community of meaning, the missionaries actively added a Christian flavor to the Kiswahili vocabulary. As Christianity continued to be a day-to-day reality in this community, the context became even more multireligious.

As a language, therefore, Kiswahili evolved to serve relations between individuals and communities, making mutual understanding and enrichment possible within a context of religious pluralism. The language has not existed to serve exclusively one religious tradition. As Ali Mazrui and Pio Zirimu put it:

> Kiswahili is becoming less Islamic and more African because of its very success. Two trends have made it less Islamized. One is its evolution into an ecumenical language—a medium of worship and theology for Christianity and indigenous African religion, as well as Islam. Kiswahili is now the language of a Christian hymn, of an Islamic sermon, and of funeral rites in African traditional creeds. . . . The *ecumenicalization of Kiswahili* is part and parcel of its universalization.[15]

This multireligious aspect of Kiswahili is often obscured by an undue focus on its otherwise undisputed links with Arabic and Islam. The skewed focus has its roots in an initial failure to give sufficient attention to African religions. It is also shaped by debates among some missionaries and colonial administrators from their earliest days in Eastern Africa. For instance, unlike Bishop Rayston, whose favorable comment is cited above, Bishop Tucker in Uganda abhorred Kiswahili. "That there should be one 'language' for Central Africa is a consummation devoutly to be wished," said Tucker, "but God forbid that it should be Swahili." Preferring English to the object of his phobia, the bishop argued that "the one means the Bible and Protestant Christianity, the other Mohammedanism, sensuality, moral and physical degradation and ruin."[16] Like Tucker, some German officials described Kiswahili as "irredeemably mixed with Islam" and campaigned for the obstruction of their joint penetration.[17] These concerns culminated in changing written Kiswahili from Arabic to Roman script.

In some quarters Christians have a lingering fear of a Kiswahili-Islam link, probably best articulated by Ralph Tanner.[18] By failing to celebrate diversity, this fear paralyzes dialogue. The very thriving of Kiswahili amid such reservations redounds to its cosmopolitan credentials, especially as marked by absence of xenophobia and its openness to desirable foreign material. As language and context, therefore, Kiswahili bears witness to localized historical receptivity to multiple religions. Here dialogue must not be approached as if between those who belong and those seeking to belong, as might be the case in the West, but between members of one community of meaning who hold in trust the same multicultural and multireligious heritage. In this context the role of dialogue is not so much to create a community of mutual understanding, but, like salt, to add desirable flavor to human relationships in an already existing community and so preserve it from current theologies of hatred and violence.

A Pastoral Case for Theologizing in Kiswahili

It would be idle to deny that Christian theologizing, like Christianity itself, retains an air of newness in the Kiswahili context just described. There is still significant ground to be covered before Christianity can become fully inculturated into this multireligious region. In the first steps toward that full inculturation members of the church will have to deepen their faith and, by so doing, afford the church the evangelization it needs before it can more credibly evangelize the Kiswahili world.[19]

The question of credibility is important in this region where a significant number of people are not Christians, not so much because they have not heard the Christian message, but because they have not decided to become followers of Christ. To these spectators Jesus Christ appears to be "an answer to questions a white man would ask, the solution of problems and needs a *mzungu* feels."[20] This attitude can only be reversed by a lively atmosphere where local questions, especially those based on experiences within multireligious communities, are brought to bear on theological discourse. For, however lofty our theological concepts may be, if they are radically contradicted by lived experiences, they will be disregarded by the courageous or simply kept superstitiously by the fearful. God reveals God's self through the language of experience. As Karl Rahner reminds us, "the real argument against Christianity is the experience of life, this experience of darkness." Any serious theologian must pay attention to this real argument. And when experience constitutes "the proof of the contrary," theologians must translate it into "the argument of Christianity."[21]

In Africa, questions regarding "the experience of life" are many: What does it mean to be childless in a context where children are almost the only security one can have in old age? What does it mean to be a nuclear family in a context where, as the experience of HIV/AIDS has harshly revealed, the extended family remains the surest source of support in times of need? What does it mean to be a woman convert to Christianity from a successful, supportive, and happy polygamous union that has lasted for years? Or what does it mean to view one's good relatives who have gone on to the afterlife as pitiable souls perpetually in need of prayers of the living, rather than as good ancestors on whose intervention the living can depend? Is the Christian heaven accessible to men and women of ordinary flesh and blood? Clearly, most Africans have found it difficult to reconcile themselves with the radical divide between the living and the dead that Christianity introduces into their world view even as it confirms their robust indigenous faith in the afterlife.

These and similar concerns place dialogue first and foremost within the church itself, making it an intra-church exercise. Such experiential questions must inform theological discourse in a non-patronizing way. The African is not the eighteenth-century "noble savage" whose imagined superior mores fascinated those sick of their stiffening civilizations. If this is to become an era marked by African Christianity, African experiences must never be treated as specimens to be experimented on in foreign theological laboratories, but as subjects for a lively discourse in which those who own the experiences can fully participate. Ultimately, Africans must choose for themselves which of their best traditions to preserve, which desirable values to accept from the outside, and which foreign "spiritual toxic waste" to reject. Here lies the link with my linguistic concerns: it is hard to see how this kind of participatory discourse can be promoted within the context described above without actually using Kiswahili as its medium. A discourse taking place in a foreign language will necessarily become elitist, and its resultant theology might even alienate the universal church from its local flock.

More positively, in seeking reconciliation, justice, and peace, the African church must ensure that its flock does not simply consume but also produces theology. This means empowering even the least member of the community so that his or her most basic experiences and reflections can influence theological—and indeed doctrinal—trends. This does not mean turning every Christian into a professional theologian. Rather, it is to reverse a trend that characterized early African scholarship, theology included, that sought to justify African experiences and concepts by citing equivalents in the West.

At the very least, professional theologians in the suggested reverse trend will perform three tasks. First, they will help members of the local church to contemplate "ever more deeply, under the guidance of the Holy Spirit," the contents of the faith of the church, and thus empower them to articulate its reasonableness to inquiring neighbors.[22] This, in a way, is a service theologians in Africa will render to the universal church, as they help to communicate its faith with increasing clarity. And if the targeted flock is Kiswahili speaking, it is only reasonable that such a service be rendered in Kiswahili.

This first task may entail some translation and all the problems that go with it. But these problems should be faced as challenges, not debilitating obstacles. Happily, not everything would have to be translated. Not all members of the Kiswahili-speaking faithful will want to read the *Summa Theologiae* at all, let alone to read it in Kiswahili. And professional theologians writing in Kiswahili are likely to read the *Summa* in its original Latin. A professional theologian who practices in Kiswahili will have to be multilingual, conversant with English, French, German, Greek, Hausa, Hebrew, Kimasai, Kirundi, Latin, Luo, Zulu—the only limit being the fatality of Babel. Monolingual theologians, be they in Tanzania, England, or Russia, are tragically limited in scope. They are doubly handicapped in their ability to take part in a wider, all-embracing discourse and in their practical usefulness to local communities.

The second theological task is to articulate local experiences in a language at once representative of those who own the experiences and comprehensible to the universal church. The articulation will be representative if it is accurate, especially if those whose experiences it claims to express can have access to what is said of them, confirming or even rejecting it, as the case may require. It is in this sense that the ordinary man and woman will actively participate in the making of theology. Obviously, the use of a local language remains critical. Then, that same articulation will be comprehensible to the rest if, after a careful consideration of the faith, a non-adversarial proposition is presented as an offering to the universal church.[23] In this way the professional theologian will have once again rendered invaluable service to the church, especially to the Magisterium, which, "benefiting from the work of theologians, . . . refutes objections to and distortions of the faith and promotes, with the authority received from Jesus Christ, new and deeper comprehension, clarification, and application of revealed doctrine."[24]

The third task is to consider the cost of producing theology. In Africa the purchase of books "is not given high priority when individual and family incomes are low and affected by inflation," which is Ralph Tanner's irrefutable argument against theology in Kiswahili.[25] Publishing in Kiswahili can hardly guarantee a theologian maize meal and *sukuma-wiki* (a vegetable) because the target readership is small and poor. For this reason local theologians are likely to publish in languages of bigger audiences with available cash for books. Valid though this practice may be, it carries with it a temptation to respond to Western curiosity about Africa, which may diminish the care required to represent African experiences accurately in the manner suggested above. Moreover, the poor deserve the attention of the church as well, including the services of its theologians. It is for local churches to lay bare the pastoral need and motivate theologians to publish in the languages of their flock. Special funds should be established to support authors and subsidize publications. It may be time that the church in Africa looks to India for lessons on how to lower publication costs.

Conclusion

The audacity of the Wanyamwezi in rejecting what they judged ungodly is a trait Africans are being urged to recover. Such boldness will be a useful tool in making Christianity in Africa even more African. The theme of the second African Synod makes it clear that African Christianity must be marked by reconciled lives flavored by justice and preserved in peace within multireligious communities. By focusing on the historical multireligious disposition of the Eastern African Kiswahili context, it is clear that there are existing cultural and linguistic resources relevant for the realization of the synod's dialogic objectives. At the heart of such resources is a community of meaning in which language and other cultural symbols, which are shared among practitioners of African religions, Muslims, and Christians, facilitate communication across the creedal divide. Kiswahili offers such a linguistic possibility in Eastern Africa, which makes its use in theology paramount.

In an effort to make more practical proposals, the second part of this essay focused on dialogue within the church. In Eastern Africa the pastoral need for an empowering intra-church dialogue further strengthens the case for theology in Kiswahili. Such a contextualized theology would enable the faithful actively to take part in discourses that reflect on their experiences. In this way ordinary Christians will become agents of dialogue at the grassroots—where it is most urgently needed. They will thus be empowered to give a confident account of their faith within their multireligious community and in a language known to their neighbors. In this theological enterprise the role of professional theologians remains indispensable: they explain the faith of the church to the faithful; they articulate grassroots experiences and liaise with broader theological discourses; and by transforming compelling experience into the Christian argument, they help the Magisterium to deepen the comprehension, clarification, and application of doctrine on the basis of specifically African experiences. Thus will the dialogue envisioned by the second African Synod become all embracing and more fruitful.

Notes

[1] The Wanyamwezi (members of the Nyamwezi ethnic community in western Tanzania) were famous as porters in the nineteenth-century Eastern Africa long-distance trade.

[2] A. Le Roy, "The Religions of Primitive Races," in *Lectures on the History of Religions,* 5 vols. (London: Catholic Truth Society, 1911), 5:31, emphasis in original.

[3] John Paul II, Post-Synodal Apostolic Exhortation, *Ecclesia in Africa* (Yaoundé, September 14, 1995), no. 48.

[4] "Intervention of Mons. Augustine Shao, Bishop of Zanzibar (Tanzania)," *Vatican Radio* (2009). Available on the radiovaticana.org website.

[5] John Paul II, Apostolic Letter *Novo Millennio Ineunte* (January 6, 2001), no. 55.

[6] See Abdulaziz Y. Lodhi and David Westerlund, "African Islam in Tanzania," *Islam for Today* (1997). Available on the islamfortoday.com website.

[7] Lamin Sanneh, *Translating the Message: The Missionary Impact on Culture* (Maryknoll, NY: Orbis Books, 1989), 211–38.

[8] Imtiyaz Yusuf, "An Analysis of Swahili Exegesis of Sûrat al-Shams in Shaykh Abdullah Saleh al-Farsy's 'Qurani Takatifu,'" *Journal of Religion in Africa* 22, no. 4 (1992): 352, 360.

[9] Tanganyika Government, *Tanganyika Reports* (London: Her Majesty's Stationery Office, 1920–1960), (1920), 30, and (1921), 7.

[10] Ludwig Krapf, *A Dictionary of the Suahili Language* (London: Trübner and Co., 1882), vii.

[11] Edward Steere, ed., *A Handbook of the Swahili Language as Spoken at Zanzibar* (London: Society for Promoting Christian Knowledge, 1917), vii–viii.

[12] "Invitation from the King of Chagga," *Church Missionary Intelligencer—New Series* 3 (1878): 448–49.

[13] A. Le Roy, *Au Kilima-Ndjaro: Histoire de la fondation d'une mission catholique en Afrique orientale* (Paris: Procure Générale des PP. du Saint-Esprit, 1928), 274, 186, 186–92.

[14] "Bishop Royston at Frere Town," *Church Missionary Intelligencer—New Series* 3 (1878): 717.

[15] Ali A. Mazrui and Pio Zirimu, "Secularization of Afro-Islamic Language: Church, State, and Marketplace in the Spread of Kiswahili," *Journal of Islamic Studies* 1 (1990): 26, emphasis in original.

[16] Alfred R. Tucker, *Eighteen Years in Uganda and East Africa*, 2 vols. (London: Edward Arnold, 1908), 2:216.

[17] Marcia Wright, *German Missions in Tanganyika, 1891–1941: Lutherans and Moravians in the Southern Highlands* (Oxford: Clarendon Press, 1971), 113.

[18] See Ralph Tanner, "Theology in Swahili: Problems in Developing an Ecumenical Language," *Studia Missionalia* 54 (2005): 195–211.

[19] See *Ecclesia in Africa*, no. 47.

[20] M. D. Odinga, "Decolonizing the Church in East Africa," *East African Journal* 4, no. 4 (1967): 12. *Mzungu* is Kiswahili for white man/woman.

[21] Karl Rahner, "Thoughts on the Possibility of Belief Today," *Theological Investigations* 5, trans. Karl-H. Kruger (Baltimore: Helicon, 1966), 5–6.

[22] Congregation for the Doctrine of the Faith, *Instruction on the Ecclesial Vocation of the Theologian* (24 May 1990), no. 5.

[23] Ibid., no. 11.

[24] Ibid., no. 21.

[25] Tanner, "Theology in Swahili," 203–4, and more generally, Ralph Tanner, "Economic Factors in East African Ecumenism," *Journal of Ecumenical Studies* 10, no. 1 (1973): 51–69.

4

The Word of God
as Transformative Power
in Reconciling African Christians

PAUL BÉRÉ

At the cusp of the first African Synod in 1994 the Rwandan genocide erupted. Among those invited to speak at the second African Synod in 2009 was a Rwandese victim of the genocide, Sr. Geneviève Uwamariya. She told the synod a moving story on reconciliation; it sounded like a song of redemption. A Catholic women's association named Dames de la Divine Miséricorde (Ladies of Divine Mercy), devoted to helping killers and (escaped) victims meet and engage in a process of healing, arranged for Sr. Uwamariya to meet the person who confessed to having killed her father. That person had been so close to the family that she could hardly believe her eyes and her ears. Yet she was blessed with words of reconciliation as she spontaneously responded to the situation, saying to the killer, "You are and will remain my brother!"

Looking back on her experience of reconciliation and forgiveness, Sr. Uwamariya appealed to church leaders to take more seriously the mission of reconciliation:

From this experience I drew the conclusion that reconciliation is not so much bringing together two people or two groups in conflict. Rather, it means re-establishing each into love and letting inner healing take place, which then leads to mutual liberation. And here is the importance of the Church in our countries since her mission is to give The Word: a Word that heals, sets free and reconciles.[1]

The last words quoted above caught my attention and prompted me to explore the link between the Word of God and reconciliation in the African world view.[2] My principal question may be framed as follows: How can the Word of God be effective as a transformative power that operates on the

48

wounded heart of an African Christian in particular? The scope of the inquiry is to work out the conceptual yet effective relation between the Word of God and reconciliation, so as to facilitate the process of restoring broken relationships. In order to answer the question, I would first like to state briefly the centrality of the *word* in both scripture and Africa. Second, I will discuss two complex notions: on the one hand, the Word of God in our theological understanding and, on the other, reconciliation from an African perspective. From there, I will explore ways of conveying the Word of God to the world of the African through a genuine process of reconciliation that takes an African route.

Restating the Centrality of the "Word" Both in Scriptures and in Africa

The Word of God is a metaphor that adopts the most fundamental element of Israel's anthropology to portray God's action and self-revelation in history. Indeed, through the Word, God created the universe (Gn 1), communicated God's will through the prophets (Heb 1:1), as we can hear in the formula: "Thus says the Lord." And according to Isaiah, God's Word that goes out from God does not return empty; it must fulfill its mission (see Is 55:11). Any Word from God aims at keeping alive with integrity the relationships within the covenant community. And with such an understanding, it appears clearly that the performative or effective character of the Word of God not only reveals Israel's conception of words, but it also captures the African use of the word.[3]

Several studies have been done to demonstrate the centrality of the word in (many) African societies.[4] Like blood in the human body, the African community is nurtured in all its components by the word: "the power of the word, spoken or unspoken, the word as dramatized in dance or mime or symbolized in art; the 'word' understood as action or 'behavior.'"[5] The palaver, the well-known African practice of communication, conversation, and dialogue, stems from the Portuguese *palavra*, which means "word."[6] This genre of conversation has already been classified according to structure, function, and meaning, and has been researched in various works.[7] According to Eboussi Boulaga, the palaver functions as a "logotherapy."[8] Bénézet Bujo shares a similar view: "Particular importance attaches here to awareness of the function of the word, for otherwise one cannot understand completely the African palaver praxis."[9]

Bujo goes on to draw an interesting parallel between the biblical world and the African world view: "People in Africa feel very close to the biblical message: the word is understood in the Bible as genuinely accomplishing what it was sent to do."[10] For him, "people in the palaver are like ruminants: they must again chew a word that was received, eaten, or drunk long ago, before it can be transformed into flesh and blood. This means that the word of the individual is tested, so that the entire community can either confirm or reject it based on whether it is good or life-giving."[11]

To sum up, it is important to keep in mind that "the African palaver aims at creating, strengthening or restoring relationships for the sake of 'the fullness' of life of the community through fellowship among all three dimensions of the community [the living, the dead, and those not yet born]."[12]

Despite the fact that the word functions as a ground common to the biblical world and to Africa, the former has some specific tones that must be highlighted in order to explore and open new paths for African Christians to tread on and to reach a deep and genuine reconciliation made possible by the divine Word. Indeed, when human words wreak havoc on the community and individuals, conflicts signal brokenness and the need for reconciliation.

Unfolding Two Complex Notions:
The Word of God and Reconciliation

It is not uncommon to assume that *Word of God* refers to nothing other than the Holy Bible. Similarly, the term *reconciliation,* as used during the African Synod, draws primarily on the biblical notion and barely echoes the African understanding of the term. One may say that the task is left to theologians to bridge the gap, creating avenues for the powerful message of the Word of God to fertilize the listening heart of the African person.[13] Such an anthropological endeavor should involve the whole person and integrate all aspects of what it means to be an African. Therefore, the process of reconciliation, which is the main concern of this essay, needs some rethinking. If the Word of God is expected to fulfill its transformative mission, room should be made within our approach to reconciliation to incorporate its anthropological and societal aspects.

The Word of God: A Multichannel Metaphor

To what does the expression *Word of God* actually refer? As noted above, it is a metaphor. Simply equating it with the Bible narrows its scope and pays little attention to the channel through which God continuously speaks to us. While there is a direct historical link between the second African Synod (2009) and the first African Synod (1994), participants at the 2009 synod also correlated use of the "Word of God" with the Synod on the Word of God in the Life and the Mission of the Church (2008), which outlined multiple ways in which God speaks to humanity. In the understanding of this synod, Christians must learn to recognize, listen to, and obey God as God speaks to us through five "channels."

1. *God speaks through the cosmos.* Galileo Galilei (1564–1642) once said that "nature is a book written in the language of mathematics." Those

who are educated in this science can read it. The same can be said of God in relation to the cosmos. The whole creation can be compared "to an immense page opened up before all of humanity, in which a message from the Creator can be read":

> The heavens are telling the glory of God; and the firmament proclaims his handiwork. Day to day pours forth speech, and night to night declares knowledge. There is no speech, nor are there words; their voice is not heard; yet their voice goes out through all the earth, and their words to the end of the world. In the heavens he has set a tent for the sun, which comes out like a bridegroom from his wedding canopy, and like a strong man runs its course with joy. (Ps 19:1–5. NRSV)[14]

Accordingly, Paul can write to the Romans: "Ever since the creation of the world his eternal power and divine nature, invisible though they are, have been understood and seen through the things he has made" (Rom 1:20).

2. *God speaks through historical events.* According to Norman Frye, the Bible is "*Le Grand Code.*"[15] This phrasing may not suffice to point out that it tells stories through which we gain access to Israel's reading of history, whereby the experience of salvation is revealed: "I have observed the misery of my people. . . . I have heard their cry on account of their taskmasters. Indeed, I know their sufferings, and I have come down to deliver them . . . and to bring them up out of that land to a good and broad land, a land flowing with milk and honey" (Ex 3:7–8). The divine is therefore present in human events that, through the action of the Lord of history, are inserted in the greater plan of salvation for "everyone to be saved and to come to the knowledge of the truth" (1 Tm 2:4).[16] God therefore speaks to us in words and in deeds.[17]

3. *God speaks through the scriptures.* The metaphorical nature of the Word of God is manifest in its written form. Known in the New Testament as *Graphè* or *Graphai*, the scriptures bear witness to the divine communication with the people of Israel. They convey God's thoughts wrapped in human words, with their socio-historical limits, in the canonical and literary frame.[18] Although the scriptures are the regulating principle that cannot in turn be regulated by anything else, the Word of God exceeds the written word, as I have indicated above. Furthermore, Christianity cannot be reduced to being the religion of the "Book," for at the center one encounters the person of Jesus Christ.

4. *God speaks in Jesus Christ.* As the Prologue of the Gospel of John marvelously proclaims, Jesus is "the Word made flesh" (1:14). "This is why our faith is not only centered on a book, but on a word of God made flesh, man and history."[19] Jesus is no longer the messenger, but the message itself. Jesus is the revelation of God in what he says (Jn 1:11) and is (Jn 12:45). Thus, Jesus Christ becomes for us "the image of the invisible God, the first-born of all creation" (Col 1:15). This faith statement lays before us, disciples

of Jesus, the same challenge Jesus himself had to live up to, namely, that we too must live a life that becomes the revelation of the person of the invisible Jesus (see Jn 1:18: the Son revealed the Father whom nobody ever saw). Therefore, as disciples, we are to make visible the face of Jesus (see Jn 8:1ff.; Lk 23:34ff.).

5. *God speaks through human conscience.* A longstanding tradition holds that God speaks to each person through his or her conscience. For the Second Vatican Council, "his conscience is man's most secret core, and his sanctuary. There he is alone with God whose *voice* echoes in his depths" (*Gaudium et Spes*, no. 16, emphasis added). Elsewhere, it affirms that in "all his activity a man is bound to follow his conscience in order that he may come to God, the end and purpose of life. It follows that he is not to be forced to act in a manner contrary to his conscience, nor, on the other hand, is he to be restrained from acting in accordance with his conscience, especially in matters religious" (*Dignitatis Humanae*, no. 3). I am aware of the unresolved question on the origin of this inner voice. For the purposes of analysis here, I would put it in God.

The ongoing considerations raise a few questions that we will have to deal with: What does it mean concretely to listen to God when, as we have noticed, God speaks through various channels? How can we let ourselves be reconciled with God who comes to us in many ways? These puzzling questions become more complex when we realize that for an African, the notion of reconciliation is not as simple as it may appear.

The African Notion of Reconciliation

As mentioned above, the first and foremost source of reconciliation emphasized by the African Synod is God. That is why the synod called "on all the people of Africa": "'*We beseech you on behalf of Christ, be reconciled to God*' (2 Cor 5:20). In other words, we call on all to allow themselves to be reconciled to God. It is this that opens the way to genuine reconciliation among persons."[20] What the synod pointed out represents the most important end of a continuum, for the concept of reconciliation in Africa involves many facets. An integral reconciliation includes both the invisible (God, spirits, ancestors) and the visible worlds (community of the living, the cosmos).[21] Therefore, in the mind of African Christians, reconciliation with God through the sacrament of penance necessarily entails other components to be effective and to bring back harmony and wholeness.

1. *Reconciliation with oneself.* It is often argued that reconciliation in Africa lacks a personal dimension because of the heavy emphasis on community. This position misses the point. In fact, "the well-being of the person is the criterion for good. The person is of ultimate significance. In African belief and practice the person is sacred and significant."[22] A close look at reconciliation rites reveals that the process of restoring harmony starts from within oneself; the heart must be engaged and pure, and that means that the

performance of the rite requires compliance with certain ethical demands. This can be understood from the vantage point of the restoration of life as the central concept of African Religion. Yet being at peace within oneself, though very important, is but the beginning of the process of regaining full communion and harmony. The person must go further and become reconciled with both the visible and the invisible worlds to which he or she already belongs.

2. *Reconciliation with the visible world.* In the African world view the individual is never isolated from the community. Considered in this context, reconciliation naturally includes a communal act or rite such as eating together or sharing a drink. The scope of this community varies: family (husband, wife, and children), extended family, clan, village, and so on. A Xhosa proverb says *umuntu ngununtu ngabantu*—a person is a person through other persons. We find a similar proverb among the Moose people of Burkina Faso: *Ninsaal ya a to tiim*—a person is another person's remedy. John W. De Gruchy comments on the Xhosa proverb, saying: "The emphasis is on human sociality, on inter-personal relations, on the need which each person has for others in order to be herself or himself. This is the root of African humanism, and it relates well to biblical anthropology, Trinitarian theology, and the idea of Christian community."[23] As Desmond Tutu puts it, "In the spirit of *ubuntu*, the central concern is the healing of breaches, the redressing of imbalances, the restoration of broken relationships, a seeking to rehabilitate both the victim and the perpetrator, who should be given the opportunity to be integrated into the community he has injured by this offence."[24] Sr. Geneviève Uwamariya's powerful example, noted at the beginning of this essay, suffices to illustrate what both authors intend.

Furthermore, the physical environment (cosmos) in which the community lives is never conceived as completely external to a person's life. Nature, according to a Senegalese poet, is the dwelling place of the dead, or rather, the "living dead." The Moose people of Burkina Faso call the earth *D Ma a Tenga*, which means "our Mother Earth," for she nourishes and protects all living beings. In the African religious world view, Earth serves as the habitat of our ancestors and the spirits of the invisible world as well.[25]

3. *Reconciliation with the invisible world.* Since in African indigenous religions God is the source of life, God must be included in the process of reconciliation that aims at restoring life in its fullness by neutralizing within the person(s) that which impedes life from flourishing. This deeply rooted conviction views all living beings (human beings, animals, and nature) as continuously receiving life from God. Like communicating vessels, they are all interconnected for good and for bad. So "the community's ancestors and other spiritual forces are directly involved in the clan's [reconciling] activities."[26]

The above analysis has shown that the two key notions, namely, the Word of God and reconciliation, are complex and should be understood analytically before trying to correlate them. Thus the metaphor Word of

God has a fivefold understanding and must be held together: God speaks through the cosmos, historical events, in scriptures, in Jesus Christ (the Son of God), and in one's conscience. Viewed from an African perspective, reconciliation is understood as a process of restoring harmony, which is necessary for life to flow; it starts from oneself, but it involves the whole community and the cosmos (visible world), as well as God, the ancestors, and the nonhuman spirits (invisible world). Considered in the context of liturgical rites, the African understanding shows the incompleteness of the church's sacrament of penance as a rite of reconciliation, and, on the other hand, the difficulty of bringing all the components of the metaphor Word of God—which means God speaks!—within the process of reconciliation in order to make it effective. Bridging this gap is a task worth attempting.

How Can the Word of God Operate to Reconcile?

The primary aim of this section is to correlate the various components of the two notions discussed in the preceding sections. Genuine reconciliation starts from within, from the heart. What is usually referred to as the heart can be understood as a microcosm wherein reconciliation takes places and involves the community, the ancestors and the spirits, nature, and God.[27] I suggest five steps to be conceived as necessary components of the process:

1. *God speaks to the penitent's conscience.* Here reconciliation takes place in the encounter between God and self. This fundamental step is what the church has oftentimes emphasized. It takes place where no one else has access, in the inner sanctuary of the person's conscience. For this reason the Baluba of the Democratic Republic of Congo say, *Munda mwa mukwenu kemwelwa kuboko, nansya ulele nandi butanda bumo!* (None may put his arm into his neighbor's inside, not even when he shares his bed).[28] And when God enters that sanctuary, nobody knows when and how it happens. Nevertheless, it depends on us. Many Christians still need to grow in understanding how to listen to their conscience, how to discern right from wrong, especially when it comes to very delicate and subtle situations (pandemic corruption for instance). Formation of a Christian conscience should therefore be thought of as an integral part of the process of reconciliation, so that contrition in the sacramental rite of penance may be effective. This requirement is hardly fulfilled in the present practice of a quick examination of conscience or a shallow preparation before the celebration of the sacrament of reconciliation, usually in Holy Week.

2. *God speaks to the penitent in Jesus Christ.* When the person becomes aware of his or her need to move forward and get rid of his or her sin, then comes the encounter with Jesus Christ through the minister in the sacrament of penance. If the minister is to facilitate true encounter with Christ, this moment should exemplify the way Jesus welcomed sinners in the gospels. Therefore, the minister of reconciliation must offer an example of a

personal and continuous encounter with Jesus in order to model Christ's compassionate response to the penitent. In other words, a minister is to be a listener of the Word of God, a person who radiates the goodness, love, and mercy of God, thus becoming a living sacrament of God's kindness (see Lk 15:11ff.). The sacrament then effects the expected healing in the penitent's heart. The gospel narratives should not be heard as outdated stories; rather, they should be confirmed by the actual life experience of the faithful. The person of the minister should bear the presence of Jesus Christ the Word, who communicates with the penitent through the words of the rite and brings about healing.

3. *God speaks to the penitent through historical events.* The first African Synod advocated the creation of Small Christian Communities (SCCs) as a way of coping with the challenge posed by large parish communities in which people feel the leaders (parish priests) do not have enough time for them. If we think of the SCCs as our Christian clan, then one can imagine the SCC as a place where spiritual guidance is received. There Christians learn to listen to the voice of God through the unfolding historical events of their lives. Carefully chosen wise women and men, whom we might call elders, may exercise the ministry of reconciliation. These elders can help the penitent in his or her effort to repair the brokenness (even in an invisible way) his or her sin provoked. At this level God speaking through history can be the visible part of the process with the help of the elders of the community, the SCC.

4. *God speaks to the penitent through scriptures.* In an ordinary fashion any act of reconciliation should lead to the healing of all the relationships involved. Healing the relationship with the ancestors can be considered through the Word that they have handed down to us. Here, the penitent should commit himself or herself to listening to the Word of God by reading and/or hearing the Bible. The Western conception of the Bible as Holy Writ wiped out its understanding as *Miqra'ôt Gedoloth*, often translated as "the Great Scriptures" instead of "the Great Proclamations." With the Psalmist, he or she must confess: "I will open my mouth. . . . I will utter . . . things that we have heard and known, that our ancestors have told us. We will not hide them from their children; we will tell to the coming generation the glorious deeds of the Lord, and his might, and the wonders that he has done" (Ps 78:2–4). By so doing the penitent proclaims the glory of the Lord and reclaims his or her place within the community of the faithful.

5. *God speaks to the penitent through the cosmos.* Our African ancestors taught us that whatever we do can disturb the cosmos. Although often erroneously considered fetishist and animist, African indigenous religions promote respect for creation. This attention to the *life* of the cosmos evokes the words of Paul to the Romans: "We know that the whole creation has been groaning in labor pains until now; and not only the creation, but we ourselves, who have the first fruits of the Spirit, groan inwardly while we wait for adoption, the redemption of our bodies" (Rom 8:22–23).

For Paul, therefore, sin has permeated the whole fabric of God's creation. It is Adam's sinfulness that we continue to brew in our own sinful
actions. The cosmos suffers from the sin of the world and awaits liberation
from Christ. We can take part in that process of liberation by protecting the
environment as a way of repairing the damage our sin has caused: planting
or watering a tree, for example. Each time we feel we have broken our
relation with Mother Earth by a sinful action, imagine that we decide to
plant an indigenous tree, for instance. What would be the outcome of such
an idea in this age of global warming?

Conclusion

This essay has focused on the two challenges that the second African Synod
has laid before Christians: first, the link between the African Synod and the
Synod on the Word of God; and second, the power of the Word of God in
bringing about reconciliation. An examination of the complexity of both
notions—the Word of God and reconciliation—in the African indigenous
religions suggests five steps in the process of reconciliation using the fivefold understanding of the Word of God.

In all five steps the various relations of the penitent (God, ancestors/
spirits, community, cosmos, self) are addressed by God, who speaks to the
person's conscience, through the historical events of his or her life, through
Jesus seen in the actions of the minister (sacrament), through scripture, and
through the cosmos. The most central element that runs through these steps
remains the Word. Reconciliation therefore takes on a new meaning and
significance as a form of a conversation with or a celebration of the Word
at various levels.

The importance of the Word in African cultures makes it a tool that can
properly foster a genuine reconciliation both within and outside of individuals and communities.[29] The Word is performative: it destroys if one
curses; it creates if one blesses. An experience of reconciliation rooted in the
living Word of God re-creates in the penitent what has been damaged within
the person, and through him or her it repairs, restores, renews, and re-
creates the entire community, both living and dead members, visible and
invisible ones.

Notes

[1] "De cette expérience, je déduis que la réconciliation n'est pas tellement vouloir
ramener ensemble deux personnes ou deux groupes en conflit. Il s'agit plutôt de
rétablir chacun dans l'amour et de laisser advenir la guérison intérieure qui permet
la libération mutuelle. Et c'est ici l'importance de l'Eglise dans nos pays puisqu'elle
a pour mission d'offrir La Parole: une Parole qui guérit, libère et réconcilie."

[2] The fact that the second Synod for Africa (October 2009) comes after the Synod on the Word of God in the Life and the Mission of the Church (October 2008) makes the link even more compelling.

[3] To avoid any misunderstanding, I would like to alert the reader to the risk of equating the "word" with orality, or opposing it with literacy. Biblical Israel had a written legacy, and yet it functioned as a word culture. This means that unless the written is read out (see De 31:24ff.; Neh 8), it does not come to life; it may even sink into oblivion (2 Kgs 22:8ff.). For recent discussions, see, for example, Simon Battestini, ed., *De l'écrit africain à l'oral: Le phénomène graphique africain* (Paris: L'Harmattan, 2006); Paulin J. Hountondji, ed., *L'ancien et le nouveau: La production du savoir dans l'Afrique d'aujourd'hui* (Porto-Novo: Centre Africain des Hautes Etudes, 2009).

[4] See, for example, Marcel Griaule, *Dieu d'eau: Entretiens avec Ogotemmêli* (Paris: Editions du Chêne, 1948); Dominique Zahan, *La dialectique du verbe chez les Bambara* (Paris: Editions Mouton, 1963).

[5] Laurenti Magesa, *Anatomy of Inculturation: Transforming the Church in Africa* (Maryknoll, NY: Orbis Books, 2004), 161.

[6] See Jean-Godefroy Bidima, *La Palabre: Une jurisdiction de la parole* (Paris: Michalon, 1997), 9–10.

[7] See Fabien Eboussi Boulaga, *Les conférences nationales souveraines: Une affaire à suivre*, 2nd ed. (Paris: Karthala, 2009 [1992]), 154–56. For a select bibliography, see Bidima, *La Palabre*, 125–26; in connection with the latter, see an elaboration of the "palaver in the praxis of healing" in Bénézet Bujo, *Foundations of an African Ethic: Beyond the Universal Claims of Western Morality* (Nairobi: Paulines Publications, 2003), 68–88, 184–94.

[8] Eboussi Boulaga, *Les conférences nationales souveraines*, 154.

[9] Bujo, *Foundations of an African Ethic*, 184.

[10] Ibid.

[11] Ibid., 186.

[12] Magesa, *Anatomy of Inculturation*, 161.

[13] Bujo compares listening to fertilization: "Special emphasis is laid on the resemblance between the ear and the sexual organs, so that this may be transformed into life, so the ear receives the word which is equipped with seed, in order to transform it into life" (Bujo, *Foundations of an African Ethic*, 185).

[14] See Synod on the Word of God, *Message*, 1.

[15] Northrop Frye, *Le Grand Code: La Bible et la littérature* (Paris: Seuil, 1984).

[16] Synod on the Word of God, *Message*, 2.

[17] See Laurent Monsengwo Pasinya, "Le cadre littéraire de Genèse 1," *Biblica* 57 (1976): 225–41.

[18] Synod on the Word of God, *Message*, 3.

[19] Ibid.

[20] Synod for Africa, *Message*, 8, italics in original.

[21] See Pete Henriot, "The Second African Synod: Challenge and Help for Our Future Church," *Hekima Review* 41 (2009): 12. One might be tempted to add neighbor, spirits, and so on, but for the purposes of this essay I will stick to the basic elements.

[22] David W. Shenk, *Justice, Reconciliation, and Peace in Africa*, 2nd ed. (Nairobi: Uzima Press, 1997), 12.

[23] John W. De Gruchy, *Christianity and Democracy: A Theology for a Just World Order* (Cape Town: David Philip, 1995), 191; see Ngindu Mushete: "Devenir une personne humaine, dans la perspective africaine, c'est devenir un nœud de relations interpersonnelles, soudant son sujet à la communauté humaine et à la totalité du cosmos" ("Eléments d'une spiritualité libératrice," in *Spiritualité et libération en Afrique*, ed. Engelbert Mveng [Paris: L'Harmattan, 1987], 56).

[24] Desmond Tutu, *No Future without Forgiveness* (New York: Doubleday, 2000), 54–55.

[25] See Birago Diop, "Souffles" (poem). www.site-magister.com/orphee.htm.

[26] Laurenti Magesa, "Theology of Democracy," in *Democracy and Reconciliation: A Challenge for African Christianity*, ed. Laurenti Magesa and Zablon Nthamburi (Nairobi: Acton Publishers, 1999), 124.

[27] Heart *(ib)* plays a symbolic and significant role in the most ancient form of African indigenous religions, that is, Egyptian mythologies. See Théophile Obenga, *La philosophie africaine de la période pharaonique 2780–330 avant notre ère* (Paris: L'Harmattan, 1990), 169–85.

[28] Quoted in Shenk, *Justice, Reconciliation, and Peace in Africa*, 16.

[29] See Boulaga, *Les conférences nationales*, 147–61.

5

Small Christian Communities

Promoters of Reconciliation, Justice, and Peace in Eastern Africa

JOSEPH G. HEALEY

Today there are over ninety thousand Small Christian Communities (SCCs) in the eight AMECEA[1] countries of Eastern Africa.[2] Kenya alone has over thirty-five thousand SCCs. Increasingly, SCCs are promoting reconciliation, justice, and peace, the three main themes of the second African Synod. While the English text of the *Lineamenta* published in 2006 used the term "living ecclesial communities," the English text of the *Instrumentum Laboris*, published in 2009, uses the more common term *Small Christian Communities* that continues in the Propositions of the synod itself.

SCCs are mentioned twelve times in the *Instrumentum Laboris* and twice in the footnotes. This is significantly more often than in the *Lineamenta*, in which living ecclesial communities are mentioned three times in the document and twice in the questionnaire. This increase in the importance given to SCCs is clearly due to the many responses from the episcopal conferences in Africa and to other answers to the thirty-two questions of the original questionnaire.

The conclusions of the synod itself, the *Message of the Bishops of Africa to the People of God*, states, "Here we would like to reiterate the recommendation of *Ecclesia in Africa* about the importance of Small Christian Communities" (no. 22; see *Ecclesia in Africa*, no. 89). SCCs are mentioned seven times in the *Final List of 57 Propositions*. Key is Proposition 35:

The Synod renews its support for the promotion of Small Christian Communities (SCCs) that firmly build up the Church-Family of God in Africa. The SCCs are based on Gospel-sharing, where Christians gather to celebrate the presence of the Lord in their lives and in their midst, through the celebration of the Eucharist, the reading of the Word of God and witnessing to their faith in loving service to each other and their communities. Under the guidance of their pastors and catechists, they seek to deepen their faith and mature in Christian witness, as they live concrete experiences of fatherhood, motherhood, relationships, open fellowship, where each takes care of the other. This Family of God extends beyond the bonds of blood, ethnicity, tribe, culture and race. In this way SCCs open paths to reconciliation with extended families that have the tendency to impose on Christian nuclear families their syncretistic ways and customs.

SCCs are "a place for concretely living out reconciliation, justice and peace" (Proposition 37). SCC members are active agents of reconciliation, justice, and peace, not just subjects (see no. 22; Propositions 36 and 44).

Our research has been tracking the slow, gradual shift of SCCs in Eastern Africa from small prayer groups that are inwardly focused to active small faith communities that are outwardly focused on justice and peace issues. Many, however, are still prayer groups that are not concerned with the wider social issues; other SCCs shy away from justice and peace concerns. The top challenge to SCCs in Eastern Africa is to become more involved in justice and peace and social action.

One major change in Kenya since the post-election violence in January 2008 is the increasing use of a pastoral theological reflection process such as the Pastoral Circle to help SCCs reflect more deeply on the challenges of their context. This process, starting from concrete experience, uses the well-known "see, judge, and act" methodology. Now more and more SCCs in Africa are using various reflection processes and methodologies to reflect pastorally and theologically on their experiences, often using the tools of social analysis to identify the new signs of the times and to respond creatively to them.

One of the original architects of the SCC plan in Eastern Africa, Patrick Kalilombe, formerly bishop of Lilongwe, Malawi, emphasizes that in the different stages of growth in SCCs, the final stage is the transformation of society. This means going beyond superficial changes to tackle the structural and systemic changes in our society. A contemporary example would be the underlying tribal and ethnic group tensions in Kenya today.

Many statements from the second African Synod documents refer to and recommend the regular use of the *Compendium of the Social Doctrine of the Church* as a source of Catholic social teaching. The AMECEA delegates who participated in the second African Synod emphasized the "centrality of the Small Christian Community" in this regard:

We have experienced that a properly trained and led SCC adds great value to the promotion of reconciliation. This is because deeper biblical reflection and more regular use of the Pastoral Circle empower our Christians to engage effectively in the social life around them.

Here formation in Catholic Social Teaching (CST) at all levels must be a priority.[3]

Research shows that during the growth of SCCs in Eastern Africa, priorities have shifted from emphasizing the importance of the two steps of Bible sharing/Bible reflection and practical action to focus more on training SCC leaders to use these two steps more systematically so that the resulting practical action, especially social action, is more concrete and effective. The training of trainers process eventually involves other SCC members in the implementation of these steps. Formation is important for everyone involved in SCCs—bishops, priests, religious, and laity. A practical example is the urgent need to train SCCs facilitators in Kenya to use the "see, judge, and act" methodology in their weekly meetings during the annual Kenya lenten campaign.

Increasing Involvement in Justice and Peace Issues

SCCs in Africa use two starting points for their weekly Bible sharing/Bible reflection: (1) a deductive approach that begins with the Bible (for example, the Gospel for the following Sunday) or a particular teaching of the Catholic Church); and (2) an inductive approach that begins with daily life (especially critical concrete experiences, examples, and stories). John Paul II's Apostolic Exhortation *Ecclesia in Africa,* under the heading of "Living (or Vital) Christian Communities," states that small Christian communities should "reflect on different human problems in the light of the Gospel" (no. 89). In courses on SCCs taught at Hekima College and Tangaza College in Nairobi in February 2010 and in a SCC workshop at St. Thomas Aquinas Seminary in Nairobi in April 2010, we asked this question: "What are the different human problems in Kenya and the rest of Africa that we should reflect on in our SCC meetings in the light of the Bible?" Specific answers included those listed below:

Abortion
Alcoholism
Atheism
Bad/poor governance
Bad/poor leadership
"Brain drain"
Clericalism
Corruption
Deforestation
Degradation of the
  environment

Deplacement of people
Disease
Divorce
Drug abuse
Gap between the rich
  and poor
Gender imbalance
Greed of politicians
HIV/AIDS
Homosexuality
Human trafficking

Hunger
Illiteracy
Injustice
Insecurity
Laziness
Malaria
Malnutrition
Natural disasters
Neglecting ecology
  and
  environment

Neglect of elderly	Refugees	Tribalism/negative
people	Selfishness of leaders	ethnicity
Orphans	Street children	Unemployment
Pollution	Slums in Kibera,	Unequal distribution
Poverty	Nairobi	of
Premarital sex	Substance abuse	resources
Prostitution	Torture	War

The most frequently cited were corruption and tribalism/negative ethnicity. We divided these forty-five problems into three categories: ten problems apply to society in general, including the political world; two problems apply to the Catholic Church; and thirty-three problems apply to both.

In various classes and workshops at Hekima and Tangaza we divided into SCCs to reflect on specific problems. Three SCCs chose abortion, three SCCs chose bad/poor leadership (in the government and the church), one SCC chose alcoholism, one chose divorce, and one chose hunger. Participants found corresponding Bible passages and then discussed possible solutions to the particular problem. For example, the SCC that reflected on abortion chose many Bible passages from the Old and New Testament, including "I have set before you life and death, the blessing and the curse. Choose life, then, that you and your descendants may live" (Dt 3:19, AB) and "I came so that they might have life and have it more abundantly" (Jn 10:10, AB). The participants then discussed how Catholics can influence the final wording in the section on "Right to Life" in the Proposed Constitution of Kenya, which was endorsed in a referendum on August 2, 2010.

Later Santiago Rodriguez Serrano (a student in the SCC course at Hekima College) and I participated in the weekly meeting of the St. Joseph SCC of the Deaf in Our Lady of Guadalupe Parish in Nairobi. It was a powerful and moving experience to be with this first SCC for deaf Kenyans. We looked at justice and equality in the Catholic Church in a new way. The deaf members want to be included as equals and even start other SCCs for deaf people.[4]

The equality of women is a related challenge to SCCs, although a new vocabulary that includes terms such as *gender justice* and *gender equality* is emerging.

SCC Involvement in the Kenya Lenten Campaigns in 2009 and 2010

Recent research[5] shows that 95 percent of the SCCs in Kenya are neighborhood groups connected to parishes (parish-based SCCs are the most common model in Eastern Africa[6]). The remaining 5 percent are specialized SCCs for groups such as nurses at Kenyatta Hospital, teachers who live on the compound of the University of Nairobi–Kenya Science Teachers Campus, Christian Life Communities, St. Joseph SCC of the Deaf in Our Lady of Guadalupe Parish, and "extraterritorial or floating SCCs" composed of Catholics who live outside the geographical boundaries of the parish but who want to stay connected by meeting as a SCC before or after Sunday mass. Other types of specialized SCCs in Eastern Africa include Catholic professional peer groups (doctors, lawyers) and small groups in the Christian Professionals of Tanzania. Recently it was proposed to start a SCC of Catholic members of Parliament in Kenya, which would bridge the gap between the Catholic Church and the government.[7]

From 2006 to 2010 both neighborhood SCCs connected to parishes and the specialized SCCs had unique opportunities to promote justice, reconciliation, and peace, especially during the annual Kenya lenten campaigns. They were also involved in the reflection process of the second African Synod on the ministry of ecology and care of the environment.

Jesuit Peter Henriot, a Zambia-based adviser to AMECEA at the second African Synod in Rome, pointed out that the topic of environmental concern was surprisingly absent from the *Instrumentum Laboris* of the second African Synod published in March 2009. It did not treat issues such as climate change (global warming), ecological integrity, lifestyle adjustments, and industrial pollution by new investors coming to the African continent (such as those in the extractives sector). Aside from one passing reference to multinational corporations not paying adequate attention to the environment, this topic was not in the forefront of the problems and challenges.

However, during the preparations for the synod in Eastern Africa, Henriot identified the specific theme of the "ecological context for reconciliation":

> Increasingly in Africa (and all over our world!) we are recognizing that we humans belong to the community of creation, the wider environment that nourishes and sustains all human life. However, we have not always respected that truth, with the disastrous ecological consequences that we now face every day and in every place. How can we reconcile with Mother Earth?[8]

All this changed at the synod in Rome. Ecology and care of the environment emerged as priorities in the short interventions of the bishops and other delegates and in the small-group discussions. The *Message to the People of God of the Second Special Assembly for Africa of the Synod of Bishops* includes quotations such as "science and technology are equipping humanity with all that it takes to make our planet a beautiful place for us all"; "multinationals have to stop their criminal devastation of the environment in their greedy exploitation of natural resources"; and "God has blessed Africa with vast natural and human resources." In the end, the *Final List of*

57 Propositions of the second Africa Synod includes Proposition 22 ("Environmental Protection and Reconciliation with Creation"), Proposition 29 ("Natural Resources"), and Proposition 30 ("Land and Water").

The Kenya lenten campaigns of 2009 and 2010 were promoted by the Catholic Justice and Peace Commission of the Kenya Episcopal Conference.[9] The 2009 booklet in English and Swahili focused on the theme "Justice, Reconciliation, and Peace"[10] to coincide with the second African Synod and covered the weeks of Lent 2009. The "see, judge, and act" process drew on the experience of SCCs with justice and peace-related themes and issues, and the proposed action directly involved the SCCs.

SCCs throughout Kenya used these themes, scripture readings, and questions in their weekly meetings during Lent. The following case study is drawn from one of the SCC discussions.

St. Kizito SCC, Waruku (an informal settlement near Kangemi) in St. Austin's Parish, Nairobi, Kenya, on Sunday afternoon, March 8, 2009, from 2 to 4:15 p.m. Total of 17 participants: 10 women, 7 men. Mixed ethnic groups. We used the reflection process of Week Three of Lent in Swahili on "Kutunza Mazingira" (environmental care) of the *Kenya Lenten Campaign 2009* booklet. The booklet, calendar, and poster were distributed to SCC members.[11] We read Ezekiel 36:23–25 from the African Bible, emphasizing verse 25: "I will sprinkle clean water upon you." It was read twice, with silence in between. We also read the Gospel of the Third Sunday of Lent (Jn 2:13–25) and the *Dibaji* (Preface) of the booklet from Archbishop Peter Kairo, the chairperson of the Kenya Catholic Justice and Peace Commission. There was good group discussion on the meaning of the drawing on page 38, which depicted eight examples of harming or destroying the environment and seven examples of helping or caring for the environment.[12]

In Step Three (act) our SCC encouraged members to get involved in cleaning up the garbage and trash in the Waruku informal sectors. After the 7 a.m. mass on Sunday, March 15, 2009, Washington Oduor will lead the first clean-up team at 10 a.m., and Anastasia Syombua will lead the second clean-up team at 10:30 a.m.

Evaluation: 1¼ hours spent on Week Three. The lenten materials are a great help, but the booklet was demanding for ordinary SCC members. SCCs need to be specifically mentioned in the text; they cannot be assumed or presupposed. The sequence on page 40 of the Swahili text in the booklet (Step Two—judge) was hard to follow, and the key Ezekiel quotation was left out.

What was the outcome? The good news is that between 10:15 a.m. and noon on Sunday, March 15 (the beginning of Week Three, "Environmental Care"), twelve members of the St. Kizito SCC took turns collecting the trash and then burning it in small fires at the main dump in

Waruku. We successfully cleaned up the whole area. This related to an important universal proverb on ecology that we had been discussing: "If each person sweeps in front of his or her own house, the whole world will be clean" (based on German and Russian proverbs). Throughout this process the lay Christians of St. Kizito SCC experienced that "we are the church" and that we can take responsibility as a small community.

Class discussions at Hekima College and Tangaza College in Week Four, "Food Security and Empowering Farmers," revealed the valuable use of social analysis. The 2009 Kenya lenten campaign booklet describes the efforts of the Kenya government and the Food and Agricultural Organization "to strengthen the capacity of farmers, especially the poor, to maximize food production and reduce poverty and hunger."[13] But after the post-election crisis in January 2008, which was deeply connected to tribalism and ethnicity, many farmers were displaced from their farmlands. Recent statistics show that the government of Kenya has been slow to resettle these farmers on their productive farms, especially in the Rift Valley, which is known as the Bread Basket of Kenya for its food crops of corn and wheat. Food production is down, and there is starvation, especially in northern Kenya. It was recommended that through fasting during the season of Lent, SCC members can have practical solidarity with millions of hungry people in Kenya and throughout the world.

The 2010 Kenya lenten campaign booklet, "Towards Healing and Transformation," focused on many issues related to ecology and the environment. Week Three was titled "Environmental Care." Step One (see) began with a story, "Changing the Face of the Mountain." Step Two (judge) provided a situational analysis of the ecological crisis in Kenya, especially encroachment on water catchment areas, desertification, and deforestation. This was followed by the three readings for the Third Sunday of Lent. In the Gospel of Luke 13:6–9 Jesus tells the parable of the barren fig tree and challenges us to recognize our interconnectedness with all creation or perish.

The five questions in Step Three (act) asked participants to

1. Reflect on the story "Changing the Face of the Mountain" and identify two concrete issues that remind you of a similar situation in the context of your family, workplace, SCC, or any other community to which you belong. Share your reflection with someone else.
2. Organize a gathering of people within your family, workplace, or SCC to discuss one issue from the "judge" section and plan how you as a group will tackle it to change the face of Kenya in a positive way.
3. Like the old lady in the story, commit yourself and your SCC or any other group to plant and care for at least three indigenous trees during this lenten season.

4. There is a Kenyan saying that goes "You must treat the earth well. It was not given to you by your parents. It was loaned to you by your children." What does this mean to you in terms of care of the environment?
5. Select as many Bible verses as you can that tell of Jesus' familiarity with nature and reflect on them throughout this week.

Each week the booklet included quotations from the relevant Propositions of the second African Synod. For Week Three the specific recommendations included the following:

1. Promote environmental education and awareness.
2. Persuade local and national governments to adopt policies and binding legal regulations for the protection of the environment and promote alternative and renewable sources of energy.
3. Encourage everyone to plant trees and treat nature and its resources with respect for the integrity of all creation and the common good of all.

SCCs throughout Kenya used these themes, scripture readings, and questions in their weekly meetings during Lent 2010. A case study of another SCC meeting notes the results:

St. Kizito SCC, Waruku in St. Austin's Parish, Nairobi, on Sunday, February 28, 2010, from 11 a.m. to 4 p.m. The previous day a team of four SCC members bought twenty-six large seedlings of five varieties of indigenous trees in Kenya (some of which have bark, leaves, and roots that are used for traditional herbal medicine). First, twelve members planted trees at the Waruku Primary School. Then, a larger group planted trees at the Sons of St. Ann Congregation Novitiate. One member planted a smaller seedling in his individual plot. Then we gathered in Joseph Kahara's home for our weekly meeting. Total of twenty-five participants: fourteen women, nine men, two children. Mixed ethnic groups. We used the reflection process of Week Three of Lent in Swahili on "Utunzaji wa Mazingira" (environmental care) of the *Kenya Lenten Campaign 2010* booklet. The booklet and poster were distributed to SCC members. We read Luke 13:6–9, with many members mentioning a word or phrase that struck them. Good group discussion on the meaning of the drawing of the old woman planting trees on the side of the mountain on page 16 and the five questions.

We discussed how we SCC members can get involved in changing the face of Waruku itself during this lenten season. This includes taking care of the seedlings that we planted (including our number-one obstacle— keeping the roaming goats away!) and the general cleanliness of the grounds and dumps.

Involving Youth in Small Christian Communities

Given the importance of youth in the demographics of both the general population and the Catholic population in Africa, the second African Synod did not give enough attention to this group. A single section (no. 27) in the *Message to the People of God of the Second Special Assembly for Africa of the Synod of Bishops* treats youth—after priests, religious, lay faithful, Catholics in public life, families, women, and men. It states: "You are not just the future of the Church: you are with us already in big numbers. In many countries of Africa, over 60% of the population is under 25. The ratio in the Church would not be much different." The message could have said much more. Proposition 48 treats youth in a problem-centered way, noting that the synod participants "are deeply concerned about the plight of youth," and proposes various recommendations. Much more could have been said about the great potential of young people in the Catholic Church and in the general society in Africa.

Since youth do not normally participate in adult SCCs in Eastern Africa, it is crucial to form specific SCCs for young Africans. A very good example is St. Stephen Youth Small Christian Community in St. Joseph the Worker Parish in Kangemi, Nairobi. It meets on Sundays for announcements and planning and then choir practice with the other parish choir, and on Thursdays for a variety of activities: Bible sharing/Bible reflection; mass; adoration of the Blessed Sacrament; sports like football and darts; discussions on various topics; and music, singing, and dancing. This youth SCC emphasizes social outreach, and its members have joined with other youth in the parish to bring foodstuffs and other gifts to a camp of internally displaced persons outside Nairobi.

One "thinking outside the box" solution is to encourage Kenyan youth to use Sheng in their meetings. Sheng, the short form of Swahili and English, is a common language of interaction among youth, especially in Kenyan cities. It is a blend of Swahili, English, and other local Kenyan languages such as Gikuyu, Luo, Kamba, and so on. This will send a message that the Catholic Church is interested in youth, young adults, and their unique worlds. Using Sheng could also help overcome tribalism and specific ethnic loyalties. A related development is the emergence of young married couples' SCCs and young married families' SCCs.

To attract more youth and young adults to SCCs we are challenged to use the new media and social networking sites. Proposition 56 states, "In a globalized world, the improved use and greater availability of the various means of social communication (visual, audio, web, and print) are indispensable for the promotion of peace, justice and reconciliation in Africa." Thus we started a Facebook page on our Small Christian Communities Global Collaborative website. It is noteworthy that, after China and India, Facebook is the third-largest "nation" in the world, with 500 million users.

Of the first 358 fans on our SCCs Facebook page, 79 percent are between eighteen and thirty-four years old. The majority of fans are from Kenya, followed by fans from the United States, South Africa, India, and the United Kingdom.

Some comments on our Facebook page include the following:

> At the end of the Second African Synod of Bishops held in Rome, the *Message to the People of God* uses the African proverb that goes: *An army of well organized ants can bring down an elephant.* SCCs are an army of well organized Christians who can help alleviate evil in society.

> The SCCs can be an avenue for environmental care. "Going green" has been a slogan in many commercials. SCCs can make their neighborhood "go green."

> SCCs should play the role of reminding our government leaders and appeal to them for security of life and alleviating poverty. Life is sacred and must be protected and secured. Let's stand up and talk without fear about the lack of good order. If we don't talk who will talk?

> Today's challenge: How do we use the NEW MEDIA for evangelization especially in Small Christian Communities?"[14]

Young people appear to love text messaging. Members of SCCs in Kenya can get daily Bible readings on their cell phones/mobile phones by simply texting the word *reading* to 3141. The response includes a description of the saint of the day and the Old Testament, New Testament, and Gospel texts. This is especially helpful for SCC members who want to prepare the Gospel of the following Sunday in advance. This and other methods of social networking help to get youth more involved.

SCCs as Facilitators of Reconciliation, Justice, and Peace in Africa

The sections on SCCs in the documents of the second African Synod break new ground. First, the SCCs themselves are described as "places" for concretely living out reconciliation, justice, and peace. Second, SCC members are challenged to be active agents of reconciliation, justice, and peace, not just subjects. This is a loud and clear call for SCCs in Africa to continue to be a new way of being church on the local grassroots level. As this new model of church, SCCs can emphasize deeper biblical reflection and more regular use of the Pastoral Circle to engage effectively the pastoral and social life around them. As facilitators of reconciliation, justice, and peace, SCCs can be very important in the future of the Catholic Church in Africa.

Notes

[1] AMECEA is an acronym for the Association of Member Episcopal Conferences of Eastern Africa. It is a service organization for the National Episcopal Conferences of the eight countries of Eastern Africa: Eritrea (1993), Ethiopia (1979), Kenya (1961), Malawi (1961), Sudan (1973), Tanzania (1961), Uganda (1961), and Zambia (1961). Somalia (1995) and Djibouti (2002) are affiliate members.

[2] While this essay focuses on Eastern Africa, SCCs are important in many parts of Africa. One highlight of South Africa is the Lumko Institute's influential program, known through the world for forming SCC leaders.

[3] "Statement (Position Paper) from Bishops of the Association of Member Episcopal Conferences of Eastern Africa (AMECEA) Who Are Delegates to the Synod of Bishops' Second Special Assembly for Africa in Rome in October, 2009," *Catholic Information Service for Africa (CISA) Email News Bulletin* 096 (September 29, 2009).

[4] For more information, see Cornelius Ssekitto, "Deaf Ministry at Our Lady of Guadalupe Parish in Nairobi, Kenya." Available on the SmallChristianCommunities.org website.

[5] This research clearly indicates that the dominant model in Eastern Africa is that of pastoral, parish-based SCCs. These SCCs are an integral part of the pastoral life, activities, and structures of the outstation and parish starting from below, from the grassroots. But in other parts of the world, such as Europe (examples are France and Italy), parishes are losing membership and influence, and the new movements are emerging as a different style of participation and involvement in the Catholic Church. Many of these new movements have a small-group component. For interesting case studies, see the "Europe" section in *Small Christian Communities Today: Capturing the New Moment*, ed. Joseph Healey and Jeanne Hinton (Maryknoll, NY: Orbis Books, 2005; Nairobi: Paulines Publications Africa, 2006), 71–95. The "Latin America" section describes the distinctive basic ecclesial communities (BECs) model of church.

[6] Especially in rural areas, SCCs are composed of members of extended families living in the same geographical location.

[7] At the AMECEA Plenary Meeting in Nairobi, Kenya, in July 1976, President Jomo Kenyatta made the now famous statement: "The Church is the conscience of society, and today a society needs a conscience. Do not be afraid to speak. If we are wrong and you keep quiet, one day you may have to answer for our mistakes" (quoted in the Kenya Bishops' pastoral letter "Family and Responsible Parenthood" [April 27, 1979] and in *The Conscience of Society*, ed. Rodrigo Mejia [Nairobi: Paulines Publications Africa, 1995], 50).

[8] Pete Henriot, "Hopes for the Second African Synod," Hakimani *e-Newsletter* (September 2009): 3. Available on the jesuithakimani.org website.

[9] The annual Kenyan lenten campaign is one of the most widely known and appreciated activities of the Catholic Church in Kenya. The themes of previous years include "With a New Heart and a New Spirit" (2008) and "Kenya's Good Governance, My Responsibility" (2007).

[10] This word order is different from the theme of the second African Synod, which is "Reconciliation, Justice, and Peace." It depends on the specific context and circumstances, and the local interpretation. In general, I think that this is a process in which justice comes first, and then this leads to reconciliation and finally

to a more lasting peace. Peter Henriot presents interesting distinctions in "Justice, Peace, Reconciliation, and Forgiveness: Theological and Conceptual Underpinnings and Linkages," in *AMECEA Synod Delegates Workshop: Shaping the Prophetic Voice of the Region* (Nairobi: Privately printed, 2009), 37–49.

[11] These visual materials were very important in the overall campaign. The drawing on the poster highlighted reconciliation and unity, and the full-year calendar encouraged people to live out the campaign throughout the year. Many religious organizations produced creative calendars in 2009 on the theme of justice, reconciliation, and peace.

[12] A SCC member spotted that the farmers were barefoot (bad) in the top half of the drawing, while the farmers were wearing shoes and boots (good) in the bottom half of the drawing. No one else in the various SCCs that I visited had noticed this.

[13] Kenya Lenten Campaign, *Justice, Reconciliation, and Peace* (Nairobi: KEC Catholic Justice and Peace Commission, 2009), 21.

[14] Small Christian Communities Facebook page, http://www.facebook.com/pages/Nairobi-Kenya/Small-Christian-Communities/279921983315.

Part II

The Mission of the Church in the Public Sphere

6

Inventing Creative Approaches to Complex Systems of Injustice

A New Call for a Vigilant and Engaged Church

ELIAS OMONDI OPONGO

In preparation for the second African Synod, the Association of Member Episcopal Conferences of Eastern Africa (AMECEA) invited me to address a plenary session of the group's bishops in June 2008. My main task was to analyze the current sociopolitical situation in Africa, particularly in the AMECEA region, in relation to conflicts and the church's response. In addressing the two hundred bishops, the image that came to mind was the story of the disciples on the road to Emmaus (Lk 24). In this story Jesus Christ walks along with the disciples in their moment of distress; he brings them hope and opens their minds to see creatively the reality beyond the immediate suffering and fear. It is this process—creatively reading the reality differently and acting upon it, not in fear and hopelessness, but with inventive strategies grounded in faith, courage, and confidence—that will bring the Emmaus experience to the church in Africa.

Emmaus is a place where we recognize Jesus in the breaking of bread and experience conversion through the transformation of our hearts. It is a place where we are invited not to worry about the historical sufferings of our time but instead to be channels of life and hope, founded in the resurrection of Christ. The economic and political development in Africa in recent years demonstrates that there is tremendous hope for change, especially if mechanisms can be put in place to guarantee the equitable distribution of the benefits to all levels of society.[1]

The church in Africa is faced today with complex interactive systems of injustice that call for vigilance and full engagement in the very structures that assail human conditions of life. Political and economic progress has been undermined by the complexity of these systems of injustice. Evidence

73

of these unjust systems includes unsustainable global economic systems that often disadvantage the poor; internal conflicts that are ethnic, religious, or resource based; and poor governance. According to research conducted by the Overseas Development Institute (ODI), the global financial crisis had a negative impact on developing countries through "declining private financial flows, trade, and remittances. By the end of 2009, developing countries may have lost incomes of at least $750 billion—more than $50 billion in sub-Saharan Africa."[2] And development "solutions" do not always work. Corporate propaganda that genetically modified foods are a solution to the African food crisis has been proven wrong by a group of four hundred scientists who assert that food sustainability lies in small-scale farming.[3]

In the political arena, as several contributors to this volume show, most conflicts in Africa are complex and tend to be resource based. For example, in the Democratic Republic of Congo (DRC), while the war seems to be based on regional and political differences, "foreign governments and multinational companies, greedy for the natural resources found in the DRC, are in cahoots with the militias and they too are responsible for the plunder and the killings."[4] In relation to governance, as pointed out by Gabriel Mmassi in this volume, the cost of corruption mainly affects the poor and subsequently weakens the credibility of governance structure and national stability.

The complex nature of these issues poses a strong challenge to the church to invent new approaches to change. The traditional response of the church, which has largely been reactive, needs to be replaced by an active approach that seeks to find ways of engaging agents of power in a process of dialogue for change. For its theme the second African Synod adopted "The Church in Africa in Service to Reconciliation, Justice, and Peace: 'You are the salt of the earth. . . . You are the light of the world' (Matthew 5:13)." The synod acknowledges that our continent has been ravaged by conflicts that generate widespread poverty, unemployment, marginalization, and economic and political injustices. The synodal process offers a timely opportunity to increase the level of the church's participation in reconciliation, social justice, and peace as a means of bringing genuine change to Africa.

In this essay I argue that the challenges that Africa faces today call for a church that is not only prophetic but also strongly vigilant, engaged, and constantly in solidarity with God's people. To be prophetic is to be present to the people of God, guiding them through the path of peace, reconciliation, and justice. *Vigilance* refers to the capacity to anticipate the signs of the times and advocate immediate actions that have a future positive impact on social transformation. *Engagement* is the ability to be part of the various processes responsible for the well-being of the human person, whether in the sphere of politics, economy, agriculture, trade, or sciences. The church ought to engage itself aggressively in these sectors in order to become both a partner and an active agent of change. To be in *solidarity* with the people of God implies participating in the daily struggles of the people to bring positive change for sustainable peace.

A New Beginning: Transition from the First to the Second Synod

The first African Synod in 1994 emphasized the model of church as a family of God. This ecclesiology is founded on the shared humanity or *ubuntu* that unites all believers and their mutual responsibility to safeguard human dignity. There is a clear transition from the first to the second synod. Two contradicting events in Africa marked the period of the first synod: on the one hand, South Africa was witnessing the end of apartheid and the election of its first nonracial government; on the other hand, genocide in Rwanda was approaching close to 800,000 deaths.

These two events, of hope for change and of conflict, mirror the ongoing history of Africa. Several situations of *conflict* on the continent underscore the need for reconciliation, justice, and peace—in northern Uganda, the Jos region in Nigeria, the DRC, South Africa, Darfur, in the Ethiopia-Eritrea tensions, in uncertainties of the impact of the referendum results in Sudan, and in the reform processes in Kenya following the post-election crisis in 2008.

Yet moments of hope are evident in efforts to build a new society founded on genuine reconciliation through post-conflict reconstruction—in Rwanda, Sierra Leone, Burundi, and Liberia. The second synod is therefore timely and responds to the needs of the African countries emerging from conflict or still experiencing conflict. The church today must echo the words of the Psalmist in working for reconciliation in order to create a new spirit of hope and mutual understanding: "Create in me a clean heart, O God, and renew a steadfast spirit within me" (Ps 51:10, NIV). This new spirit can only be effective if we let the peace of Christ rule in our hearts (Col 3:15) through the love of one another expressed in efforts toward positive social change, democratic participation, and economic development.

However, in order to achieve these objectives, the church has to understand the complexities involved in the systems of injustice that have become very subtle. This is more important today when people are subjected to a multiplicity of different ideologies in discourses on politics, poverty, wealth, conflict, or peace, subsequently rendering their Christian faith vulnerable to misleading interpretations.

The Current Social-Political Situation in Africa

The slowly expanding democratic space and economic development marked by improved livelihood have brought new hope into many countries in

Africa. The results of research on 203 presidential and parliamentary elections in Africa indicate considerable improvements in democratic participation.[5] According to the *World Fact Book*, in 2008, there were significant economic growth rates in several countries: Angola (13.2%), Ethiopia (11.2%), Rwanda (11.6%), Equatorial Guinea (10.6%), and Niger (9.5%).

There has also been a renewed awareness of the people's right to participate in the social organization and political governance of their country. However, despite such encouraging indicators of progress, Africa still faces the daunting task of responding to the challenges of unemployment, increased poverty, poor governance, social-economic marginalization, and HIV/AIDS. For example, "the world's GDP in 2008 was $60.6 trillion; of that amount, Africa created a mere $987 billion."[6]

In order to understand the current challenges of injustice, it is important to identify the various multiple transitions that African countries have experienced. In the post-independence period most African governments enjoyed *liberalist* and *populist* governments. The center of power was mainly vested in the government, and the focus was to increase literacy through formal education, to tackle poverty through creation of job opportunities, and to reduce the death rates by improving health services. These objectives remain illusive for many African governments.

The transition from *military* to *democratic* governments has seen some military "liberationists" formalize their governments through "democratic processes" that are often tailored to favor the liberationists. Several countries—such as Uganda, Burundi, Rwanda, South Africa, Zimbabwe, Angola, and Nigeria—have experienced military resistance to independence or military coups that transitioned into some semblance of democracy. It is often difficult for liberationists to cede power, given that they still live in a liberationist frenzy and are unwilling to accept that democracy involves checks and balances on the quality of leadership. This is the case in Uganda, Ethiopia, Guinea-Conakry, Eritrea, and Zimbabwe.

From a spiritual perspective we note that Africa is a continent experiencing spiritual thirst. Many Africans are in search for a deeper expression of their faith. As Paulinus Odozor shows in his contribution to this volume, the continent leads in the growth of Christianity. A recent study by the Pew Forum on Religion and Public Life in nineteen African countries indicates that between 1900 and 2010 the number of Christians soared "almost 70–fold from about 7 million to 470 million. Sub-Saharan Africa is now home to about one-in-five of all the Christians in the world." The Pew survey asserts that in most countries both Christians and Muslims coexist peacefully.[7] However, as Odozor demonstrates, politicians have taken advantage of multiplicities of religious faiths and coopted the latter into partisan politics. Several countries have witnessed interreligious tensions, sometimes leading to the loss of lives such as in the Jos region in Nigeria, where perennial interreligious clashes have led to hundreds of deaths.

The consequences of economic growth for many African countries have sometimes been unchecked. Contrary to promises of poverty reduction and development in the 1990s, globally "the actual number of people living in poverty has actually increased by about 100 million. This occurred at the same time that the total world income increased by an average of 2.5 percent annually."[8] Most mining and investment contracts with multinational companies have largely favored foreign investors. The concerns over Africa's right to control and manage its own resources have been emphatically raised by Peter Kanyandago in this volume.

Another factor is the increasing economic relationship between Africa and China. China has turned to Africa for resources such as oil, minerals, and food; trade through export of its products; and investment opportunities in exchange for loans and construction of infrastructure. Given that China is the fastest-growing economy today with an average annual growth rate of 8 percent and has turned from oil exporter to the second-largest oil importer after the United States, the interests of China in Africa bear further scrutiny. In fact it is "estimated that the Chinese demand for oil will increase by 156% between the years 2001 and 2025."[9]

The universal church has played a critical role in creating an alternative prophetic voice that challenges poor political leadership and calls for responsible governance based on the values of the gospel. The church's loyalty to building the kingdom of God on earth remains central to its commitment to the social transformation of unjust structures. In his homily to the participants at the second African Synod, Pope Benedict XVI acknowledged that despite the many problems the continent faces, "moving testimonies have shown us that, even in the darkest moments of human history, the Holy Spirit is at work and transforms hearts of the victims and persecutors so that they recognize each other as brothers."[10] However, in order to transform the situation of conflict and unjust structures of our continent, there is urgent need for a renewed commitment on the part of the church.

I now turn to four critical characteristics that the church must integrate if it is to make a significant impact in the process of transformation of our continent to a more just society. These characteristics refer to the church as prophetic, vigilant, engaged, and in solidarity with the people.

The Prophetic Church and the Witness of Action

The term *prophetic church* is common in ecclesiastical and theological parlance. However, the prophetic role of the church has been limited to proclamations against injustices through pastoral letters, homilies, and witness to the gospel. These components are still very important because they allow the church to be the "salt of the earth" and "the light of the world" in the conviction that we all have an obligation to transform the situations of injustice in our midst. However, there is a need to be more strategic in realizing the prophetic role of the church. Pastoral letters alone are not enough. There has to be a "witness of action," as advocated by Pope John Paul II in the encyclical letter *Centesimus Annus*: "Today more than ever, the Church is aware that her social doctrine will gain credibility more immediately from *witness of action* than as a result of its internal logic and consistency" (no. 57). Two major characteristics define how the witness of action can be prophetic.

First, the church has to develop its identity through integral evangelization that considers justice and peace as intrinsic components of its prophetic role. Pope John Paul II's post-synodal exhortation, *Ecclesia in Africa*, reinforces this point: "According to the Synod Fathers, the main question facing the Church in Africa consists in delineating as clearly as possible what it is and what it must fully carry out, in order that its message may be relevant and credible" (no. 21). The response to this question demands that the church revise its approach to evangelization, not only in the philosophical, theological, and pastoral preparation of seminarians and lay collaborators, but more crucially in its commitment to justice and peace. The work of justice and peace should therefore not be seen as an addendum to the commitment to evangelization, but rather as "integral part of the task of evangelization, (and) it follows that the promotion of these values should also be a part of the pastoral programme of each Christian community" (no. 107). A direct engagement in the understanding of the complex systems of injustices is therefore urgently needed.

Second, the formation of justice and peace commissions (JPCs) in many dioceses in Africa has been a positive step toward this commitment. Although some JPCs have performed extremely well, a good number have lagged behind. From personal experience of training and interacting with the various JPCs in Africa, it is clear that most of them lack resources, capacity, and pastoral support from the diocesan structures, unlike the better-funded non-diocesan nongovernmental organizations. It is not enough to appoint "good" people to run the JPCs; their personnel have to be well trained and committed to the work of peace and justice. For this to happen, "each Bishop must put issues of reconciliation, justice and peace high up on the pastoral agenda of his diocese."[11] However, as Odomaro Mubangizi argues in his contribution to this volume, the work of JPCs ought not to be limited to JPCs alone; it should also be extended to Catholic universities that can engage in research and analysis of the sociopolitical and economic situations of Africa.

The Vigilant Church: Reading through the Signs of the Times

Transformation of the structures of injustice is critical to ensuring sustainable peace. The church ought to be *vigilant* not only in reading the signs of our times, but also in reading *through* the signs to address issues of injustice.

This calls for a more anticipatory approach to conflict transformation. In most cases pastoral letters have been written as a reaction to given situations of injustice. While this is commendable, given the boldness and the courage it takes to stand against oppressive regimes, it is equally critical for the church to anticipate and analytically project potential conflicts and situations of injustice.

Vigilance requires foresight in anticipating the impact of political, economic, and religious policies on the population. However, in order for such vigilance to be effective, there has to be a continuous and thorough analysis of the context and the challenges and opportunities for positive change. In this process the church has to cooperate with lay professionals and people of good will in order to come up with a comprehensive plan of action. For example, in the period leading up to the December 2007 parliamentary and presidential elections in Kenya, religious groups formed an interreligious forum to address issues of social concern such as insecurity, violence, and inflammatory statements by politicians.[12] In Zimbabwe, three Christian bodies—Zimbabwe Catholic Bishops Conference, Zimbabwe Council of Churches, and the Evangelical Fellowship of Zimbabwe—came together to respond to the crisis in Zimbabwe in the form of a *National Vision Document*. This eventually led to a visioning process that produced the document *The Zimbabwe We Want: Towards a National Vision for Zimbabwe*, which provoked a national discussion on social engagement.[13] While the document was not fully agreeable to the government, it expressed the boldness of the church's determination to transform the structures of injustice. David Kaulem observes in this volume that the violence in Zimbabwe rendered truth the first casualty, hence making it difficult for the public to trust the state.

Participants at the second African Synod were candid in underscoring the fact that in order to effect change in our society, the church must seek transformation. Transformation implies, among other things, that there has to be unity among the bishops and the people of God. The synod reemphasized its commitment to remaining united and to be a symbol of Christ's body in a divided society: "As Bishops, we challenge ourselves to work in unity in our various Episcopal Conferences and Assemblies giving our nations a model of reconciled and just national institution, ready to offer ourselves as artisans of peace and reconciliation, whenever and wherever we are called upon."[14]

It has been disheartening to witness divisions among the conferences of bishops and the people of God. During the post-election violence in Kenya the churches were divided and sometimes implicated in propagating ethnic hatred and violence. A number of churches later came forward and asked for public forgiveness for taking sides along ethnic and political lines during the election and post-election events. Part of the struggle for the church in Kenya today is regaining its credibility in the aftermath of such partisanship. Churches, therefore, need to demonstrate that they can rise above the various social, ethnic, economic, and political divisions among the Kenyan people.

The question of unity and observance of justice and peace within the church is further underlined in the responses that came from the faithful in preparation for the second African Synod: "The Church-Family of God is called upon to establish mediation groups at various levels" (*Instrumentum Laboris*, no. 109). This will strengthen the church as a community of faith.

An Engaged Church

The church has both the liberty and the obligation to intervene against societal and government practices that violate human dignity. As expressed by Vatican II in *The Church and the Modern World,*

> Whatever insults human dignity, such as subhuman living conditions, arbitrary imprisonment, deportation, slavery, prostitution, the selling of women and children as well as disgraceful working conditions, where men and women are treated as mere tools for profit, rather than as free and responsible persons; all these things and others of their like are infamies indeed. (no. 27)

Transformation of structures of injustice entails the commitment of the church to analyze strategically the root causes of conflict and divisions and to identify responsible actors in order to work out points of entry for initiatives for change. In some cases the church has rushed to condemn without understanding the complexity of the issues at hand. There have been efforts in a number of JPCs to establish a Catholic Parliamentary Liaison Office. The essay by Anthony Egan shows that the South African Catholic Bishops' Conference has perhaps registered the most remarkable success in this area; it is now able to offer training to other JPCs that are interested in establishing such an office. The South African Catholic Bishops' Conference works closely with parliamentarians and parliamentary committees in advocating for just institutional structures through policy reforms and informed interventions on parliamentary bills. The director of the Catholic Parliamentary Liason Office for the South African Catholic Bishops' Conference, Peter John Pearson, observes that,

> the Church in South Africa realized very early, in the process of South Africa's reconstruction, that if the ravages of the apartheid were to be reversed then a major focus of that process would lie in the creation and implementation of just policies and legislation. It understood quite categorically that just as parliament and the laws which it issued was a major location for shaping evil so in the new South Africa the same institution had the potential to be a focus for good.[15]

Such initiatives, though very technical, have allowed the church to be a proactive agent in structures of governance rather than a reactionary player who after the event denounces an injustice that could have otherwise been prevented.

Solidarity through Forgiveness and Reconciliation

The church has to live in *solidarity* with its people as an agent of conflict resolution, forgiveness, and reconciliation. The 2008–2009 Africa Development Bank report indicates that between 1990 and 2005 Africa accounted for half of the number of conflicts worldwide.[16] However, despite the decrease in the number of conflicts on the continent, still more people die from diseases, malnutrition, and starvation. Under such circumstances, as a community of solidarity, the church has the responsibility to intervene in conflicts in Africa from two different but related fronts: conflict resolution and reconciliation, and transformation of the structures of injustice.

In divided African societies the concept of living the image of God across cultures has turned out to be a difficult endeavor. Identity is primarily attached to family, clan, ethnic group, and then nation. As in European and American wars, Africa has experienced conflicts that have sidelined Christian faith as a value rather than embracing it as a guide to human action. In fact, in most African conflicts Christians have "faced off" against other Christians or people of different religious faiths, making their Christian identity secondary to ethnic or national identities. For example, in Rwanda the statistical preponderance of Christianity as a national religion did not prevent the occurrence of a horrific genocide that claimed 800,000 lives. In Kenya, where more than half the population is Christian, the post-election violence divided the country along ethnic lines, leading to the death of thirteen hundred people. Similar situations have been witnessed in Burundi, Ethiopia, Sierra Leone, and other countries. Evidently, Christian identity is often submerged by the social, economic, and political threats that prioritize identities based on manipulated fears created by politicians and the subsequent unjust structures in place.

Interventions for change in periods of conflict and post-conflict ought to occur through an integral process of forgiveness and reconciliation that seeks to heal the wounds of conflict. Important here is the model of Jesus Christ, which counters the evil of domination and oppression with the gospel of love, because a "just society cannot be achieved without the component of love" (*Lineamenta*, no. 50). In fact, while justice is a necessary prerequisite to peace, it ought to be administered within the whole framework of forgiveness and reconciliation. Most African cultures advocate restorative justice that seeks to "rehabilitate both the victim and the perpetrator."[17] This goal is carried out through rituals of retribution, forgiveness, and reconciliation, making the entire process meaningful, engaging, and binding. The concept of the church as family of God denotes a deliberate effort to embrace the "other," who could be different but is united by the fact of a shared humanity and created in the image of God. Hence, "to shed a brother's or a sister's blood is to shed one's own blood, the Blood of Christ" (*Lineamenta*, no. 39).

Conclusion

I have proposed a radical reevaluation of the church's strategy for changing social situations of injustice. The future of the African church is founded on a commitment to a reconciliation process that restores relationships with one another, the environment, and God; stands up for justice for the poor and marginalized; and promotes true peace founded on gospel values of love of God and neighbor. In his message on the World Day of Peace in 2010, Pope Benedict XVI reiterated the need for ecological integration: "Sad to say, it is all too evident that large numbers of people in different countries and areas of our planet are experiencing increased hardship because of the negligence or refusal of many others to exercise responsible stewardship over the environment" (no. 7). Such is true of many conflicts in Africa that are due to competition for limited resources.

However, for the church's social mission to achieve better results in a more complex world, it is vital to initiate new approaches that promote full human development. We African Christians face the challenge of proclaiming a gospel that transforms the world by understanding the local and international networks that marginalize the majority but similarly engaging with multiple initiatives that seek to dialogue with these systems and change them for the good of humanity. The task and focus of the church ought to be about bringing God's kingdom on earth: "Seek first the kingdom of God and all shall be given to you" (Mt 6:33, NIV).

Notes

[1] The 2010 Kenya economic survey demonstrates that the Kenyan economy has a projected growth of 2.6 percent. But this has not been the experience of many poor people. The survey acknowledges that "food inflation of 12.6 percent recorded between 2008 and last year was the highest in the consumer goods and services basket" (Jeff Otieno and Dave Opiyo, "Kenya Predicts a Positive 2010," *The East African* [May 20, 2010]; available on the theeastafrican.co.ke website.

[2] Dirk Willem Te Velde, "The Global Financial Crisis and Developing Countries: Taking Stock, Taking Action," *ODI Briefing Papers* 54 (2009). Available on the odi.org.uk website.

[3] Institute of Science in Technology (ISIS), "GM-Free Organic Agriculture to Feed the World," *ISIS Report*, April 4, 2008. Available on the i-sis.org.uk website.

[4] Phumlani Majavu, "Africa: The Role of Natural Resources in Civil Wars," *Towards Freedom* (May 3, 2010). Available on the towardfreedom.com website.

[5] Staffan I. Lindberg, "The Democratic Qualities of Competitive Elections: Participation: Competition and Legitimacy in Africa," *Journal of Commonwealth and Comparative Politics* 42, no. 1 (2004): 61–105. Available at http://ssrn.com/abstract=1013646.

[6] World Bank, "Key Economic Indicators," December 10, 2009. Available on the worldbank.org website.

[7] Pew Forum on Religion and Public Life, "Tolerance and Tension: Islam and Christianity in Sub-Saharan Africa," April 15, 2010. Available on the pewforum.org website.

[8] Joseph Stiglitz, *Globalization and Its Discontents* (New York: Norton, 2002), 5.

[9] Judith Van de Looy, "Africa and China: A Strategic Partnership?" ASC Working Paper no. 67 (2006): 14.

[10] "Courage! Get on Your Feet, Continent of Africa"—Homily of His Holiness Benedict XVI at the closing mass of the African Synod, October 25, 2009; and *Message to the People of God of the Second Special Assembly for Africa of the Synod of Bishops*, no. 5. Available on the vatican.va website.

[11] "Courage! Get on Your Feet, Continent of Africa," no. 19.

[12] Philomena Njeri Mwaura and Constansia Mumma Martinon, "Political Violence in Kenya and Local Churches' Responses: The Case of the 2007 Post-Election Crisis," *The Review of Faith and International Affairs* 8, no. 1 (2010): 42–43.

[13] David Kaulem, "The Role of Religion in Societal Transformation: The Case of Zimbabwe," in *Peace Weavers: Methodologies of Peacebuilding in Africa*, ed. Elias Omondi Opongo (Nairobi: Paulines Publications, 2008), 54–55.

[14] Quoted in ibid., 16.

[15] Peter John Pearson, "Parliament as a Place of Conversation: The Church's Ongoing Role in Parliamentary Debate," in Opongo, *Peace Weavers*, 66.

[16] Africa Development Bank, "African Development Report 2008–2009, 8th April 2009," xi. Available on the afdb.org website.

[17] Desmond Tutu, *No Future without Forgiveness* (New York: Doubleday, 1999), 55.

7

Toward a New Social Configuration?

The Role of the Catholic Church in the Public Sphere

YVON CHRISTIAN ELENGA

*The Church cannot and must not take upon herself the political battle
to bring about the most just society possible. She cannot and must not
replace the State. Yet at the same time she cannot and must not remain on the sidelines in the fight for justice. She has to play her part
through rational argument and she has to reawaken the spiritual energy without which justice, which always demands sacrifice, cannot
prevail and prosper. A just society must be the achievement of politics, not of the Church. Yet the promotion of justice through efforts to
bring about openness of mind and will to the demands of the common
good is something which concerns the Church deeply.*
—DEUS CARITAS EST, NO. 28

To rethink the role of the Catholic Church in the public sphere calls for a
consideration of this concept as it has been developed quite frequently in
constitutional law, public policy, political theology, and the social teaching
of the church.[1] Is there a univocal idea of *public sphere* that is operative
beyond the interrelations of contexts? In simple terms, the public sphere
delineates the social, economic, and political space where multiple groups
of individuals, institutions, and disciplines interrelate in view of political
action. Analysis of the historical and political character of the public sphere
shows the complexity of the relationship between the religious and the political. Indeed, the political theories of the public sphere approach this debate
from the angle of philosophical critique of religion and ongoing secularization.

As German philosopher and sociologist Jürgen Habermas has noted, the
idea of a public sphere lies between the normative understanding of the

society and the empirical experience of democracy.[2] He identifies the origin of this model in the Athenian city-state, where the householder organized the assembly. Hannah Arendt framed the notion of public sphere by looking back to the Greek *polis* as the place where the excellence of the public good is exposed. Though her conception can be seen as an elitist model, it does not extend to the way that society organizes economic life and interest.[3] The arguments can be read against a background of the commonly discussed theories of ideological legitimization, namely republican, biblical, and liberal.

In terms of the Catholic Church, two levels of interpenetration among church, state, and society are at work. First, theology as the public discourse of a community of faith has to find a means of self-recognition and of public argument with the rest of the society. Second, as an organized institution the church is definitely concerned with political transformations that affect people's lives, and it takes practical steps to effect such transformations. That is why, as stated in the introductory quotation by Benedict XVI, the church must play an important role in the preservation of values and ideals in society.

Though the involvement of the church in the public sphere is not new in Africa, there is an aggressive desire of church leaders to be heard. This has been evident throughout the continent since Vatican II, which did not clearly bridge the gap of church-state separation. However, the council did initiate a change in thinking about church-state relations, religious freedom, and political participation in the world. The rise of democratization has opened up the public sphere and has provided space for a much more organized civil society. The church itself is not at the margin of this process, but its involvement has been described as reactive instead of active.

My purpose in this essay is to locate the role of the church at three levels: (1) as an ecclesial community, (2) as a part of a society in which its voice must be heard, and (3) as a role player in social transformation.

The second African Synod presents an opportunity for the church to contribute productively to the construction of a society that embodies the values of reconciliation, justice, and peace in Africa. Several documents elaborate on the triple theme of the synod, including the *Lineamenta*, the *Instrumentum Laboris*, the *Message of the Synod*, the *Propositions of the Synod*, and various articles and commentaries.

Building an Ecclesial Community in the Public Sphere

The ecclesial boundaries of the church are within the community that shares a common faith and a set of beliefs. The primary goal of its institutional and ministerial praxis is the ongoing effort to found and build a church nourished by the Spirit. This understanding of the nature and meaning of the church corresponds to the traditional ecclesiology that remains open to social and political realities. This openness is encapsulated in the church's tradition of Catholic social teaching.

Since the end of the nineteenth century the church has constantly paid attention to economic, social, and political issues. Until then, the councils were the primary means for expressing this concern. The inaugural, systematized, and determinative statement of the tradition of Catholic social teaching came with Pope Leo XIII's *Rerum Novarum* (1891), which blazed the trail for successive papal documents on socioeconomic and political issues.[4]

From its inception Catholic social teaching has found its roots in the scriptures, where the Law and the prophets, on one hand, and Jesus' ministry, on the other, provide a substantial body of instructions and directions for community life. The interpretation and reappropriation of this foundation inspired discourses by theologians such as Basil of Caesarea, John Chrysostom, Ambrose, Augustine, and Aquinas, to mention a few.[5] "The examples could be easily multiplied, citing other biblical and patristic texts. The point is that the early Church was always cognizant of the political realm but tended not to develop political theories as much as pastoral strategies."[6]

Arguably the most important component of this tradition is the body of papal statements and encyclicals that engages the church in the public debate and defines the arguments of its involvement in political life. From Leo XIII to Benedict XVI, Catholic social teaching offers an understanding of democracy that coincides with or echoes the reflections proposed by philosophers and political theorists. Yet the church has not always been an enthusiastic promoter of democracy.[7] The classic case is the 1832 encyclical *Mirari Vos* of Pope Gregory XVI, which, as Manuel, Reardon, and Wilcox point out, opposed "elected assemblies, freedom of the press, freedom of conscience and the separation of Church and state."[8]

Against this historical background the body of texts now available confirms the Catholic commitment to a fruitful role of the church in the public sphere. The multiple challenges it confronts determine its mission and orient its action in a variety of contexts—national entities, international agencies, civil society, nongovernmental institutions, and so on. The Catholic Church has found ways to assert the importance of its involvement and presence in the public realm. Typically it advocates for human rights, the political participation of all citizens, and the involvement of different groups in promoting the common good.[9] As stated in the *Final List of Propositions:*

> The evangelizing mission of the Church-Family of God in Africa draws on several resource materials, prominent and foremost among which is the Scripture, the Word of God. But, as observed at the Synod ("*Relatio ante disceptationem*," p. 6), the conduct and character of the Church's ministry are enhanced by several "supports events and

material," "*subsidia fide*," such as *The Compendium of the Social Doctrine of the Church*, a very comprehensive guide on the Church's mission and self-expression in the world and its social order as "teacher" and "leaven." (no. 18)

This view of the church as teacher and leaven resonates with the approach to church-state relations adopted by Vatican Council II. The council's *Pastoral Constitution on the Church in the Modern World (Gaudium et Spes)* was an attempt by the church to discuss the contemporary issues that affect world peace and the economic order. The proposed image was that of "a helpmate to all persons of good will, whether Catholic or not, whether Christian or not, and as beacon of hope for a better world."[10] This effort to make clear the church's involvement in the world's expectations is a significant response to questions about the role of the church in the public sphere. In resolutely confronting themes such as economic life, political community, and peace among peoples, the church understands her mission as that of an institution involved in the fate of the world.

In elaborating the conditions for genuine human development and a better political community, *Gaudium et Spes* emphasizes principles that promote the building of human society. Its fourth chapter firmly states:

The Church and the political community in their own fields are autonomous and independent from each other. Yet both, under different titles, are devoted to the personal and social vocation of the same men. The more that both foster sounder cooperation between themselves with due consideration for the circumstances of time and place, the more effective will their service be exercised for the good of all. For man's horizons are not limited only to the temporal order; while living in the context of human history, he preserves intact his eternal vocation. The Church, for her part, founded on the love of the Redeemer, contributes toward the reign of justice and charity within the borders of a nation and between nations. (no. 76)

In fact, ever since the council, the church has relentlessly initiated peacebuilding reflections on the basis of its Christian worldview. Although Vatican II was the beginning of a movement of renewal, the ecumenical assembly produced, to use Kenneth Himes's term, "an array of images for self-understanding" of the church's mission.[11] From this perspective the ecclesiological proposition of Vatican II adequately matches the conscious demands of today's world. By its theological aspirations and its concerns for a dialogue with contemporary society, the church remains attentive to possible changes occurring in human existence. Indeed, the development of its teaching is founded on the conviction that its mission to achieve reconciliation, justice, and peace is a response to the demand of the gospel of Jesus Christ. Acknowledging such a challenge is to avow at the same time that the service of the church is God's service. Since our world is marked by a lack of reconciliation, stained by injustice, and torn by violence, the service of the church is oriented *ad extra* and *ad intra*—mission and communion.

Back to the Synod:
The Service of Reconciliation, Peace, and Justice

The church understands itself as playing an important role in the world. Its mission exposes the dynamics of its commitment and makes public the elements of profound engagement for a more transformative presence in the public sphere. It does not overstep its boundaries when it takes action in the service of reconciliation, justice, and peace. The theological foundation of these three concepts should be noted: the subtitle from the Gospel of Matthew is "You are the salt of the earth. . . . You are the light of the world" (Mt 5:13, 14).

Reconciliation, Justice, and Peace: Bridging the Gaps

Reconciliation can be understood through its connection with the biblical idea of restoring communion. The breaking of the covenant with God or the unity among the sons and daughters of Israel creates an urgent need for reconciliation as faithfulness to the word of God who promises to be faithful to his people.[12] The Book of Genesis narrates stories of how humankind breaks its relationship with God (Gn 3) and how Joseph, once sold by his brothers, was eventually reconciled to them (Gn 37:12–28; Gn 45:7). Furthermore, the *Lineamenta* of the second African Synod includes explicit quotations and clear biblical orientations connected to the general theme of the assembly.

The panoramic view of the African continent presented in the first chapter of the *Lineamenta* is echoed by Cardinal Peter Kodwo Appiah Turkson, then archbishop of Cape Coast (Ghana), who was in charge of the *Relatio ante Disceptationem*, the preliminary report to the synod. In his well-elaborated report during the first general meeting of the synod, Cardinal Turkson argued that reconciliation is a passage from hostility to peace, from alienation to communion. The whole process must guide us to justice (2 Cor 5:21; Gal 3:13; Rom 8:5). Founded on Christ's gift of "abundant life," reconciliation must be sought for the communion it realizes. The sacramentality of the church defined as family should help in building up the communion of brothers and sisters, overcoming the limitations of human contingences. The same point was made by Archbishop Laurent Monsengwo Pasinya (Kinshasa) when he presented an assessment of the reception of *Ecclesia in Africa*, the post-synodal exhortation of John Paul II after the first African Synod:

This is why the ideal of Christian reconciliation, pardon and love transcends all human efforts. It needs the force of the Holy Spirit to live, grow and perfect itself, that Spirit of love that spreads in our hearts (cf. Rom 5:5, 8:15) through the sacramentary economy of the Church: "You must therefore be perfect, just as your heavenly Father is perfect" (Mt 5:48). Perfect reconciliation is deployed and lived in the Church–Family of God inasmuch as the Sacrament of God's salvation is the place and instrument of reconciliation and pardon.[13]

Reconciliation, however, is unachievable without justice. The notion that reconciliation and justice go hand in hand is rooted in the building of the kingdom of God. Justice for the kingdom goes far beyond respect for the law. According to the *Instrumentum Laboris*, the kingdom of God, based on the reign of justice and peace, promotes the ethical dimension of the human need for a better world (nos. 44–47). Ways to reconciliation, justice, and peace are paved by human efforts to achieve these goals. Yet such efforts cannot be successful if they are not nourished by a seed planted by God. This is the specific mission of the church: it is called to serve. This service is exemplified by the model of church proposed by the first African Synod, namely, the church as God's family.

For the Service of Humankind: Koinonia *and* Diakonia

The association of these two ecclesial dimensions is in perfect harmony with the commonly articulated ecclesiology of communion and service. This terminology is very appropriate for the specific community of the universal church we are addressing, namely, the church in Africa. For almost half a century the theology of the church has been approached in a new methodological manner. Until Vatican II, systematic theology suggested that to understand the nature of the church fully, an ecclesiology of the mystical body was important. Even rigid approaches that had shaped speculative ecclesiology for centuries were abandoned in favor of a more communal understanding.[14] Yet the notion of the church as communion is not reducible to a single understanding or model. Church as communion can be understood from various perspectives: the sacraments, the people of God, the body of Christ, and so on. The reason for this is clear: "Communion refers first to the *causa* or the very *thing* of the Church, its *res*. Communion is not the structure of the Church, but its essence; as stated by the council, its mystery."[15] Thanks to the flourishing development of doctrine since Vatican II and the encouraging appropriation of the social sciences (*Gaudium et Spes*, no. 62), we are now well equipped to explore new, effective, and more adequate ecclesiologies for our time.

So, how does the ecclesiology of the church as family of God contribute to the mission of the church in the public sphere, which is made of various and diverse entities? Both the first and second African synods presuppose this question in all its complexities. Anthony Egan's essay in this volume raises a similar question in regard to the particular situation of South Africa. In my attempt to answer this question, I first explain why the configuration of the church in Africa, corresponding to the whole Catholic Church, bears a historically grounded vision and a speculative and idealistic approach. Second, I locate the ecclesiology of the church as family of God as a specific form of an ecclesiology of communion. Third, I suggest that this approach is not definitive or without limitation. The use of images or symbolic language always bears this limitation since the sign never totally discloses the signified.

The ecclesiological stand of this second African Synod clearly affirms the servant model of the church. This understanding situates the church both within and without the boundaries of the ecclesial community. In this context the work of reconciliation, justice, and peace can be characterized as one that brings the church into the midst of all the collaborative effort within the human community. Avery Dulles writes:

> The theological method accompanying this type of ecclesiology differs from the more authoritarian types of theology that have become familiar to us in the past centuries. This method may be called "secular-dialogic": secular, because the Church takes the world as a properly theological locus, and seeks to discern the signs of the times; dialogic, because it seeks to operate on the frontier between the contemporary world and the Christian tradition (including the Bible), rather than simply apply the latter as a measure of the former.[16]

According to the *Lineamenta* of the second African Synod, the understanding of the church as family opens up the real meaning of the life of the community. The mission of the church is to instill communication among its members. The *Lineamenta* refers unambiguously to the ecclesiological model of the church as servant as it describes the social, political, economic, and cultural priorities that fall within its purview: the challenges of good governance, management of public affairs, and the need to save African cultures in the global context of our time (nos. 10–17). The servant or diaconal dimension of the church as family is based on the exemplary love of Jesus for his disciples (Jn 13:15) and the testimony of the Good Samaritan (Lk 10:29–37). In recognizing human suffering we also recognize our hope that the kingdom of God provides an alternative to the current situation. As a servant of reconciliation, justice, and peace, the church calls all its members to a deep *metanoia* or conversion (Mk 1:15).

It is striking that the *Lineamenta* mentions the experiences of national conferences or truth and reconciliation commissions in exploring paths in the service of reconciliation, justice, and peace. The visibility of this service is truly the expression of ministry at the service of humankind. As a sign and instrument of reconciliation, justice, and peace, the church is called to operate in coherence with the prophetic identity of its service—salt of the earth, light of the world.

The service of reconciliation, justice, and peace is a work of solidarity with people who are suffering; it should be a lived experience of mutual help. If the contribution of the church in Africa is to announce the gospel of Christ, the fruitfulness of this ministry ought to be visible in the lives of all believers. Throughout the past decades the church has striven to meet these various challenges, at times by the traditional affirmation of its mission and at others by new imperatives to reframe the church's efforts to promote human dignity. *Gaudium et Spes* highlights this point when it states that it is all about the salvation of the human person, the renewal of human society (no. 3).

The Church in Democratizing Societies

As noted above, the involvement of the church in the public sphere and its engagement with social, political, and economic issues facilitates the sharing of Catholic social teaching. There is an evident desire today to revitalize this mission of the church in Africa and the church's rich legacy of Catholic social teaching. As the relationship between the church and the African democratizing societies has become more and more collaborative, we have become aware that the foundation of this understanding of the church's mission is based on the legacy of Vatican II.

The council's documents articulate quite comprehensively the need for the church to be part of the changing world. The *Lineamenta* and the *Instrumentum Laboris* contain many references not only to *Gaudium et Spes*,[17] but also to the *Decree on the Church's Missionary Activity (Ad Gentes Divinitus)*,[18] the *Declaration on the Relation of the Church to Non-Christian Religions (Nostra Aetate)*, and the *Declaration on Religious Liberty (Dignitatis Humane)*. In particular, the church's interest in politics is explained by the shift initiated by *Gaudium et Spes*.

The church, which cannot be indifferent, tries to go beyond the traditional thesis/hypothesis method for assessing church-state relations. On the basis of this method

the thesis was that the Catholic Church, as the institutional expression of the one, true religion, ought to be given a privileged public role in the life of the nation. The hypothesis was that exceptions to the thesis could be made if implementation of the thesis would lead to civil unrest and severe animosity toward the Church and its members.[19]

It is undoubtedly *Dignitatis Humane* that allowed a workable recon-
ceptualization of the relation between church and modern society. Becoming
a real partner with civil society thrust the church forward in the search for
peace and justice.

In 1971 the General Synod of Bishops called attention to justice in the
world. Many analysts acknowledge that this event marked a turning point.
The synod's final document, *Justice in the World,* stated, "Action on behalf of justice and participation in the transformation of the world fully
appear to us as a constitutive dimension of the preaching of the Gospel, or,
in other words, of the Church's mission for the redemption of the human
race and its liberation from every oppressive situation" (no. 6).

In response to the challenge of this new configuration, especially given
current political trends in various African countries, the church has been
present as active participant in the democratic process. In the words of
M. A. Garreton, "Christianity is prophetic: it fights against injustice in
order to put an end to it. Politics is the art of the possible. It fights against
injustice in order not to be destroyed by it. This is the drama that links, yet
distinguishes, these key components of . . . [human] societies."[20] Undeniably, the role of mainstream religious leaders in Africa's democratization
process has been decisive. It has brought support and collaboration to political action to forge a framework within institutions.[21] This is not to suggest
that what I call a new configuration is a groundbreaking trend in the church
mission. Instead, it refers to the decisive but as yet unachieved mission that
appeals to the collaboration of the church and the state.

The transition to democracy in Africa in the 1990s has changed the
political culture and framed new relationships between church and state
in Africa. Now that the church has committed itself and considers itself
an important partner with the state, it must also affirm its autonomy in
regard to the state's comprehensive authority. Catholic social teaching
always insists on the distinction between the state and society. The democratic authority of the state comes from service to the community.
Practically speaking, the political community comprises many other small
communities whose legitimacy in the political realm relies on their contribution to the common good of all. But, as Vatican II affirms in *Gaudium
et Spes:* "The practical ways in which the political community structures
itself and regulates public authority can vary according to the particular
character of a people and its historical development. But these methods
should always serve to mold men who are civilized, peace-loving, and well
disposed toward all—to the advantage of the whole human family" (no.
74).

As the second African Synod affirms, the church in Africa as part of
society contributes to the defining task of the state through the work of its
members. It recognizes and affirms both the authority and the responsibility of the state in the promotion of reconciliation, justice, and peace.[22]

Conclusion

In the African context the public debate on the role of the church in the public sphere remains open. From place to place various situations need to be studied carefully and with specific nuances. Yet trends since the democratization process of the 1990s indicate that the church is firmly engaged in this (re)evolution. Such a process definitely questions and clarifies its attitude in regard to the public sphere.

Thanks to Vatican II and subsequent work, the church in Africa today has found its way between two seeming opposites: fidelity to the universal church and creativity according to local context and culture. From the first African Synod to the second African Synod, both of which are grounded in the legacy of Vatican II, the mission of the church in the public sphere reveals its theological self-understanding and allows for better participation in the promotion of reconciliation, justice, and peace. This mission calls for a prophetic engagement of the church with the state and with society.

Notes

[1] See Michael J. Perry, *Religion in Politics: Constitutional and Moral Perspectives* (New York: Oxford University Press, 1997); Mark Tushnet, "The Limits of Involvement of Religion in the Body Politic," in *The Role of Religion in the Making of Public Policy*, ed. James E. Wood, Jr., 191–220 (Waco, TX: Baylor University Press, 1991); Jürgen Moltmann, *God for a Secular Society: The Public Relevance of Theology* (Minneapolis: Fortress Press, 1999); and Zablon Nthamburi, "Theology and Politics in Africa," in *Democracy and Reconciliation: A Challenge for African Christianity*, ed. Laurenti Magesa and Zablon Nthamburi, 135–62 (Nairobi: Acton Publishers, 2003).

[2] Jürgen Habermas, *The Structural Transformation of the Public Sphere* (Cambridge: Polity Press, 1989).

[3] Hannah Arendt, *Crises of the Republic* (New York: Harcourt, 1972).

[4] See *Le discours social de l'Eglise catholique: De Léon XIII à Benoît XVI.* Documents réunis et présentés par le CERAS (Montrouge: Editions Bayard, 2009); Conseil Pontifical, *Justice et Paix: Compendium de la doctrine sociale de l'Eglise* (Città del Vaticano: Libreria Editrice Vaticana, 2005); and *Propositions of the Synod*, no. 18.

[5] Saint Basil, *Homélie 6 contre la richesse.* PG, 31, 277; Jean Chrysostome, *Homélie 10.* PG, 61, 86; Augustine, *De Trinitate*, I, 14, ch. 9. PL, 42, 1046; Thomas Aquinas, ST II, II, q. 66, a. 2.

[6] Kenneth R. Himes, "Vatican II and Contemporary Politics," in *The Catholic Church and the Nation-State: Comparative Perspectives*, ed. Paul C. Manuel, Lawrence C. Reardon, and Clyde Wilcox (Washington DC: Georgetown University Press, 2006), 16.

[7] See Manuel, Reardon, and Wilcox, *The Catholic Church and the Nation-State*, 7.

[8] Ibid.

[9] *Propositions of the Synod,* nos. 5 and 15.

[10] John W. O'Malley, *What Happened at Vatican II?* (Cambridge, MA: The Belknap Press, 2008), 233.

[11] Himes, "Vatican II and Contemporary Politics," 17.

[12] See Paul Béré's analysis of the biblical notion of reconciliation in this volume.

[13] Laurent Monsengwo Pasinya, *Rapport sur Ecclesia in Africa,* §4.5. Available in English on the zenit.org website.

[14] Benoît-Dominique de La Soujeole, "'Société' et 'Communion' chez saint Thomas d'Aquin: Etude d'Ecclésiologie," *Revue thomiste* 90 (1990): 587–662; and "L'Eglise comme société et l'Eglise comme communion au deuxième concile de Vatican," *Revue thomiste* 91 (1990): 219–58.

[15] Walter Kasper, "L'Eglise comme communion: un fil conducteur de l'ecclésiologie de Vatican II," *Communio* 12, no. 1 (1987): 18, my translation. See also Jean Rigal, "Trois approches de l'ecclésiologie de communion: Congar, Zizioulas, Moltmann," *Nouvelle revue théologique* 120, no. 4 (1998): 605–19.

[16] Avery Dulles, *Models of the Church,* exp. ed. (New York: Doubleday, 1987), 92.

[17] *Lineamenta,* nos. 44, 45, 48, 58, 62, and 71, and *Instrumentum Laboris,* no. 120.

[18] *Instrumentum Laboris,* no. 148.

[19] Himes, "Vatican II and Contemporary Politics," 25.

[20] M. A. Garreton, quoted by Laurenti Magesa, in "Celebrate Catholic Social Teaching," *New People* (January-February 2007), 7.

[21] See Jeff Haynes, *Religion and Politics in Africa* (Nairobi: East African Educational Publishers; London: Zed Books, 1996), 104–33; Paul Clifford, *The Christian Churches and the Democratization of Africa* (New York: E. J. Brill, 1995).

[22] See *Message to the People of God of the Second Special Assembly for Africa of the Synod of Bishops,* nos. 34–35; and *Propositions of the Synod,* nos. 24–25. Available on the vatican.va website.

8

Governance beyond Rhetoric

The South African Challenge to the African Synod

ANTHONY EGAN

As the most newly democratized state in Africa and one that is rooted in the principle of separation of religion and state, South Africa presents a test case for the second African Synod's comments on good governance. After outlining the synod proposals, I examine the particularities of government in the new South Africa to see how effective and how realistic the synod's position might be. I focus in particular on how, even before the synod, the Catholic Church engaged with the secular democratic state on matters of public policy, and then I ouline the kind of "ground rules" such engagement must inevitably follow.

The Second African Synod on Governance

The 2006 *Lineamenta* affirms the importance of a political role for the church in Africa. It stresses that the historical, political, and economic dilemmas of Africa are those of post-colonial states facing the tensions created by a past dominated by the imposition of a Western political dispensation that many national liberation movements (themselves products of the colonial system) adopted at independence. The effect was often political fragmentation and dissociation. This effect became manifest in anti-colonialism expressed in colonial language, critique, *and* imitation of the West. It was also visible in the creation of neocolonial orders that benefitted the new anti-colonial elites and had the effect of destroying indigenous cultures deemed obstacles to progress. On the eve of the African Synod, the *Instrumentum Laboris* reaffirmed the importance of these points, noting with hope the growing sense of civic consciousness and commitment to making democracy work on the continent (nos. 22–33).

The language of these documents articulates an ecclesiology of the church as family of God (the theme of the first African Synod), as sacrament of reconciliation, and as witness to the light of Christ in Africa. There is a tension inherent in these themes, themes implicitly recognized in the "social analysis" included in these documents: Africa is not a Catholic but a religiously pluralist continent. Despite its enormous role in social and educational ministry crossing Christian and faith boundaries, the church needs to tread lightly in its theological articulation of its self-identity, particularly in countries like South Africa where the church is a minority. The Catholic Church cannot unilaterally and categorically pronounce on matters of governance. An ecclesiology that is understood as triumphalist raises the specter among non-Catholics of a church using its many resources as a cover for proselytism.

Significantly, the *Message to the People of God of the Second Special Assembly for Africa of the Synod of Bishops* has played down this aspect of the church's mission, explicitly calling for cooperation between Christians and believers of other faiths to promote justice and peace on the continent. Turning to Catholics, it calls on Catholic laity involved in politics and governance to "allow your Christian faith to permeate every aspect and facet of your lives; in the family, at work, in the professions, in politics and public life" (no. 22), to study the Catechism and social teaching of the church, and to educate themselves in the faith.

Commending Catholics in public life, the synod reminds them that they are in "an apostolate to promote the common good and God's kingdom of justice, love and peace" and extols the example of Catholics like Julius Nyerere, stating, "Africa needs saints in high political office: saintly politicians who will clean the continent of corruption, work for the good of the people, and know how to galvanize other men and women of good will from outside the Church to join hands against the common evils that beset our nations" (no. 23).

In addition, the synod encouraged the local church to support public leaders spiritually and to encourage them to avoid corruption. In perhaps the most dramatic part of the text, the synod noted: "Many Catholics in high office have fallen woefully short in their performance in office. The Synod calls on such people to *repent, or quit the public arena and stop causing havoc to the people and giving the Church a bad name* (no. 23, emphasis added). These are poignant words, even if they seem limited in their scope (to corruption) and their focus (to Catholics). Questions arise: Is this anything other than rhetoric? Can it have any impact, even on Catholics involved in public life? To examine this I turn now to my case study, South Africa.

South Africa: Democracy and Dominance

South Africa emerged from the authoritarianism of apartheid in 1994. It has a multi-party democratic system, separation of powers, a constitution, and one of the most liberal bills of rights in the world. Its Constitutional Court, accessible to all who seek final arbitration in human rights or constitutional matters, is effective and well respected. Breaking away from a "winner takes all" candidate-based system, it employs a party-list proportional-representation electoral system in which voters vote for a party, not an individual. Parties draft candidate lists in order of internal popularity. The proportional representation system was created in order to favor political diversity—smaller parties have a greater chance of getting a few seats than in the old Westminster system used before 1994.[1] The advantage is that voting is clear; the disadvantage is that parties have inordinate control over who goes to parliament.

In effect, South Africa is a one-party-dominant situation.[2] The ruling African National Congress (ANC), which has never received less than 63 percent of the vote, is hegemonic: what the ANC decides, the country gets. The only significant check on the ANC is the Constitutional Court. However, the judges of the court are appointed for a fixed term by a strongly ANC-influenced Judicial Services Commission. Though many ANC-leaning judges on the court have put their loyalties aside in the interests of interpreting the constitution, it is not inconceivable that in the near future the court may itself come under undue influence from the ruling party.

The real power in South Africa, the ANC, is at once almost monolithic yet divided. Although it is a liberation movement built from its grassroots upward to its national leadership elected at regular national conferences,[3] it has never quite escaped the centralist style of government acquired during its exile years. Once elected, in between congresses, its national leadership exercises considerable control over almost every aspect of policy implementation and, most significantly, the vetting of candidates for the legislature. Central to this is the right of recall—sometimes called redeployment—of members, including parliamentarians. Given that holding office has many perks and privileges, not least the possibility of lucrative connections to economic elites close to the party, it is implicit (if not explicit) that loyalty to the party line is essential for advancement in public office. Obedience is essential, even if it is sometimes at the cost of personal convictions.

The real space for political change and opposition is within the dominant party, which is composed of a number of political tendencies—liberal, conservative, African traditionalist, Christian, and Marxist. The ANC is the dominant partner in the Tripartite Alliance, with the South African Communist Party and the Congress of South African Trade Unions. The latter groups represent a vocal opposition to the ANC's economic neo-liberal agenda. After Nelson Mandela's resignation from the presidency in 1999, the neo-liberals enjoyed nine years of dominance within the party under Thabo Mbeki.[4] Mbeki's reign came to an ignominious end when he and his colleagues were defeated at the December 2007 Polokwane ANC National Conference by a coalition of the "poor"—populists and socialists led by Jacob Zuma.[5] With new leaders in Luthuli House (the ANC's headquarters in Johannesburg), many Mbeki loyalists were not selected for the 2009 election lists. Official patronage, some cynics argue, shifted from one bloc to another.

Despite ANC hegemony, South Africa remains a politically complex entity. This complexity can be summed up as follows:

Secular yet religious: South Africa is a secular state with a significant minority of persons without religious beliefs, yet overall it is still a deeply religious and religiously conservative country. The ANC has a long tradition both of religiosity (strong support among Christians, including a tradition of active clergy members going back to its foundation in 1912) and secularism (mainly through its alliance with the Communist Party). Given the deeply fragmented nature of its Christian community, there is no possibility of a "state church," even if it were desirable.

Rich yet poor: Officially a middle-income economy, South Africa has one of the highest levels of economic inequality in the world and extensive unemployment/poverty. Since 1994 unemployment statistics have varied between 25 and 40 percent. Although black economic empowerment and affirmative action have created a sizable new middle and upper class, the poor generally have grown poorer. Poor education—a legacy of apartheid and unrealistic post-1994 schooling policies—has created a skills shortage in many sectors and a lack of skills transferability in a globalizing market. This has led to many jobs being filled by immigrants from other parts of the continent, which in turn has increased xenophobia and violence.

Reconciliation yet racism: Despite the success of the Truth and Reconciliation Commission (TRC), hailed as one of the best of its kind, there remain many unreconciled people. Victim reparations were mishandled. Many resented that perpetrators who had only to "reveal all" to be pardoned apparently escaped without punishment. A significant minority, mostly from the former white ruling class, regarded the TRC process as biased in favor of the ANC and withdrew into their privileged enclaves.[6] The upshot of it all was, for the most part, polarization and the resurgence of identity politics—both black and white.[7]

Liberal yet socially conservative: The ANC's social liberalism in matters like the equality of women, abortion rights, gay rights (including marriage), and opposition to the death penalty flies in the face of a population that is generally deeply patriarchal, homophobic, pro life, and, particularly in response to high crime rates and poor policing, broadly in favor of capital punishment. Social liberalism reflects South Africa's Constitution and Bill of Rights. While many call for parts of it to be changed to reflect real social mores, there is a fear that once such a precedent is set, it might be used to undermine democracy itself and entrench ANC rule.

Universalism in rights yet culturally mediated: Rooted in a strong Western-type universal human rights culture, South Africans are faced with multiple contestations over the nature of these human rights. Echoing Bénézet Bujo's warning—that Western values are appealed to when it suits the self-interests of new ruling elites but that tradition is trotted out to keep the masses under control, but never the other way round—we see the widespread misuse of both rights and culture in defense of sectoral interest.[8]

Good governance yet corruption: Although committed to good governance, there remain high levels of corruption. Transparency International's annual Corruption Perception Index has shown a dramatic slide in South Africa's standing for clean governance, from the top twenty to thirty least corrupt countries in 1995 to fifty-fifth in 2008.[9] The cause for this slump varies: "sweetener deals" for MPs and administration officials working with corporations (in other words, bribes posing as gifts to facilitate lucrative government tenders); misappropriation of public funds; undeclared conflicts of interests by officials owning companies dealing with the state; and so on.

In short, there is much in the new South Africa that is relevant to the kind of challenges the African Synod put forward regarding governance.

The Church Responding

Despite the relevance of the African Synod to South Africa, the ideals that this synod expresses cannot easily be effectively implemented in the country. To understand why, we need to first look at the state of the Catholic Church in South Africa and then to the way in which the church *has* in fact responded to the new democratic situation through structures that have been in place almost since the arrival of democracy in 1994.

The 1996 and 2001 national censuses reveal a highly diverse church situation in South Africa.[10] African Initiated Churches combined with Pentecostals and "other churches" effectively constitute the "mainline" churches in contemporary South Africa. African Pentecostalism is closer to the African Initiated Churches in style and theology than to historically white Pentecostalism.[11] Similarly, many mainline Protestant churches show Pentecostal/charismatic tendencies. The high levels of "refused/no religion/ not stated" in the survey (18.3 percent in 1996, 16.4 percent in 2001) suggest a high degree of secularization of South African society compared to the rest of Africa. While whites are heavily represented in this category, many blacks, including many politicians, are on record as regarding themselves as atheists or agnostics.

What is clear, however, is that the Catholic Church in South Africa is in decline. Its membership as a percentage of the "market share" of the population is dropping, despite the fact that it remains the second-largest single church in the country after the Zion Christian Church. Catholics are found across party lines, including many within the ruling ANC, rather than as a Catholic bloc. They vote according to their interests and political sympathies, not as believers. Despite a high institutional profile in the struggle period, the average Catholic has limited knowledge of Catholic social teaching and does not as a rule see the need to become educated in the faith beyond what is required for the sacramental rites of passage.

It is very difficult for the Catholic Church to influence governance in the country directly. Despite the ANC government's liberal social agenda, which the majority reject according to reliable and comprehensive surveys (for example, on abortion, gay marriage, women's equality, prohibition of capital punishment),[12] social conservatism has not translated into support for conservative parties, like the African Christian Democratic Party (ACDP). Economic interests, however imperfectly implemented by the ANC, as well as the sense that voting against the ANC would be voting against national liberation, hold sway. If the church were to align itself explicitly with the ACDP or to try to pressure its members not to vote for the ANC, the effect might be at best that Catholics would openly ignore the hierarchy or at worst would leave the church.[13] This would be particularly the case among Catholic MPs and party officials, whose careers are to varying degrees dependent on maintaining the good will of the party.

The Catholic hierarchy, while maintaining a clear and critical voice in the new South Africa, has opted for a different strategy, namely, the creation of the Southern African Catholic Bishops' Conference Parliamentary Liaison Office (CPLO). Planned as a means to help shape policy and legislation,[14] it was set up in Cape Town in 1999. Situated next door to Parliament in the archdiocesan offices, its purpose was primarily to create a "ripple effect": to engage with policy and clarify the thought of the MPs. "The idea was to open up in MPs' minds what theologian David Tracy calls discursive possibilities," commented its founder, Fr. Peter-John Pearson. "It was not, was never intended to be, occasions for Bible-thumping."[15] This involved interaction on a number of levels. By participating—together with other religious representatives—in portfolio committees, where most lawmaking is done, the CPLO has utilized the ANC government's explicit commitment to public debate over proposed legislation and made presentations and interventions on policy. The CPLO maintains good working relationships with MPs and cabinet ministers, often drawing on these relationships to organize meetings between legislators and bishops.

Through a system of "round tables" the CPLO has engaged with legislators, church persons, and wider civil society. The CPLO has used a strategic approach in selecting members to attend these meetings. Religious hardliners and "one issue" activists are not welcome. As Pearson observed, "It is no use to invite anyone interested in an issue. . . . Round tables are not the places for enraged clergy to sound off at government. We choose people who are familiar with the issues, with what parliament has been doing, and are actually working on the documents and proposals under discussion."[16]

Each round table is unique. Some are open to a range of groups, and others tend to focus on particular interested parties. Some do not even have parliamentarians present. In 2009 one such forum (in which the author was present) was set up between the churches and members of the South African

Law Commission who were investigating possible reforms of national prostitution laws. The South African Law Commission representative presented four options: maintaining but tidying up existing legislation (prostitution is currently illegal under two conflicting statutes), criminalizing solicitation but not prostitutes, decriminalization, and regulation. Participants, including Catholic, South African Council of Churches, and Dutch Reformed representatives, were invited to comment on the options and to consider the pros and cons of each.

Significantly, the tone of the debate was largely secular. As a secular democracy, the group recognized that no *explicitly* Christian or Catholic understanding would be helpful in law reform. What *did* emerge was a discourse that deeply echoed the kind of thinking associated with Catholic social teaching. Rather than asking "What does the Bible say?" or "What does God command?" the participants (Protestants included) asked, "What does this issue mean to the dignity of the human person?"

Within parliament the CPLO has contributed to issues as varied as the arms trade, black economic empowerment, child rights, religion-state relations, the budget, intergovernmental relations, and open democracy.[17] Some of its briefs have in fact been revised and incorporated into national legislation. Together with its colleagues from the South African Council of Churches, its joint People's Budget campaign has shown signs of bearing fruit in trying to encourage Parliament to take a more people-centered approach to economic growth.

Although it works primarily in the secular realm, the CPLO participates in the Southern African Catholic Bishops' Conference's Joint Agency Meeting, which meets three times a year to discuss the work of specialized Catholic agencies like the national Justice and Peace Commission, the national AIDS office, the Siyabhabha National Development Trust, the Denis Hurley Peace Institute, the Catholic Institute of Education, the Catholic Health Care Association, the Rural Education Access Program, the Rural Development Access Program, and, since 2007, the newly founded Jesuit Institute–South Africa, all organizations of the Catholic Church engaged in public and secular matters.

There are, inevitably, limits to CPLO intervention. In certain areas where the government has decided to adopt policies that go against the official teaching of the Catholic Church, the CPLO has simply reported that there is an impasse between church and state. As a movement with strong internal discipline and a commitment to implement its program, ANC dialogue partners understand the CPLO and the church perhaps better than church people imagine. This is, of course, no consolation to the church.

A positive new development has been attempts to give spiritual support to members of Parliament. During Lent 2010 the Jesuit Institute prepared email meditations for parliamentarians. While this effort was well received, particularly by the ANC, it does not as such constitute any kind of "chaplaincy." The notion of a Catholic chaplaincy itself is problematic. The ANC has long had a chaplaincy of its own, with chaplains ultimately appointed by and answerable to itself. Other parties, like the Democratic Alliance, have no such tradition. Within such a situation the space for influence is limited.

The Ongoing Challenge

In some ways the activity of the Catholic Church through the CPLO highlights not only what the church's response to government and governance in South Africa *is*, but also the limitations of church-state relations in a secular democracy. As philosopher Charles Taylor has indicated quite clearly, this is an age of secularism and one not likely to change.[18] Even though many people, including politicians, still believe in God, God and God's official representatives no longer have the direct influence or the authority they once had.

Is this trend reversible, and what is the value of such reversibility? Taylor doubts secularism will be cast aside, particularly in secular democratic states. Although some fundamentalists attempt to reverse the trend, it is unlikely they can succeed in the long term. Whether such states would be tolerable to the rest of the world, or to their own populations, is doubtful. Recent events in Iran show that even established fundamentalist states seem to have in-built limitations and weaknesses: protest against electoral fraud may have been suppressed this time around, but it seems that popular discontent will not forever be silenced. The de facto failed states of Somalia and Afghanistan remind us of the human cost of trying.

Simplistic statements and moral fulminations now fall on deaf ears in many countries, and even on co-religionists in public life. There is a need, only partly realized in the documents of the second African Synod, to develop a new approach to dealing with governance. This is particularly true in states like South Africa where dominant political party structures are strong, popular, and highly influential in the wider political and economic society.

Under the foregoing circumstances the challenge for the church is twofold. First, it has to confront and overcome its long, historical unease with democracy. Quite rightly, the church and figures like Pope Pius IX recognized that democracy would undermine religious authority. It did, and it has. However, one looks in vain for other systems of government that are less harmful than the democratic dispensation. The South African churches recognized this when they joined the struggle against apartheid, although they probably did not anticipate the liberalism of the state they helped to birth.

Second, the church has to play by a new set of ground rules, what Robert Audi calls the three guiding principles for church-state relations.[19] The *libertarian principle* affirms that the state has a duty, within the limits of civil-criminal law, to tolerate any and all religions to function within its borders. The *equalitarian principle* insists that no preference can be given to any religion over another. The *neutrality principle* insists that the state should neither favor nor disfavor religion as such. Audi insists that these rules apply equally to both religions and the state. He does not, however, claim that religions should stay out of the public arena. Rather, their engagement cannot simply be based on moral claims rooted in internal religious doctrines alone; they need to be expressed fully or partly in secular terms comprehensible to any secular person.

Such a view as Audi's seems close to the tradition of Catholic social thought and indeed is reflected in the documents of the African Synod. Even here, however, we must beware of basing our secular reasoning on—by secular definition unverifiable—religious presuppositions, for example, our notions of personhood that are at root religious but couched in secular language.

Audi's insistence that "reason without intuition [read: faith] is at best too formal to guide everyday life" but that "faith requires sufficient reason to interpret its objects and human life in general" offers us a way forward for Catholic engagement with secular democracy in South Africa, Africa, and elsewhere.[20] Closer attention should be given as to *how* the church might communicate its moral message about democracy. The African Synod opens the debate and offers some insight, but stirring rhetoric is not enough.

Notes

[1] Bertha Chiroro, *Electoral System and Accountability: Options for Electoral Reform in South Africa*, Policy Paper 3 (Johannesburg: Konrad Adenauer Stiftung, 2008).

[2] Hermann Giliomee and Charles Simkins, eds., *The Awkward Embrace: One-Party Domination and Democracy* (Cape Town: Tafelberg, 1999).

[3] Vincent Darracq, "The African National Congress (ANC) Organization at the Grassroots," *African Affairs* 107, no. 429 (2008): 589–609. For a less sanguine, more realistic, analysis, see Tom Lodge, "The ANC and the Development of Party Politics in Modern South Africa," *Journal of Modern African Studies* 42, no. 2 (2004): 189–219.

[4] For an account of Mbeki's presidency, see Mark Gevisser, *The Dream Deferred: Thabo Mbeki* (Cape Town: Jonathan Ball, 2007); and William Mervin Gumede, *Thabo Mbeki and the Battle for the Soul of the ANC* (London: Zed Books, 2007).

[5] For analyses of the significance of Zuma and his rise to power, see Xolela Mangcu, *To the Brink: The State of Democracy in South Africa* (Pietermaritzburg: University of KwaZulu Natal Press, 2008); Roger Southall and John Daniel, eds., *Zunami! The 2009 South African Election* (Johannesburg: Jacana Media/ Konrad Adenauer Stiftung, 2009); and Somadela Fikeni, "The Polokwane Moment and South Africa's Democracy at the Crossroads," in *State of the Nation: South Africa 2008*, ed. Peter Kagwanja and Kwandiwe Kondlo, 3–34 (Cape Town: HSRC Press, 2009).

[6] For examples of the literature, see Terry Bell and Dumisa Buhle Ntsebeza, *Unfinished Business: South Africa, Apartheid and Truth* (London: Verso, 2003); Alex Boraine, *A Country Unmasked: Inside South Africa's Truth and Reconciliation Commission* (Cape Town: Oxford University Press, 2000); James L. Gibson, *Overcoming Apartheid: Can Truth Reconcile a Divided Nation?* (New York: Russell Sage Foundation, 2004); and Deborah Posel and Graeme Simpson, eds., *Commissioning the Past: Understanding South Africa's Truth and Reconciliation Commission* (Johannesburg: Witwatersrand University Press, 2002).

[7] See Adrian Hadland, "'I Am an African'—But You Are Not," *Cape Times* (October 16, 2007), 9; and Ivor Chipkin, *Do South Africans Exist? Nationalism, Democracy and the Identity of "The People"* (Johannesburg: Witwatersrand University Press, 2007).

[8] Bénézet Bujo, *The Ethical Dimension of Community: The African Model and the Dialogue Between North and South* (Nairobi: Paulines Publications, 1998), 156.

[9] See details on the transparency.org website.

[10] These statistics in this section are based on analyses in H. J. Hendriks, "Religion in South Africa: Census '96," *South African Christian Handbook 2001/2002* (Tyger Valley: Christian Network Media/TM, 2001); and H. J. Hendriks and J. Erasmus, "Religion in South Africa: The 2001 Census Data," *Journal of Theology for Southern Africa* 121 (2005): 88–111. The observations in this section are based on research conducted for my essay "Kingdom Deferred: The Churches in the New South Africa, 1994–2006," in *State of the Nation: South Africa 2007*, ed. Sakhela Buhlungu, John Daniel, Roger Southall, and Jessica Lutchman, 448–69 (Cape Town: HSRC Press, 2007).

[11] Observed in A. H. Anderson and S. Otwang, *Tumelo: The Faith of African Pentecostals in South Africa* (Pretoria: UNISA Press, 1993).

[12] See Udesh Pillay, Benjamin Roberts, and Stephen Rule, eds., *South Africa Social Attitudes: Changing Times, Diverse Voices* (Cape Town: HSRC Press, 2006).

[13] I base this on my observations of the decline of white Catholics during the 1970s and 1980s when the church took a strong stance against apartheid and alienated many of its white members, a considerable number of whom joined Pentecostal/charismatic churches or stopped attending church altogether.

[14] Michail Rassool, "The Catholic Voice in Parliament," *The Southern Cross* (January 2006), 25–31.

[15] Peter-John Pearson, interview with author, February 27, 2006, quoted in Egan "Kingdom Deferred?" 463.

[16] Ibid.

[17] The scope of the CPLO involvement can be gauged by the columns Pearson writes fairly regularly in the Cape Town Archdiocese's bi-monthly newsletter, *Archdiocesan News*.

[18] Charles Taylor, *A Secular Age* (Cambridge, MA: Belknap Press, 2007).

[19] Robert Audi, *Religious Commitment and Secular Reason* (Cambridge: Cambridge University Press, 2000).

[20] Ibid., 215.

9

Agent of Reconciliation, Justice, and Peace

The Church in Africa in an Era of Globalization

ODOMARO MUBANGIZI

The universal church is taking Africa seriously by offering the continent a second opportunity to address the challenges that the African church faces. The first African Synod of 1994 came up with a new vision of church as family. But even as the synod deliberated on the meaning of this model of church, genocide erupted in Rwanda, raising questions about the depth of evangelization in Africa. Years later, at the time of the second African Synod in 2009, challenges facing the African church have become even more complex, requiring new pastoral strategies.

While African Catholics busied themselves with the *Lineamenta* in preparation for the second African Synod, Kenya and Zimbabwe were still nursing wounds inflicted on the population during electoral violence. Besides, the eastern Democratic Republic of Congo (DRC) remains fragile as various rebel groups claim legitimacy against the government. Sudan negotiates the delicate process of deciding whether to allow the southern part of the country to become autonomous from the Khartoum government. The *Statement of the Eastern African Bishops-Delegates to the African Synod* described the new context for the church as marked by the global economic crisis, poor governance marked by electoral violence, corruption, the environmental crisis, violent conflicts, the persistence of HIV/AIDS pandemic, a lack of self-reliance, and the need for capacity-building on the side of church personnel and institutions.[1]

In spite of the many challenges facing the African church, the contemporary phenomenon of globalization offers great opportunities for the church as a global actor to further its agenda of promoting justice, peace, and reconciliation. The success of this agenda requires a sustained focus on five

105

critical areas, namely, justice, peace, and reconciliation; sustainable development; health care; higher education for social transformation; and good governance. By integrating these issues into its ecclesial praxis, the church in Africa will fulfill its prophetic role and be a credible witness in a world yearning for change.

A social ethic and a theology that will guide the church in addressing Africa's complex social, economic, health, political, and educational needs will have to adopt a new methodology. The old method of theologizing grounded in Scholastic philosophy needs to be reassessed. The new methodology will have to embrace a social ethic and a theology that reflect on the African context by critically examining the social, economic, and political realities in Africa.[2] In addition to relying on philosophy as a "handmaid of theology," as has been the dominant model for theological reflection, the new paradigm for theological reflection in a global context will also have to take the social sciences seriously. This attention to the social sciences will help discern the logic and dynamics of sin and grace at work in social, economic, and political institutions, and serve as a basis for designing appropriate pastoral strategies.

After looking at the African context, I turn to the issue of globalization, which offers opportunities for the church to play a significant role in the public sphere, as a mixed blessing for Africa. I then argue that there is a pastoral imperative for the church in Africa to promote justice, peace, and reconciliation by focusing on the priority areas listed above. These areas serve as practical ways of living the vision of the second African Synod.

A Critical Look at the African Context

The challenges that face the African church can be discerned from the current social, economic, political, cultural, and pastoral context of the continent. Only after analyzing this context can appropriate pastoral strategies be designed, informed by a faith vision and mission.

On the socioeconomic front Africa is still marginalized. The economic structural adjustment programs of the 1980s and 1990s failed to lift Africa out of poverty. Even the institutions that had prescribed these reforms, the World Bank and International Monetary Fund, have admitted the abysmal failure of their policies. In the area of economic and social development Africa has made limited progress since the 1950s and 1960s. The *Lineamenta* of the second African Synod concurs with this assessment, naming

> deterioration in the standard of living, insufficient means of educating the young, the lack of elementary health and social services with the resulting persistence of endemic diseases, the spread of the terrible scourge of AIDS, the heavy and often unbearable burden of the international

debt, the horror of fratricidal wars fomented by unscrupulous arms trafficking, and the shameful, pitiable spectacle of refugees and displaced persons. (no. 15)

As a result of the above factors, the percentage of people who live on less than US$1 a day has remained as high as 30 percent in most African countries. Martin Meredith describes the reality of underdevelopment in Africa of the 1980s as follows:

> By the mid-1980s most Africans were as poor or poorer than they had been at the time of independence. Crippled by debt, mismanagement and collapse of tax revenues, African governments could no longer afford to maintain proper public services. Roads, railways, water, power and telephone systems deteriorated; schools, universities and hospitals were starved of funds; scientific facilities and statistical offices became early casualties. At every level the capacity of governments to function was fast diminishing.[3]

One serious consequence of such economic and social decline that has further worsened Africa's situation is "brain drain." It has been estimated that as many as 100,000 professionals left Africa between 1960 and 1987 to look for greener pastures abroad, while about 50,000 to 60,000 managers left Africa between 1986 and 1990.[4]

The consequences of such high levels of poverty are obvious: lack of basic education, health, nutrition, and decent shelter, as well as high infant mortality, low life expectancy, and general insecurity. A church that lives by the principle of living life to the full cannot ignore these issues of basic survival and claim to be preaching the good news of salvation. Salvation in such contexts would also mean liberating people from oppressive forces such as poverty, preventable deaths, and insecurity.

In such extreme situations of deprivation and misery, the church has a prophetic mandate to continue the mission that Jesus Christ announced in the Gospel of Luke: "The spirit of the Lord is upon me, because he has anointed me to preach good news to the poor. He has sent me to proclaim release to the captives and recovering of sight to the blind, to set at liberty those who are oppressed, to proclaim the acceptable year of the Lord" (4:18–19, RSV). This mission of Jesus covers the main priorities that are to be discussed in this essay. Preaching good news to the poor, proclaiming release to the captives, and setting at liberty those who are oppressed clearly fall under the priority of justice, peace, and reconciliation, as well as sustainable development. Restoring sight to the blind is clearly an issue of health, but it can also include the provision of education, since knowledge clarifies vision and perception. If we reread the gospels from an African social and political perspective, we recognize how radically empowering the teachings of Christ can be.

For this new perspective to become a reality, there is a need for a theology or ethic of social and political commitment that looks at the social political realities with the eyes of faith enlightened by the prophetic word of God, as Paul Béré argues in his contribution to this volume. This approach is consistent with what the *Lineamenta* proposed to the local churches of Africa: "to meditate on these three dimensions—socio-political, socio-economic and socio-cultural, and to make suggestions on how to remedy situations through reconciliation, justice and peace" (no. 16).

Several African countries have been caught in various forms of conflict right from the time of independence—conflicts over resources, identity, boundaries, and contested elections. As the case in Sudan demonstrates, some conflicts are based on religion and race. Lasting solutions to these conflicts remain elusive despite well-meaning efforts of church-based peace and justice commissions and the African Union.

There is no doubt about the statistical growth of the church in Africa. The number of priests and religious is growing exponentially as is the number of baptized Catholics. Multiple successes have been registered in the provision of education at all levels, healthcare delivery, and relief services. More remarkable are the new initiatives in critical areas such as care for those affected and infected by HIV/AIDS.

One area worth underlining is that of higher education. The interest in higher education by the church, as experience in other parts of the world has shown, stems from the recognition that primary and secondary education are necessary but not sufficient when it comes to the social transformation of society. What can considerably transform a society are the intellectual and practical skills acquired by a university-level education. A university that is a center for research, inquiry, and rigorous reflection is the best locus for reflection on critical issues that shape the direction of society.

Globalization: A Mixed Blessing for Africa

Even though scholars do not agree on the precise definition of *globalization,* there are a few elements that can help us grasp its salient features. David Korten offers a neo-liberal perspective of corporate globalization as an attempt "to integrate the world's national economies into a single borderless global economy in which the world's mega-corporations are free to move goods and money anywhere in the world that affords an opportunity for profit, without governmental interference."[5] Another key element of globalization highlighted by Roland Robertson is "global connectivity . . . and fast expanding and intensifying reflexive global consciousness."[6] Robertson's conception of globalization brings out the elements of communication and culture—aspects that are of great relevance for the church. Accordingly, the *Lineamenta* views globalization as a "process which encompasses not only the economic integration of markets, production, and capital, but also harmonization of political systems for the desired management of a globalised economy and the uniformity and standardization of cultures and social systems" (no. 17).

An increasingly globalized world, with its excellent facilities of travel, media, information and communication technology, global economy, global solidarity, and innovative forms of governance, offers unprecedented opportunities for the church in Africa to promote peace, justice, and reconciliation. Hitherto, major actors in international relations have been mainly multinational corporations and nation-states. With globalization new actors have asserted their role on the world scene in form of nongovernmental organizations (NGOs), faith-based organizations—and terrorist groups.

Joseph Nye's discourse on the innovative theory of "soft power" describes NGOs as a part of postmodern development that is skeptical of authority and that has created alternative centers of power: "Some NGOs enjoy more trust than governments do, and though they are difficult to control, they can be useful channels of communication."[7] The World Social Forum is an example of organizations that have carved out some space for themselves in the global governance architecture, which is still taking shape, as they mobilize across borders to shape world policies and promote social justice and solidarity.[8] Some of the campaigns that have helped to champion the African cause, such as debt relief, were organized by Jubilee 2000, a Catholic international NGO. Numerous NGOs and foundations are involved in the process of democratization and in efforts to combat HIV/ AIDS in Africa.

The new conceptual framework that has emerged after the end of the Cold War in 1989—perhaps best conceived as a "global civil society"— brings with it new initiatives described by Mary Kaldor as "the demand for autonomy, self-organization or control over life—and the global content of the concept."[9] In Africa this demand for autonomy and the right to self-determination was demonstrated in the 1990s by the church's increasing role in influencing public life through raising awareness on issues of constitution reform in Uganda and regime change in Malawi and Zambia. Kaldor summarized the new political space created after the 1989 revolutions that has consequently paved the way for the church's global public role:

> The 1989 revolutions legitimated the concept of civil society and consequently permitted the emergence of global politics—the engagement of social movements, NGOs and networks in the process of constructing global governance. And the coming together of peace and human rights gave rise to the new humanitarian discourse that is challenging the geopolitical discourse of the centralized war-making state.[10]

In terms of theological possibilities, the rapid growth of NGOs involved in charitable work and other forms of humanitarian assistance offers an opportunity for new theologies to emerge. By undergoing careful reflection, moments of crises can stimulate creative theological discourse about compassion and global solidarity. There is a sense of collective global vulnerability that calls for concerted efforts from all parts of the world. Whether earthquake or terrorist attack, we are all vulnerable.

The presence of Al Qaeda networks in Somalia and Sudan and other suspected parts of Africa has brought Africa into the orbit of the global war on terrorism. The latter has generated a new discourse on the potential of religion to promote both conflict and reconciliation. In some of the most religious countries, such as Uganda, religious symbols and concepts have been manipulated to advance armed conflicts: "In the postcolonial era one can point to Uganda's civil strife in which Alice Lakwena's Holy Spirit Movement and Joseph Kony's Lord's Resistance Army waged war in the name of restoring the ten commandments."[11] It is instructive to note that Joseph Kony's Lord's Resistance Army is included among the U.S. list of terrorist organizations.

Clearly, states can no longer claim to have a monopoly over the use of force or violence. Religious organizations have entered the sphere of armed violence, which indicates that any strategies for bringing about peace must include them as major actors.

Some scholars of international relations have even identified a unique role that religions can play in a new kind of peacebuilding known as "faith-based diplomacy."[12] The characteristics that such faith-based practitioners have include spiritual principles and resources, spiritual authority, a pluralistic heart, a transcendent approach, and ability to persevere amid hardships.[13] These characteristics or qualities are virtues that are developed over time and through gradual religious formation, and they are not characteristics that most people associate with diplomacy. The new paradigm of faith-based diplomacy has policy implications for both the church and the state. Resources need to be invested in cultivating the above qualities for peacebuilding by both the state and the church. In this type of faith-based diplomacy, the example of the lay Catholic Community of Sant'Egidio is commended in countries such as Uganda and Mozambique.

One great benefit of globalization is the social and ethical awareness that has been created with regard to global poverty and inequality. This fact is acknowledged by Peter Singer with regard to the United States, and he recognizes the moral responsibility that comes with this awareness: "We can take practical steps to expand our concern across national boundaries by supporting organizations working to aid those in need, wherever they may be."[14] The global awareness that globalization has facilitated is best demonstrated in the 2000 UN Millennium Summit at which world leaders agreed on the minimum goals to be achieved for the world's poor: "To halve the proportion of people who suffer from hunger, or who live on less than $1 per day; to see that all children have a primary education; to reduce by two-thirds the under-five child mortality rate; to halve the proportion of people without access to safe drinking water; and to combat HIV/AIDS, malaria, and other diseases."[15] The benchmark for meeting these goals is 2015—if the rich nations can afford to give a total of $40 to 60 billion a year.[16]

Some critique from an African perspective is needed of the list of the Millennium Development Goals (MDGs). They are a good starting point, but they seem to be mainly focused on economic development and health. Other major challenges facing Africa are governance and armed conflict. Some African dictators will easily accept the MDGs and ignore the call for democracy and respect for human rights.

The call for the rich nations to contribute to alleviating the suffering of the poor nations is grounded on the Catholic social doctrine traced from Thomas Aquinas, who argues that "whatever a man has in superabundance is owed, of natural right, to the poor for their sustenance."[17] The doctrine that created goods are for the satisfaction of human needs has very radical implications, but regrettably it has not been popularized or emphasized in church circles.[18] However, this principle of the universal destination of created goods should not be taken as an argument in favor of more aid for the developing countries. Aid alone will not lift Africa out of poverty. Aid has been flowing to Africa for decades, but unfortunately there is little to show for it. Factors for the failure of aid are not hard to discern. Aid given to dictatorial regimes has been diverted to private accounts. Oftentimes, aid was put into what are popularly known as white elephant projects. Stories are told of governments that have invested donor funds into hydro-electric power projects, only to discover later that there was not sufficient water to operate the dams.

At the Service of Justice, Peace, and Reconciliation

Justice, peace, and reconciliation are to be considered not as some specialized functions suited only to those specially trained, but as part of a deeper process of evangelization. Some participants at the second African Synod expressed dismay at the fact that Catholics could participate in politically motivated ethnic conflicts and in the abuse of public funds.[19] The need for a faith that does justice is all the more urgent, and this can be possible only if formation in Catholic social teaching is done at all levels of Christian life and institutions, as the second African Synod recommended. Unfortunately Catholic social teaching still remains the church's "best kept secret." Incorporating Catholic social teaching in Catholic primary, secondary, and higher education institutions is the best way to develop awareness on social concerns among citizens.

While the justice and peace commissions within the Catholic Church seem to be fairly organized and well funded at the level of episcopal conferences, there is less commitment and availability of resources at diocesan, parish, and small Christian community levels. One concrete task that justice and peace commissions need to take up is the forming of truth, justice, and reconciliation commissions in post-conflict countries such as Rwanda, Burundi, Zimbabwe, Uganda, and Sudan. Other tasks include the creation of parliamentary liaison offices and representatives at regional and continental bodies such as the African Union.

Sustainable Development

Even though the Catholic Church has taken a leading role in providing charity and relief globally through agencies such as Caritas International, Catholic Relief Services, and Jesuit Refugee Services, the issue of sustainable development has not been fully embraced in the pastoral plans of most dioceses across Africa. Relief and humanitarian aid is by and large considered the work of foreign donor agencies. This partly explains why for decades foreign aid has not managed to eradicate poverty; instead, it has created a spirit of dependency.

The much praised doctrine of the preferential option for the poor should entail setting up programs for poverty eradication in which the poor take an active part, so that it is not just "option *for* the poor" but "option *by and with* the poor." Such a commitment also entails some work in advocacy and lobbying for good policies that favor the well-being of the marginalized. As was noted in the discussion of the African context above, poverty and conflict are partly caused by structural and systemic injustices. Sustainable development is as much about giving development aid as it is about advocating for fair international policies in the global system.

Higher Education for Social Transformation

With renewed interest in higher education as a priority for the church in Africa, there is hope that the complex issues affecting Africa will be well analyzed, and appropriate pastoral strategies will be designed. If the church is to offer credible and efficient alternatives to what the governments have offered so far, it has to invest in the academic formation of the agents of evangelization (lay, religious, and clergy) at the university level. Attention has to be paid to the pastoral areas identified: health, justice, peace, reconciliation, development, and higher education. It is not helpful to identify these areas as priorities and then fail to train competent personnel for them.

Any mention of higher education for religious and clergy is usually met with doubt and even suspicion, with the claim that primary and secondary education are the foundation for a prosperous society. Even governments support this claim, hence the mantra of "universal primary and secondary education." Yet it is evident that no society has ever made considerable and lasting progress without a good number of university-level skilled citizens.

Even if the much praised policy of universal primary and secondary education, supported both by African governments and the World Bank, was justified to lower levels of illiteracy, the implementation of this policy needs highly qualified primary and secondary schoolteachers who require tertiary education. It is not clear how one can increase the primary and secondary levels of student enrollment without a corresponding increase in the number of teachers at these levels.

The type of higher education that is needed is not the type that develops "white collar" professionals, but rather the kind that equips citizens with life skills for social transformation. It is not a secret that the type of education operating in most African countries was designed by the colonial state to produce law-abiding citizens who would sustain the colonial political economy and become civil servants. No wonder that decades after independence, universities still produce graduates for whom there is no employment. Since the existing state universities, products of the colonial education policy, are not willing to reform their curricula, the church needs to set up its own institutions of higher education informed by the vision and mission of promoting a just society. This is the same philosophy that informs the establishment of Catholic primary and secondary schools.

Since the second African Synod is keen on specific pastoral strategies, with regard to higher education, one concrete strategy would be to elevate existing major seminaries to the level of universities. The newly established Catholic universities in Kenya, Uganda, Sudan, South Africa, and elsewhere on the continent seem to be heading in the right direction in terms of relevant disciplines that will contribute to the realization of the vision of the second African Synod. These disciplines include health sciences, governance and peacebuilding, peace studies and international relations, and development studies and management. Such courses also pose a challenge for religious and speculative sciences such as theology and philosophy; that is, they must be relevant to the African context.

The new context of the African church as identified by the second African Synod demands that new theological disciplines be designed to reflect the new challenges that face the African church. Such courses would include theology or philosophy of HIV/AIDS, theology or philosophy of health care and ministry, theology or philosophy of reconciliation and peace, theology or philosophy of interreligious dialogue, theology or philosophy of development, and theology or philosophy of globalization. Initiatives such as the publications by the African Jesuit AIDS Network on the pastoral and theological dimensions of HIV/AIDS are a great contribution to the emerging contextual African theology.[20]

Such innovative courses will pose new methodological challenges, since they have to be in dialogue with natural and social sciences instead of Scholastic philosophy and theology, but they are well worth exploring. Such a methodology would in fact help to bridge the gap between secular and sacred disciplines, a gap that might be partly responsible for the growing secularism and materialism that is increasingly associated with the educated middle class all over the world. Donal Dorr describes the new theologies that are needed as "a different way of theologizing, resulting in the different kind of theology, one that is much closer to life, affecting all our commitments, our attitudes, and even our feelings."[21]

Good Governance

The greatest challenge with regard to good governance in Africa is the absence of stable democratic institutions, especially electoral systems and human rights institutions. The church can play a key role in forming leaders and responsible citizens who will shape the public sphere. Most Catholics still consider politics a dirty game; there are numerous Catholic schools that train responsible citizens who nonetheless neglect their political responsibilities. The second African Synod also decried the fact that some Catholic-trained politicians engage in corrupt practices, both economically and politically. Training good leaders who respect the rule of law, human rights, and democracy should be part of the church's apostolic commitment. This can be done by specialized centers of social policy, social concern, and theological reflection.

The question of whether the church should get involved in public affairs keeps arising, particularly during election time. The issue is not *whether* the church should get involved in public or political affairs, but rather *how* it should do this. Clearly the church as an institution should not get involved in partisan politics, but the church has a right and a duty to take part in civic education, election monitoring, constitutional reform processes, and peaceful protests against injustices. Individual Catholics are also free to be actively involved in party politics. There is even room for clergy and religious to take an active part in politics if circumstances, such as a period of transition, demand this special option and if it is established that there are no competent lay people who can lead.

Conclusion

With better means of communication and travel, a heightened awareness of human rights, more available resources, and more cultural and political interactions, the church in Africa is in a better position to take advantage of these aspects of human progress and advance its mission. The second African Synod identified critical areas that need urgent attention: healthcare, peace, justice, reconciliation, higher education, good governance, and development. While the church has been addressing these issues for quite some time, it has not done so in a systematic and sustained manner, and definitely not at all levels of ecclesial organizations.

If the church in Africa takes up this challenging yet exciting new paradigm of ministry at this time in history, marked by globalization, it will not only be a credible prophetic voice, but it will also renew its dynamic presence in a world that is thirsting for change. For this new model of ministry that fully engages political, economic, and social issues to succeed, however, the states and the existing international system have to be fully supportive of the church's initiatives and see them as complementary in promoting the common good. The new approach required is that of collaboration rather than confrontation.

Notes

[1] See "Kenya: Statement of Eastern African Bishop-Delegates to Africa Synod," nos. 2–3. Available at http://www.mafrome.org/cisa18_synod_africa.htm.

[2] For examples of this new methodology, see Agbonkhianmeghe E. Orobator, *From Crisis to Kairos: The Mission of the Church in the Time of HIV/AIDS, Refugees, and Poverty* (Nairobi: Paulines Publications, 2005); and idem, *The Church as Family: African Ecclesiology in Its Social Context* (Nairobi: Paulines Publications, 2000).

[3] Martin Meredith, *The State of Africa: A History of Fifty Years of Independence* (New York: Free Press, 2005), 368.

[4] Ibid.

[5] David Korten, "When Corporations Rule the World: Global Corporate Power vs. Global People Power." Available at http://livingeconomiesforum.org/power-struggle.

[6] Roland Robertson, quoted in John A. Coleman SJ, "Making the Connections: Globalization and Catholic Social Thought," in *Globalization and Catholic Social Thought: Present Crisis, Future Hope,* ed. John A. Coleman and William F. Ryan (Maryknoll, NY: Orbis Books, 2005), 13.

[7] Joseph S. Nye, Jr., *Soft Power: The Means to Success in World Politics* (New York: Public Affairs, 2004), 113.

[8] Mary Kaldor, *Global Civil Society: An Answer to War* (Cambridge: Polity Press, 2003), 101.

[9] Ibid., 76.

[10] Ibid., 77.

[11] Paul Tiyambe Zeleza, "Introduction: Causes and Costs of War in Africa: From Liberation Struggles to the 'War on Terror,'" in *The Roots of African Conflicts: The Causes and Costs,* ed. Alfred Nhema and Paul Tiyambe Zeleza (Oxford: James Curey, 2008), 25.

[12] For a detailed discussion of faith-based diplomacy, see Douglas Johnston, ed., *Faith-Based Diplomacy: Trumping Realpolitik* (New York: Oxford University Press, 2003), 3–29.

[13] Ibid., 16–17.

[14] Peter Singer, *One World: The Ethics of Globalization* (New Haven, CT: Yale University Press, 2004), 185.

[15] As stated in ibid., 184.

[16] Ibid.

[17] Thomas Aquinas, as quoted in ibid., 185.

[18] Ibid., 185–86.

[19] See "Kenya: Statement of Eastern African Bishop-Delegates to the African Synod," no. 4.

[20] Two publications that narrate the activities of HIV/AIDS programs in Africa and offer some theological and spiritual reflections on the pandemic are AJAN, *Linked for Life: African Jesuit AIDS Network* (Nairobi: Paulines Publications, 2007); and Michael J. Kelly, SJ, *HIV and AIDS: A Social Justice Perspective* (Nairobi: Paulines Publications, 2010).

[21] Donal Dorr, *Spirituality and Justice* (Maryknoll, NY: Orbis Books, 1984), 36.

Part III

Ecclesial Leadership and Gender Justice in Church and Society

10

"Woman, You Are Set Free!"

Women and Discipleship in the Church

ANNE ARABOME

Now he was teaching in one of the synagogues on the sabbath. And just then there appeared a woman with a spirit that had crippled her for eighteen years. She was bent over and was quite unable to stand up straight. When Jesus saw her, he called her over and said, "Woman, you are set free from your ailment." When he laid his hands on her, immediately she stood up straight and began praising God.
—LUKE 13:10-13, NRSV

This seemingly simple text from the Gospel of Luke echoes the desperate cries and yearnings of African women for the healing touch of Jesus to bring them to wholeness as disciples of Christ. African women in general, and Nigerian women in particular, are bent over by a constellation of social, cultural, religious, political, and economic burdens. Waiting for the touch of Jesus, African women bear the burden of violence. While violence touches both men and women in Africa, women suffer from subjugation in a way that men do not. According to a recent United Nations study, "51 percent of African women have been victims of violence, 11 percent suffer violence while pregnant, 21 percent marry before the age of fifteen, and 24 percent experience genital mutilation."[1] Even before the second African Synod, Pope Benedict XVI, in an address in Luanda, Angola, repudiated this violence against women, "paying particular attention to ways in which the behavior and attitudes of men, who at times show a lack of sensitivity and responsibility, may be to blame."[2] The African church has a long way to go before it can say with any sense of truthfulness that women are treated with dignity and justice and recognized as equal disciples in the community called church.

For African women, no words are too strong to express the injustice that we feel. Few doorways can be opened for women, but one of those few doorways is found in the Gospels, where we experience Jesus as healing and restoring life. Jesus makes the reign of God present by showing a particular interest in women.[3] In the African church, where patriarchy is so oppressive of women, we might ask, as did Thérèse Souga of Cameroun:

> Is Jesus whom we find to be full of concern for the women of his own time also standing with African women in their particular context? Can African women understand themselves in relation to Jesus of Nazareth? Except for the Blessed Virgin, the church, which has often forgotten the role of women in the Gospels, has been the bearer of an image of women likening them to Satan. Thus in the missionary context there has developed an attitude of mistrust toward the black woman.[4]

At the second African Synod something remarkable happened. Three women religious spoke to the synod participants. Even though each statement lasted no more than five minutes, their words had a noticeable impact.

Sister Felicia Harry, OLA, from Ghana, made clear to the bishops that women religious want to be involved in the collaborative decision-making process—before decisions have been made. Using words from *Instrumentum Laboris* (no. 114), she underlined the importance of bringing our feminine "genius" of gentleness, tenderness, and openness to hearing the word and of service to others to bear on the very life of the parishes where we work. "As well as teach catechism to children, decorate parish churches, clean, mend and sew vestments we the women religious in Africa would like to be part of various parish councils . . . We just want to be equal partners in the Lord's vineyard." Sister Harry further challenged the bishops: if the church wants to bring reconciliation, peace, and justice to the African continent, then it had better begin at home! She emphasized that no one group should be dominative. At the end of her talk, she suggested to the bishops that before they went to bed that night, they take a few minutes and consider "what the church would be like without women."[5]

The life of an African woman unfolds along a trajectory of servitude: from her home, where she serves every family member, to her church, where she continues to serve at the pleasure of ordained clergy and with very limited opportunities for leadership or the recognition of her value as a disciple of Jesus Christ. Indeed, what would the African church be without women? The ordinary life of the parish would no longer be so ordinary.

Sister Pauline Odia Bukasa, FMS, from Democratic Republic of Congo, was the second woman to speak at the second African Synod. She told the synod that African women are "marginalized on all levels" and that "she is the victim of the ancestral customs and traditions while she is the one who actually carries the burden of all the armed conflicts that tear Africa apart."[6] Sister Bukasa's statement bears serious implications. Oppressive practices from the past, such as polygamous and/or forced marriages, widowhood customs that are demeaning to women, the trafficking of women and children, female genital mutilation, and use of the ritual bride price—all these practices enslave African women to traditions that cause their spiritual life-blood to be drained from their souls. There is no way that the African church can speak to the dignity of women until these chains of injustice are lifted. In addition, these practices and rituals do not begin to touch on other social problems that burden women—lack of legal rights for women, lack of access to education, lack of adequate health care, and lack of fair compensation for work.

The *Lineamenta* of the synod quotes Pope John Paul II's *Message for the World Day of Peace*, which acknowledges that in some places in Africa women are treated like slaves. In addition, many women are deprived of the human rights that are the heritage of every human being: "This is an affront to not only their dignity but also the best offerings of African tradition, which sees women as the preeminent symbol of life, a precious gift" (no. 22).

Clearly, the first step for the liberation of women is to release women from negative and oppressive practices and traditions. The *Instrumentum Laboris* notes that "in the name of culture or ancestral traditions, women are victimized and abused in matters of inheritance and rites of widowhood, sexual mutilation, forced marriages, polygamy, etc." (no. 32). The second step is to provide assistance to women in reclaiming their humanity and personhood through the provision of educational opportunities, a fair legal system, and equitable work opportunities. The third step is to accept women as full partners in the life of the family, the life of the church, and the society.

Exodus: Liberation and Partnership in the Church

In light of the African Synod's concern for justice, fairness, and equality, women are called to be equals in Christ. This means that women must not subject their identity to the men around them or suppress their gifts so that they become lost to their own humanity. New interpretations of the scripture and a Christology that empowers the women of Africa are long overdue in the church in Africa. Ghanaian theologian Mercy Amba Oduyoye holds that it is time for the African church to allow women to be partners in developing theology. In addition, women must be "fully present in decisions and operations that affect the whole church."[7] African women must be taught how to break open the word of God, which will enable them to share the gifts of scripture with other women. In this regard synod participant Sister Teresa Okure, SHCJ, a Nigerian theologian and contributor to this volume, makes an important point:

As in other walks of life, biblical interpretation up to the last three decades of our century was dominated by white, male, clerical scholars. . . . Today, in the wake of feminism, women and some men have, as biblical scholars, sought in different ways to include the women's viewpoint and approach in this "biblical science." . . .

Contemporary women's interpretation of the Bible has received different names in different racial and cultural contexts. . . .

African women theologians, to my knowledge, have not coined a terminology for their interpretative efforts.[8]

Jesus came to call all peoples to be part of the movement that was to make present the reign of God. As proclaimed by Jesus, the reign of God was meant to be particularly inclusive of the marginalized and the outcasts of society. American theologian Anthony Gittins, CSSp, proffers a striking hermeneutics of the woman who was bent over for eighteen years (Lk 13:10–17) as a symbol of/for those who are marginalized:

The bent-over woman can represent anyone who has been victimized or neglected for a long time. . . . Not only was she quite incapable of improving her situation, she was also a pariah, an outcast in the sight of her neighbors and peers. . . . This woman was socially dead. . . . And Jesus notices her. . . . "When Jesus saw her, he called her over and said, "Woman, you are set free from ailment" (v. 12). It happens in a flash, it changes her entire life, and its impact will be felt, not only by the bystanders, but even on those who encounter this woman, as Jesus did, but after a gap of two thousand years.[9]

Following the call of the African Synod, African women are invited to engage with life, especially in unjust situations, just as Jesus would encourage the raising of women's voices and allow for the full development of who they are. This is the true meaning of discipleship in Christ—to embrace the gifts that have been bestowed on us by God and to pay attention to issues that stifle growth or life in ourselves and others. Just like the woman who engaged Jesus until there was a resolution in her favor (Mt 15:21–28; Mk 7:24–30), so also African women are called to their vocation as Christian disciples; they must learn to hold on and hold up until their voices are heard and their oppressors accept conversion. As social psychologist Sister Joan Chittister, OSB, passionately asserts: "Discipleship stands naked in the middle of the world's marketplace and, in the name of Jesus, cries aloud all the cries of the world until someone, somewhere hears and responds to the poorest of the poor, the lowest of the low, the most outcast of the rejected. . . . The Church of Jesus Christ is not called to priesthood, the church of Christ is called to discipleship."[10]

Acts: Paradigm Shift

The second African Synod addresses some of the concerns about women in Proposition 47 of the synod document, although women have cause for reflection in knowing that the African bishops have placed issues concerning women into a single proposition. Since women are demographically the larger half of the human community and the church, it seems that issues concerning their well-being would be better served by integrating women's realities throughout the document. This would mean interweaving women's perspectives into sections on family and on war and on tribal conflict. Such integration would mean recognizing women's gifts as well, allowing for the influence that women might have on issues of peacemaking and reconciliation.

The goal of the above recommendation by African bishops should be a process that allows men and women to sit down together as partners at the decision-making table to consider the problems facing the church, to plan strategies for all of God's people, and, together, to engage in leadership for the Christian community. The call to follow Jesus included women who were close companions of Jesus, although they were not included among the twelve. In modern scholarship, many, including American theologian Elisabeth Schüssler Fiorenza, question "the assumption that biological maleness and masculine gender" are "intrinsic to the function and mission of the twelve." She challenges this common belief and understanding regarding the necessity of being male as a prerequisite for leadership in the community called church.[11]

The synod document notes that the participants "condemn all acts of violence against women. This condemnation includes some of the aforementioned acts of violence such as wife battering, oppressive widowhood practices, genital cutting, sex slavery, marriages that are forced and the disinheriting of daughters." (nos. 41–50). This is good as far as the statement goes; however, every single one of the mentioned instances refers to the place of women as those who are dominated and held captive to the wishes of men. The full and just recognition of women will require a paradigm shift in the thinking of both men and women.

While men may oppress women, oftentimes women themselves cooperate in their own oppression. African women must focus more on building up sisterly love among themselves, regardless of tribe, ethnic group, and social status. Growing in love and trust for self and others, women will share their struggles and common challenges. If this kind of sharing is encouraged in a loving and nonjudgmental way in Christian communities, the result will be authentic women with the capacity to love and to birth life. It is this force that must be channeled in the church—the very nature of womanhood as conceived in African culture. The kind of closeness alluded to here is "seen in the Tanzanian Sukuma proverb: 'There is always room for the person you love even if the house is crowded.'"[12]

Writing about the unique qualities of African women, Nigerian theologian Agbonkhianmeghe Orobator, SJ, draws on the imagery of *Obirin Meta* to describe the boundless nature of their gifts and graces:

> I think of a mother who could balance a big pot of water or a basket of produce on her head, with a baby strapped to her back, trying to make it home on time to prepare dinner for the whole family, taking care of all the needs of the family, and being a mother to all. In the midst of all these tasks and chores she might even be carrying another baby in her womb. It takes a special kind of woman to do this—it takes *Obirin Meta*.[13]

It is going to take this kind of woman to meet the current challenges within the church, particularly the challenge of equality in mission, service, and leadership. Women in the parish setting must join with Jesus in breaking open the boundaries of subjugation, just as Jesus broke open the boundaries that existed between him and the Samaritan woman (Jn 4). In order to be accepted as equals in Africa, women must raise educated voices against the unjust treatment of women. Protesting by African women may cause suffering for those who choose to speak the truth, but "disciples must be prepared to lose that which is of irreplaceable value to them—their very lives."[14]

In the suffering that will occur, women will find their own healing because truth will have been spoken. For African women, to hear the word of God and obey what they hear may require a great deal of risk and ridicule. Only through deep study and prayer will women be prepared for what is ahead in terms of pursuing liberation of the voices and bodies of women. It is time for women to tell their stories of suffering and of triumph, of birthing and dying, and of loving and hating.

Salt and Light:
Women as Agents of Reconciliation, Justice, and Peace

The African Synod's desire for the church to be salt of the earth and light of the world calls for efforts toward reconciliation, justice, and peace. In this task African women can play an irreplaceable role.

Sister Geneviève Uwamariya, SSMN, from Rwanda was the third Catholic nun to address the bishops at the synod. In her short presentation Sister Geneviève shared her experience of reconciliation, which Paul Béré uses to introduce his chapter on the power of the Word of God in the African context. She survived the Rwandan genocide in 1994. Her father and other members of her family were not so lucky. Her father was killed by someone she knew—a family "friend." Sister Geneviève had a lightning-bolt experience of forgiveness when she encountered her father's killer in a prison camp. Her ability to forgive this man freed her from the burden of terrible anger and resentment. In asking for forgiveness, the culprit was freed from his terrible guilt. She said,

> "From this experience I drew the conclusion that reconciliation is not so much bringing together two people or two groups in conflict. Rather, it means re-establishing each into love and letting inner healing take place, which then leads to mutual liberation. And here is the importance of the Church in our countries since her mission is to give The Word: a Word that heals, sets free and reconciles."[15]

Sister Geneviève's account of her experience underlines the fact that in the church's mission of reconciliation and healing, women should be included as partners. With a special emphasis on the acknowledgment of women's abilities, the church could begin in a natural way to make use of and manifest what has often been hidden from others—the amazing variety of gifts that women offer. This would be a timely step toward freeing women, as noted in the title of this essay. The idea that women can become healers and reconcilers at the service of the church and the message of Jesus Christ offers hope for both women and men. As with Sister Geneviève, whose heart was filled with compassion for the man who murdered her father and relatives, so women may be healed from their own wounds in reaching out in compassion to their wounded sisters and brothers.

On the theme of the second African Synod, the *Instrumentum Laboris* makes the point that "the two images of salt and light express the dual aspects of the identity of the disciple of Christ" (no. 37). The image of salt is a perfect expression of women's activity. As a mother in the family, she is the salt that can add flavor to the family life. Her very presence is the salt that "dissolves and becomes invisible," adding sweetness and transformation to the life of the family. The gifts that make the mother precious beyond compare can, likewise, be made use of in the parish and diocesan communities, drawing on women's natural abilities to bring peace and reconciliation to bear in situations of disputes and conflicts.

Such women who provide salt for the life of the church, states the *Instrumentum Laboris*, inevitably shine and provide light (no. 38). Contrary to prevailing practices, this light should no longer be covered but "placed on a lamp stand" (Mt 5:14–16) for all to see. The ecclesial community must work to become conscious of the gifts of women in the local parish so that those gifts might be identified and released into the local political and economic arenas as well. Encouraging women to shine would be a remarkable first step toward recognizing, honoring, and integrating women's gifts in the community called church.

Prophetic Actions:
Moving from Proposition 47 into the Future

As indicated above, when addressing the presence of women in the life of the church, it is necessary to remember that a massive shift in consciousness is needed for both men and women. This ground-shaking shift is of such major proportions that the church must prepare for a long and arduous journey. This journey will be painful and fraught with challenges and difficulties in the process of discovering new ways of communicating and checking unjustified assumptions. This shift in consciousness can only be achieved in the context of prayer. The ancient practices of Africa will not easily be altered and changed. Attitudes about women and the role of women are deeply ingrained in the cultures of Africa. Only through the study of the scriptures, especially the Gospels of Jesus Christ, will new light be focused on this task. Retreats and parish revivals might include this topic, and priests need to be given material that can be used to develop sermons regarding the treatment of women.

In Proposition 47 the synod suggests setting up "study commissions on women in the Church within the Pontifical Council for the Family." This commission should be composed of both men and women so that the process of study will alter the behavior and attitudes of the participants themselves. The same proposition also suggests "setting up of commissions on the Diocesan and national levels to address women's issues, to help them better carry out their mission in the Church and society." It is important to note that women's issues concern men as well. It is not possible to study women's issues without the involvement of men—husbands, brothers, fathers, bishops, and priests. Care must be taken in setting up these commissions, taking suggestions from a variety of groups as to those who should be members of these commissions.

The synod further suggests the "greater integration of women into Church structures and decision-making processes." In order for this to happen, there needs to be training—not only of women—but also of laymen and priests. Because this manner of interaction would appear foreign to many, it may be difficult at first to accept that women should participate in the decision-making process of the church. Collaboration does not come naturally to people, but styles of leadership and interaction are learned skills.

Perhaps the initiation and deepening of commitment to Small Christian Communities would be a natural place for women, together with men, to work out new collaborative styles of leadership, as suggested in the *Instrumentum Laboris* (no. 19). Studying the word of God and sharing this word would provide a prayerful setting for this experience of collaboration, as is proposed by Joseph Healey in his essay in this volume on small Christian communities. Religious formation and consciousness-raising for women can begin with a positive reinterpretation of the role of women as viewed through the prism of the scripture and the relationship of Jesus with women in scripture.

Women's groups and men's groups can be initiated. Women need to wrestle with their responsibility as women. Even if it is difficult to accept new ways of seeing their roles in the church, the exposure to new ideas is important. As for the men, it is perhaps more difficult to accept that "the ways things have been" are not healthy for women or for men. It will take a great deal of patience for men to come to new ways of perceiving women's roles.

One particular issue that the church must face in Africa is the practice of female genital mutilation (FGM). At the synod Bishop Michael Maguba Msonganzila of Musoma Diocese in Tanzania suggested that the bishops of Africa "must offer alternating rituals for helping girls mark the passage to womanhood. . . . [The church must] offer its faithful an alternative initiation rite, one that includes teaching about the value of the human body and about human rights."[16] The deplorable practice of FGM must be halted. However, this will happen only if there is a ceremony of some kind to replace it, as Bishop Msonganzila suggests. The church, as Stephen Bevans points out, must "start where the faith actually lives, and that is in the midst of people's lives."[17]

As for widowhood practices, parish women's groups could be invited to accompany any woman from the parish through this time. As Sister Rosemary Edet, HHCJ, points out, "Among most African communities, the death of a husband heralds a period of imprisonment and hostility to the wife or wives."[18] Education regarding this time must be provided to the entire Christian community. In addition, the death of a husband often bankrupts the family, which is then caught in an untenable situation for months to come, making the death of the husband and father even more difficult for the family. All of this has to do with changing attitudes and can be addressed by the local parish.

Polygamous marriage presents the African church with a highly volatile issue. "Contemporary polygamous practice is one of Nigeria's intractable gender issues, breeding low self esteem among some women."[19] This is an economic reality as well and involves not only the husband and wives, but the children. In addressing patriarchal traditional Africa, Anne Nasimiyu-Wasike writes, "Many wives and many children meant stronger 'immortality' for that family. . . . As a result . . . males enjoyed privileged and respectable positions in society. In the patriarchal system, women were valued only in relation to men."[20]

It goes without saying that the work of the local parish must involve ongoing sermons and classes on spousal fidelity. Often, male promiscuity is condoned at the expense of the marriage partner. A report from the United Nations on AIDS estimates that "60%–80% of HIV+ (positive) African women have had sexual intercourse only with their husbands. . . . While women are often perceived as bearers of HIV/AIDS, it is usually men who bring HIV into a family."[21] The natural embarrassment that comes with discussions about this issue must be overcome, because it is a matter of life and death.

In Proposition 47 the synod advocates "the close collaboration among Episcopal conferences to stop the trafficking of women." This concern must be addressed at the level of the diocesan structure. Closely aligned with this suggestion is the call for "the creation of 'shelters' for abused girls and women to find refuge and receive counseling" (also Proposition 47). These two proposals expose the situation of abuse that faces many women. The church is the ideal place for these concerns to be addressed. Women and men in parish settings must join with Jesus of the gospels to break open the boundaries of the subjugation of women. In this process, reconciliation can occur for entire families.

Finally, the synod wisely proposes "the integral human formation of girls and women (intellectual, professional, moral, spiritual, theological, etc.)" (Proposition 47). This process will require diocesan as well as local involvement. While this recommendation will take years to implement, it must not be ignored, because the education of woman is integral to her liberation.

Clearly, the African church can provide leadership to the world church by seriously addressing the above realities. Inaction or the perpetuation of the status quo is not an option. And, taking these steps together in the Christian community will not liberate only women; the sharing of discipleship with women will liberate men as well. It is in the primary relationship between man and woman that change must begin. In this context the words of Anne Nasimiyu-Wasike, acknowledging the oppressive condition of the African woman, hold true:

> The African woman's experience calls for a christology that is based on a holistic view of life. She needs the Christ who affects the whole of her life, whose presence is felt in every corner of the village and who participates in everything and everybody's daily life. She needs the Christ who relates to God, the God who can be reached through the spirits and the living dead or through direct intercession. This God, the Christ, is the one who takes on the conditions of the African woman—the conditions of weakness, misery, injustice, and oppression.[22]

Conclusion

African Catholic women are disciples of Jesus Christ. This vocation originates in their creation and dignity as people created in the image of God. It is not a privilege conferred by ecclesiastical hierarchy. It is of the utmost importance that this be understood and recognized by all in the church. African women carry the capacities of life giving and are the mothers that nurture and hold the Christian community together. It is the African woman who embraces the ancient inheritance of the ancestors and passes this on to future generations. The church can only become more beautiful when it learns to embrace women as equals in ministry as disciples of Jesus Christ. Some priorities for action can be summed up as follows:

- Learning to be collaborative will be a process of growth for clergy and laity. The discipleship of women must be emphasized, acknowledging that women are equal with men in their responsibility for the church.

- Women must be placed on local and diocesan committees and boards so as to be included in decision-making in the church.

- Women must be encouraged to undertake in-depth study of the scriptures. This entails the learning of hermeneutics so that they may contribute to the ongoing study of women's roles in the understanding of discipleship.

- Educational opportunities must be offered to women so that women grow in their capacity to express themselves, to think critically, and to understand their lives as the *imago Dei*. Their education should include courses in philosophy and theology.

- Both men and women must engage in a kind of consciousness-raising so that women's gifts are recognized and honored; also, both sexes must understand the injustice of the subjugation of women.

- The roots of violence against women must be examined by all members of the Christian community—clergy and all the families in a parish—so that domestic violence, rape, the trafficking of women and children, and punitive widow practices are seen for what they are— sinful acts by some humans against others.

At first, men in the church—both clergy and lay—may find this paradigm shift regarding women shocking and life changing. Women, however, will be deeply affected as well as they integrate their God-given gifts into the daily life of family and community. For both men and women this new way of viewing the roles of women will be a gift. Gradually, acts of violence will become unacceptable. Tribal conflicts will cease. Wars will become unthinkable. When women are recognized as equals in discipleship and leadership and seen as *imago Dei*, all people in church and society will perceive glimpses of the advent of the reign of God.

Notes

[1] Statistics quoted in John L. Allen, Jr., "Pope Extols Women's Rights in Africa," *National Catholic Reporter*, March 22, 2009.
[2] Ibid.

[3] Virginia Fabella and Mercy Amba Oduyoye, eds., *With Passion and Compassion: Third World Women Doing Theology* (Maryknoll, NY: Orbis Books, 1998), 24.

[4] Ibid., 26.

[5] Sr. Felicia Harry, NSA (OLA), superior general, Ghana. Auditor. Intervention. Vatican Radio. http://www.radiovaticana.org?EN1/Articulo.asp?c=324103.

[6] Sr. Pauline Odia Bukasa, FMS, superior general of the Sisters of "Ba-Maria," Buta Uele, Congo. Available on the missionalive.net website.

[7] Mercy Amba Oduyoye, *Daughters of Anowa: African Women and Patriarchy* (Maryknoll, NY: Orbis Books, 1995), 181.

[8] Teresa Okure, "Feminist Interpretations in Africa," in *Searching the Scripture: A Feminist Introduction*, ed. Elisabeth Schüssler Fiorenza (New York: Crossroad, 2001), 76–77.

[9] Anthony Gittins, *Encountering Jesus: How People Come to Faith and Discover Discipleship* (St. Louis: Ligouri/Triumph, 2002), 56–57.

[10] Joan Chittister, *In the Heart of the Temple: My Spiritual Vision for Today's World Discipleship* (London: SPCK, 2005), 144.

[11] Elisabeth Schüssler Fiorenza, *Discipleship of Equals: A Critical Feminist Ekklesia-logy of Liberation* (New York: Crossroad, 1993), 108.

[12] Joseph Healey and Donald Sybertz, *Towards an African Narrative Theology* (Maryknoll, NY: Orbis Books, 1999), 108.

[13] Agbonkhianmeghe E. Orobator, *Theology Brewed in an African Pot* (Maryknoll, NY: Orbis Books, 2008), 31. Orobator explains that *Obirin Meta* is applied to a woman who has the beauty, strength, character, and personality of three women. "She is a multifunctional woman of unmatched density and unbounded substance" (31).

[14] James D. G. Dunn, *Christianity in the Making: Jesus Remembered* (Grand Rapids, MI: William B. Eerdsman, 2003), 561–62.

[15] "De cette expérience, je déduis que la réconciliation n'est pas tellement vouloir ramener ensemble deux personnes ou deux groupes en conflit. Il s'agit plutôt de rétablir chacun dans l'amour et de laisser advenir la guérison intérieure qui permet la libération mutuelle. Et c'est ici l'importance de l'Eglise dans nos pays puisqu'elle a pour mission d'offrir La Parole: une Parole qui guérit, libère et réconcilie."

[16] Cindy Wooden, "Bishop Asks Synod for Initiation Ritual that Respects Girls' Bodies," October 26, 2009. Available on the catholicnews.com website.

[17] Stephen B. Bevans, *Models of Contextual Theology*, rev. ed. (Maryknoll, NY: Orbis Books, 2002), 61.

[18] Rosemary N. Edet, "Christianity and African Women's Rituals," in *The Will to Arise: Women, Tradition, and the Church in Africa*, ed. Mercy Amba Oduyoye and Musimbi R. A. Kanyaro (Eugene, OR: Wipf and Stock, 1992), 31.

[19] Chukwenye O. Ogunyemi, *African Woman Palava: The Nigerian Novel by Women* (Chicago: University of Chicago Press, 1996), 82.

[20] Anne Nasimiyu-Wasike, "Polygamy: A Feminist Critique," in Oduyoye and Kanyoro, *The Will to Arise*, 102.

[21] Statistics quoted in Rose N. Uchem, *Beyond Veiling: A Response to the Issues in Women's Experiences of Subjugation in African Christian Cultures* (Enugu, Nigeria: Snapp Press, 2002), 27.

[22] Anne Nasimiyu-Wasike, "An African Woman's Experience" in *Faces of Jesus in Africa*, ed. Robert J. Schreiter (Maryknoll, NY: Orbis Books, 1991), 77.

11

Come, Let Us Talk This Over

On the Condition of Women Religious in the Church

NGOZI FRANCES UTI

Each of us has a capacity for great good and that is what makes God say it was well worth the risk to bring us into existence.
—DESMOND MPILO TUTU, *NO FUTURE WITHOUT FORGIVENESS*

The proclamation by the second African Synod to the church in Africa to be reconciled is an invitation both particular and universal. It calls on the church in Africa and African Christians to be ministers of reconciliation. Hearing this call as an African Christian woman religious, two biblical images readily come to mind: Eden, and Christ on the cross. The first holds the hope, and the second presents the path toward its fulfillment: *koinonia* by means of *kenosis*.

The synod's call to restore "justice and the just demands of relationships" (Proposition 14) reveals the church's courageous mission to relieve our age of the burdens, betrayals, and suppressed hopes of its past. This manner of reconciliation must begin with the church. Therefore, remembering the humiliation that women religious suffer in the church and recalling the hope of our Christian faith reveal how our church stands in need of the ministry of reconciliation.

In this essay on the condition of women religious in the church, I proffer biblical justice as a way toward a reconciliation that creates a reconciled church in the nation as God's word to it. First, I examine gender justice in feminist discourse on gender equality. An acknowledgment that violence has occurred begins the process of true reconciliation, and a meeting of the victims of violence with the perpetrators of violence remains indispensable. Given these imperatives of reconciliation, I briefly examine how apostolic ministries can be contexts of gender injustice against women religious in the Catholic Church in Nigeria. Then I propose the approach of the South African Truth and Reconciliation Commission as a way to confront lies and elicit truth telling as a way toward reconciling women religious who bear marks on their bodies of the violence of gender injustice. I then offer some recommendations and draw a conclusion.

Of Gender and (In)Justice

Understood as a socio-historical construction, gender prescribes life-limiting absolute roles and values to persons by biological sex differences. Gender creates the cast that persons inhabit and from within which they acquire cultural selves. This development of persons by sex-specific categories produces gender injustice—social discrimination against one's personhood because of sex. The emergence of gender injustices in God's creation makes the earth a place for mediocrity, falsehood, fear and hiding, hostility, accusation and counter accusation, and fratricide. Unlike God, who responds to creation's groan with the best servant possible, the Beloved, we, the heirs of the received prejudice of man's superiority over woman, are limited by gender in choosing servants. As long as gender injustice exists, creation will never be justly served, because the field of search is always artificially narrowed. Some are shut out because they belong to the "other side."

In the beginning, the creator made them in God's own image and likeness: "in the divine image he created him, male and female he created them" (Gn 1:27).[1] After the fall man began to exclude and oppress, dominate and subordinate the rest of creation, in particular woman. He has not had the courage to let her be the woman according to the word of God (Lk 1:38). Woman's and man's alienation from God resulted in the further alienation of man from the flesh of his flesh and also in the enthronement of gender inequality. The woman and the man ended with obscured identities and a loss of inner dignity.

The efforts of women to unmask the falsehood of man's claim to superiority in order to restore right relations in creation have employed terms like *women empowerment, women's rights, gender equality,* and *gender mainstreaming.* Unfortunately, feminist efforts at dismantling skewed images of God used to authorize masculine tyranny have not fulfilled humanity's aspiration to set the world aright. Women remain the ones with reduced self-esteem and expression.

Arguably, gender injustice against the personal dignity of every woman belongs properly to social injustice because it developed as a consequence of the fall. The structural subordination of women to men does not belong to things as they are in themselves; it results instead from the disorder in relations that began with human beings' alienation from God. Evidence in scripture suggests that woman is man's equal as a free human being with dignity. Like the man, woman, in her "subjectivity," must assume responsibility for her life as an artisan of the culture of her society and its institutions.

Undoubtedly, the different approaches—including the tool of biblical hermeneutics—to countering the atrocities against women on the grounds of sex have helped advance discourse on gender justice. Yet the quest for justice on liberal ideological grounds alone has an intrinsic weakness in that it lacks a faith dimension and an ability to engage in self-criticism. This weakness ultimately renders it incapable of eliminating gender-based injustice.

Gender-based injustices against women continue even as efforts to secure justice for women have inspired "gender justice" as a new frame of discourse by activists and the academy. Unfortunately, the use of this term has not led to the eradication of gender disparities in the world. Cultural variations in the understandings of *rightness* and *fairness* in gender relations appear to militate against gender justice. In other words, women are at different points of awareness and understanding of what constitutes gender injustice across the globe: what is perceived as injustice to a woman in Europe may not necessarily be perceived in the same manner by a woman in Africa. The problematic of differences in the construal of rightness and fairness in female and male relations continues to thwart efforts by activists and the academy to reach a common definition of gender injustice. In my opinion, the 1999 Convention on the Elimination of All Forms of Discrimination against Women (CEDAW) offers a working definition for engaging in a constructive conversation on gender injustice. Article 1 of the convention states,

> For the purposes of the present Convention, the term "discrimination against women" shall mean any distinction, exclusion or restriction made on the basis of sex which has the effect of impairing or nullifying the recognition, enjoyment or exercise by women, irrespective of their marital status, on a basis of equality of men and women, of human rights and fundamental freedoms in the political, economic, social, cultural, civil or any other field.[2]

Those who seek a clear-cut definition that scorns ambiguity are not satisfied with CEDAW's resistance to a strict definition of gender injustice in order to promote collaborative efforts at understanding "right" and "fair."

Gender and Biblical Justice

The foregoing analysis reveals the limitations of a quest for gender justice grounded exclusively on liberal ideology or rational persuasion. Such a quest does not heed the imperative of biblical justice: fidelity to let love order relationships with others. Biblical justice, which is given by God, draws its hope and inspiration from faith. It is not foremost a matter of *suum cuique tradere*: rendering to each what is one's due. Nor is it a matter of rights and duties. Biblical justice is grounded in the experience of reconciliation that is the sign of the kingdom of God, announcing the dawn of "a new heaven and a new earth" (Rv 21:1). In this regard Ronald Rolheiser maintains that

> for a Christian, the question of social justice has not only to do with truth, but also with energy, with motivation for the quest. Not just any motivation for justice is adequate since justice is not first of all a question of politics and economics, but a question of helping God build a kingdom of peace and joy for all. Thus, for a Christian, the ultimate motivation in working for justice may never be simple ideology, irrespective of how noble that particular ideology may appear. Rather both the truth that inspires the quest for justice and the energy that fuels it must ground themselves in something beyond any ideology.[3]

The faith-rootedness of justice prohibits any separation of it from social justice. Consequently, feminists have to be just, overcoming the self to establish just relations—again *koinonia* by means of *kenosis*. The doer of justice is a minister of God's manifold gifts and receives the mission to act justly from the Spirit of God (Is 61:1–3). The feminist is a friend of God and a prophet (Wis 7:27), capable of suffering and compassion. With its faith origin, biblical justice points the way to a true ministry of reconciliation, and such reconciliation becomes discipleship. The feminist takes the world as it is and engages it as a creator of human culture with nothing less than the "greater love" of John 15:13. Consequently, gender justice becomes a demand of faith and more than a mere ideological campaign.

In the perspective of biblical justice the ultimate aim is to overcome the tragic lack of freedom that divides female and male and marginalizes the victim of injustice. In this approach the evildoer becomes the neighbor, the least of the brethren of Jesus, and a partner in the act of reconciliation. It is similar to what one encounters in the parable of the Prodigal Son and with Jesus on the cross: the father and the crucified Son overcame sin in order to establish right relations (Lk 15:11–32; 23:34). This manner of justice refuses to rest in the status quo of adversarial social relations. Instead, it inspires and energizes commitment toward social regeneration. At the core of biblical justice lies a fidelity to the love of God and neighbor and self that disposes those involved in the cause of justice to humility and truth, as they seek to create a social and political consciousness that inspires just and equitable responses to the suffering others.

In Memory of Biblical Justice

Memories and remembering belong to biblical justice. The Creator remembers and creation remembers the reason for creation's groans (see Rom 8:22). What do we remember? In the beginning the woman was "bones of my bones and flesh of my flesh" (Gn 2:23) with no fear or deceit. God spoke to woman and man face to face in the garden (Gn 3:8). Fear came after the fall, and what God had united became divided. Man and woman turned against each other and inaugurated a culture of accusation and evasion. "The woman whom you put here with me—she gave me fruit from the tree, and so I ate it" (Gn 3:12), said the man. "The serpent tricked me into it, and so I ate it" (Gn 3:13), said the woman. The rupture with God led to division within humanity and an increasing estrangement on earth. In the beginning the woman and man looked up to God for the meaning of their existence.

That woman and man are created in God's image and likeness falsifies the claim of maleness as the canon of humanity. Phyllis Trible offers a phenomenology of the origin of masculine domination:

> The woman ate; she gave to her man and he ate (3:6). At this turning point, distinctions within one flesh became oppositions. Division followed, yielding "opposite sexes." To defend himself, the man turned against the woman and betrayed her to God (3:12). Yet, according to God, she still yearns for the original unity of male and female: 'for your man is your desire." Alas, however, union is no more; one flesh is split. The man will not reciprocate the woman's desire; instead, he will rule over her. Thus she lives in unresolved tension. Where once there was mutuality, now there is a hierarchy of division. The man dominates the woman to pervert sexuality. Hence, the woman is corrupted in becoming a slave, and the man is corrupted in becoming a master. His supremacy is neither a divine right nor a male prerogative. Her subordination is neither a divine decree nor the female destiny. Both their positions result from shared disobedience. God describes this consequence but does not prescribe it as punishment.[4]

God's creating of woman and man in the image and likeness of God, according to the Priestly creation narrative, remains the theological grounding for resisting masculine tyranny and for the construction of new narratives that shape a different world and an affirmation of gender equality.

In interpreting "created in the image of God," Jesuit professor of biblical studies John R. Donahue argues that "its original context does not mean some human quality (intellect or free will) or the possession of 'sanctifying grace.'" He points out that "two interpretations enjoy some exegetical support today. One view is that, just as ancient Near Eastern kings erected 'images' of themselves in subject territory, so humans are God's representatives, to be given the same honor due God." The other interpretation argues that "created in the image of God" "means that humans were created to be God's counterpart, creatures analogous to God with whom God can speak and who will hear God's word." Donahue contends that "in either of these interpretations, all men and women prior to identification by race, social status, religion, or sex are worthy of respect and reverence."[5]

Reading the fall narrative outside Paul or other post-Pauline interpretations, Donahue argues that it "remains, however, a rich source of understanding human evil and alienation from God." In his view, the fall "explains the human potentiality of evil, no matter how gifted one may be." Furthermore, "the human person according to Genesis 2:4b—3:24 is created for life and knowledge." And "the ultimate test or temptation in this narrative is to 'be like God' (3:5), knowing good and evil, which is 'knowledge in a wide sense, inasmuch as it relates to the mastery of human existence.'" In the light of this, Donahue submits, "sin is overstepping the limits of the human condition by aspiring to divine power. It can take place through action (the woman) or through complicity (the man). Their desire to be like God sadly separates them from God."[6] Consequently, we have the use of power that is not accountable to God.

Jesus: The Image of Biblical Justice

Thus far in our remembering, we have recalled that God spoke personally with the woman and the man, who were companions and friends of God. They were God's conversation partners, just like Mary of Nazareth and Jesus of Nazareth. They remind us that women and men are persons with whom God speaks. They hear the word, and they obey.

Jesus, the truth that came to change the world, has become our way of being human in the world. Free of fears, he was a man reconciled with himself through a radical *kenosis*: "Though he was in the form of God, [he] did not regard equality with God something to be grasped. Rather, he emptied himself" (Phil 2:6–7). He acted according to the will of God, on whom he fixed his gaze and obeyed. Because he listened to God as his Abba, he encountered his fellow humankind with a listening that was both attentive and creative. He showed us how to meet the other as the real presence of the unseen God. In Jesus, God interrupted and recast human understandings of God through Jesus' life, death, and resurrection. In this man whom God raised from the dead, humanity could speak of God's love in a new light, and his friends came to understand that love is unaffected by death. In an attitude of acceptance and proclamation of the truth, Jesus reached freely across all divides, surpassing masculine domination. He revealed God's delight, "to sum up all things in Christ, in heaven and on earth" (Eph 1:10).

At Pentecost the Holy Spirit fell on all in the upper room. As it was in the beginning when woman and man were God's conversation partners, at the beginning of the church women and men received the gift of the Holy Spirit (Acts 2:1–21) in order "to complete his work on earth and bring us the fullness of grace" (Eucharistic Prayer IV).

Although these memories help us to hope, male imperialism continues to exist in sociopolitical, cultural, and economic spheres. In secular societies women are deprived of full participation in these domains because they are women, but male imperialism also subsists within the community of disciples. Taking a cue from Teresa Okure's contribution to this volume, I ask if the church should not act toward women as if every woman has received her image from God. Among people of faith, women's voices remain largely silenced in matters that affect humanity. Male domination remains a scandal in a church that exists for freedom and justice. For this reason the *Mesage to the People of God of the Second Special Assembly for Africa of the Synod of Bishops* urges local churches "to go beyond the general statement of *Ecclesia in Africa*, and put in place concrete structures to ensure real participation of women 'at appropriate levels'" in the life of the church (no. 25).

Gender (In)Justice in Context

I now turn to the relationships among bishops, priests, and women religious in Nigerian local churches. Following the decline of the religious orders after the French Revolution, the nineteenth century witnessed a new form of religious life dedicated to teaching and other forms of active apostolic life. During this period over six hundred new communities were founded.[7] In addition to imparting knowledge, the schools offered a new context for transmitting Catholic Christian doctrines to many and for winning potential members. The schools provided a context for evangelization as women religious took the lead in providing both secular and religious education to as many people as possible.

Women religious have always discerned and identified areas of need and initiated new ministries that have then received ecclesiastical approval and became part of the church's mission.[8] Such apostolic collaboration is in harmony with the oldest traditions in the early Christian community (Acts 6:1–6). Following the lament of the Hellenists on behalf of their starving widows, the community of disciples that was the church of Jerusalem elected seven men to whom they entrusted the ministry of serving at table while the twelve continued with the ministry of preaching. Although women were not mentioned among the seven men, it should be borne in mind that the early Christian communities were made up of women and men, and women ministered to the needs of Jesus and the apostles. They ministered in the churches according to the gifts given to each (see Eph 4:11–13). In *Lumen

Gentium (Dogmatic Constitution on the Church) Vatican II articulates its understanding of this community in the following terms:

> As all the members of the human body, so also are the faithful in Christ (cf. 1 Cor 12:12). Also in the building up of Christ's body there is a flourishing variety of members and functions. There is only one spirit, who, according to His own richness and the needs of the ministries, distributes His different gifts for the welfare of the church. (no. 7)

In this self-understanding of the church as an apostolic body of Christ, *Mutuae Relationes (Directives for the Mutual Relations between Bishops and Religious in the Church)* outlines terms of apostolic collaboration with members of women religious institutes (nos. 37, 40, 49, 55, 56). Also, canons 676 and 680 spell out the conditions of apostolic collaboration between the diocesan clergy and women religious. However, in spite of these guiding documents, in Nigeria the attitude and behavior of ecclesiastical leaders toward women religious are often both oppressive and contemptuous. There are cases of the outright appropriation of the properties of the congregations of women religious. In their subordination to the clergy, the clergy dictate terms and expect unquestioning compliance. This attitude falls short of the fullness of the truth of the church in the world. Undeniably, the church is divided in itself and in its collaborative ministries in the world. This false witness of the clergy undercuts its mission as salt, light, and the "powerful leaven of reconciliation" in a fear-stricken and deceit-governed nation.

Due to their quest for economic control, incompetent priests are appointed hospital secretaries, school administrators, and bursars in diocesan apostolic institutes run by and/or belonging to women religious. Priests are gradually abandoning the task of preaching the word to take over the ministries of women religious. In the past, religious women lacked the education for justice that would have awakened them to masculine oppression, even though education alone does not automatically end such oppression. In addition, their lack of education for justice made them a source of cheap labor for the clergy.

According to Tony Flannery, because the women religious had "not learned to think for themselves," they were "much more easy to control, and more inclined to think to do what they were told, so that they fitted more easily into the system." In this condition, "in general, simplicity was valued more highly than knowledge." For Flannery, this condition allowed the clergy to treat women religious "as glorified house keepers."[9] I must ask: How long will women religious be used as glorified housekeepers?

In Proposition 5, the African Synod maintained that "reconciliation overcomes crises, restores dignity to people, and opens the way to development and lasting peace among people at all levels." This statement leaves one wondering: Why talk of reconciliation when little or nothing has been said or heard of wrongdoings? On the surface, all seems well. Yet this is not the entire story. There is fear and suspicion between Nigerian women religious and the clergy because of the church's unfaithfulness to the Spirit of its Christ. "Where the Spirit of the Lord is, there is freedom" (2 Cor 3:17). In the Nigerian church it appears that God speaks only with and through the clergy and that women religious are manipulated and exploited because they are women.

The 1989 pastoral letter of the archbishop of Lubumbashi, Monsignor Kabanga, courageously represents the unjust treatment of women in the church. As recalled by Bernadette Mbuya-Beya, Monsignor Kabanga described the church's violent degradation of women's dignity thus: "Women appeared to be of no use to the Church beyond giving birth in the sacrament of matrimony to become good mothers of families or by religious profession, to become 'good sisters' as they say." Mbuya-Beya argues that Monsignor Kabanga's letter "revealed an image that many still have of women."[10] It is this conception of women, which Monsignor Kabanga repudiates, that permits and fosters the contemptuous treatment of women religious by the clergy.

Church and Reconciliation

In light of the foregoing, the verdict is clear: our church has sinned. We must listen to the synod's exhortation "to ask God for special pardon for all hurts and wounds inflicted upon each other and to reconcile offended persons and groups within the Church and the wider community" (Proposition 8.1). How might the church start on the road to healing the broken bodies and spirits of women religious? The first step is for the church to come together to talk about the silent miseries of women.

No bishop or priest can tell the story of what it means for Nigerian women religious to live a "slum" life in the church. There are women religious who do not know either, women who believe that things have always been like this and are satisfied with a degraded subsistence as members of the family of God. These humiliated women religious cannot imagine another life in the church because they do not have memories of times when women religious enjoyed relationships of solidarity as co-workers with the clergy for the kingdom of God. There are women religious who continue to live the precarious life of pretending that the status quo is acceptable. Terrified and crippled by fear they say "'Peace, peace,' when there is no peace" (Jer 6:14). Caution, not courage, rules their existence. Ruled by fear, they have exchanged the demands of faith and justice for fleeting securities.

But, as Teresa Okure shows, there are women religious who have dared to hope for another life altogether in the church. However, their anguish is a whisper. Although the church may want women religious' experiences of domination to be forgotten, they must be exposed in public and be heard.

The first step toward a transformative reconciliation is for women religious to tell their stories of violence and suffering as clearly identified individuals. As Desmond Tutu argues, besides serving as a critic of history, laying bare the nightmares in the souls of sword-pierced hearts is cathartic. Tutu used the case of Lucas Sikwepere to illustrate how telling an experience of violence to one's personhood leads to an intense inner release. Lucas, who was shot in the face and blinded by a Cape Town police officer, speaks of his release: "I feel what . . . has brought my sight back, my eyesight back, is to come here and tell the story. I feel what has been making me sick all the time is the fact that I couldn't tell my story. But now . . . it feels like I have got my sight back by coming and telling you the story."[11]

Like Lucas, women religious must tell stories of the indignity they suffered in the church in order to feel what has been making them sick all this time. Similarly, as did Mr. Nicodemus Sono, women religious must tell of their helplessness in the face of masculine bullying in the church. Nicodemus told of his fruitless attempt to save his son:

When I looked at Lolo he was in terrible state, he was shaking. . . . I started pleading again with Mrs. Mandela: "Please, won't you leave my son with me because he's already been beaten?' . . . And she totally refused that: "This is a spy." She said to . . . [the driver] again, "Pull off," so he pulled off. As he went I pleaded with her until she said to me: "I am taking this dog away. The movement will see what to do."[12]

While those who have been sinned against remember their experiences and honor those who continue to suffer multiple injustices, giving voice to what seems to have slipped into obscurity but continues to harass and shame them is vital. Similarly, those who have sinned must tell their stories in confession, as did Jerry Richardson, who recounted how he killed Stompie Seipei, a fourteen-year-old activist:

I slaughtered him. I slaughtered him like a goat. We made him lay on his back and I put garden shears through his neck and the garden shears penetrated to the back of his neck and I made some cutting motion. . . .
    I killed Stompie under the instruction of Mummy Mrs. Mandela. Mummy never killed anyone, but she used us to kill a lot of people. She does not even visit us in prisons. She used us.[13]

And after confession, those who have sinned directly or indirectly must be truly contrite, and ask for forgiveness, as did Mrs. Mandela:

I will take this opportunity to say . . . to Stompie's mother, how deeply sorry I am—I have said so to her before a few years back, when the heat was very hot. I am saying it is true, things went horribly wrong. I fully agree with that and for that part of those painful years when things went horribly wrong and we were aware of the fact that there were factors that led to that, for that I am deeply sorry.[14]

The church must take the way of vulnerability, humility, and solidarity toward reconciliation in order to overcome injustice, oppression, and evil.

Recommendations and Conclusion

In light of the foregoing analysis of the situation of women religious in the church in Nigeria and elsewhere, the following steps are vital to redress the multiple injustices women face:

- That in the spirit of the African Synod and its theme of reconciliation, justice, and peace a structure and a process be initiated that will listen to justice issues within the church, especially for women religious.

- That such a structure should include women religious who are knowledgeable in civil and canon law and not be the exclusive preserve of the clergy.

- That the documents of the church on collaboration and mutual relationships be honored to the letter.

- That religious congregations establish—unhindered—ministries that are faithful to their respective charisms and allow them to maintain and care for their members.

Within communities of disciples in history, as in this church of Nigeria, Paul's vision continues to elude us. Indeed there are slaves and the free, female and male, Ibo and Yoruba (Gal 3:26–28). Just as Adam betrayed Eve to God out of fear, fear and a lack of security continue to prevent us from living in the freedom of the children of God. We are afraid of waking up one morning and discovering that things have changed, and we will not know how to treat one another. Christ our brother revealed to us that we—woman and man—are sharers in divine nature. He taught us that fear is useless. If we heed the voice that tells us "Be not afraid" (Mt 28:5), we shall arise to become the builders of the kingdom of God, of another life altogether when we will see one another as we truly are: *imago Dei*. And like one whose body we are, the church must learn to sincerely ask women religious as historical subjects in ecclesial discourse, "What do you think?" And we will declare to the church, "Do whatever he tells you" (Jn 2:5).

Notes

¹ All scripture texts are taken from the African Bible.

² Available on the un.org website.

³ Ronald Rolheiser, *The Holy Longing: Guidelines for a Christian Spirituality* (New York: Doubleday, 1999), 173.

⁴ Phyllis Trible, *God and the Rhetoric of Sexuality* (Philadelphia: Fortress, 1978), 128.

⁵ John R. Donahue, "What Does the Lord Require?: A Bibliographical Essay on the Bible and Social Justice," *Studies in the Spirituality of Jesuits* 25, ed. John W. Padberg (March 2, 1993), 8.

⁶ Ibid., 8–10.

⁷ Helen R. Fuchs Ebaugh, *Women in the Vanishing Cloister: Organizational Decline in Catholic Religious Orders in the US* (New Brunswick, NJ: Rutgers University Press, 1993), 17.

⁸ Claire Murphy, *An Introduction to Christian Feminism* (Dublin: Dominican Publications, 1994), 282.

⁹ Tony Flannery, *The Death of Religious Life?* (Dublin: Columba Press, 1997), 21.

¹⁰ Bernadette Mbuya-Beya, "Women in the Churches in Africa: Possibilities for Presence and Promises," in *The African Synod: Documents, Reflections, Perspectives*, ed. Africa Faith and Justice Network (Maryknoll, NY: Orbis Books, 1996), 182.

¹¹ Desmond Mpilo Tutu, *No Future without Forgiveness* (New York: Doubleday, 1997), 167.

¹² Ibid., 136.

¹³ Ibid., 135.

¹⁴ Ibid., 174.

12

The African Synod for Those of Us Who Stayed at Home

David Kaulem

The second African Synod has come and gone. After several meetings and processes to prepare for the synod, bishops and participants from Africa and the rest of the world met for a month in Rome. As is customary, the *Lineamenta* was distributed in advance of the synod "to foster extensive discussion on the synodal topic."[1] Subsequently, a working document was prepared from the responses to the "Questionnaire" and included in the *Lineamenta*. These responses were used for discussions at the synod. At the end the synod bishops and other participants prepared propositions that were submitted to Pope Benedict XVI to help him prepare the post-synodal exhortation. The Preface of the *Lineamenta* explained the process as follows:

> The Questionnaire at the end of the document can serve as an assistance. Each bishops' conference is to provide translations in the local languages to encourage greater community participation in preparation for the Synod. The responses from the interested Church bodies should be submitted by the end of October 2008 for the preparation of the *Instrumentum Laboris*, the working document for the Second Special Assembly for Africa of the Synod of Bishops.

Those who were at the synod were fully committed to the process and a month later returned to their respective homes and stations. A few of the attendees have written and are still writing about the synod discussions. There is even a debate among them around the question that was also asked regarding Vatican II: Did anything happen?[2] Whatever the answers are to these debates, the synod relied on processes, activities, and attitudes that either did not take place or were not as extensive and intensive as was intended to support the synod fully. Many of those who stayed at home did not even know of the existence of the *Lineamenta* and the expectations expressed in it. Therefore, most Catholics in African countries did not answer the Questionnaire in the *Lineamenta,* and so the "extensive discussion on the synodal topic" did not happen. In short, what needed to happen for the synod to be effective simply did not occur in many places. However, this shortcoming can be corrected, at least partially, if the post-synodal processes are intensively and extensively publicized and made more participatory.

At Home, Business Remained as Usual

Many of those who stayed at home went on with their day-to-day church chores and programs before, during, and after the synod. They went to mass and attended various guild meetings, religious conferences, and workshops, with little talk of the synod. Yet all these activities were supposed to be rich opportunities to prepare for the synod. Deanery and pastoral council meetings mentioned little about the synod. Nor was their work seen as opportunities to enrich the synod. They planned and decided on pastoral strategies without considering the synod.

As a result, the synodal processes appeared mysterious to many people—almost secretive. Yet the synod assumed that its proceedings would be informed by what happened at mass in different parts of Africa; the research and teaching in Catholic schools, institutes, and universities; the formation efforts at seminaries and formation houses; and by the activities in Small Christian Communities (SCCs), lay associations, and the social, economic, and political lives of Catholics. On the whole, these Catholic institutions and processes still struggle to see the questions of the synod as legitimate and appropriate for the church to ask.

Yet, the *Lineamenta* clearly pointed out that the synod was about the lives of the people of Africa. It indicated that the theme of the synod, "The Church in Africa in Service to Reconciliation, Justice, and Peace: 'You Are the Salt of the Earth. . . . You are the light of the world'" "cannot fail to treat the causes of so much hatred, injustice and war on the continent." The *Lineamenta* continues: "In fact, the urgency of this Second Special Assembly is tied to the suffering of the African peoples, and the dehumanising and oppressive situation which persists on the continent. Africa is facing a whole set of conflicts and problems which are central to the challenges to evangelisation in Africa today" (no. 10).

Many people of faith in Zimbabwe, including bishops, priests, and religious, are still afraid to repeat such statements and to take them into account in their work, in church programs, and in their day-to-day activities. The irony is that there is an attempt to evangelize in Africa, without addressing directly and courageously "the dehumanising and oppressive situation" or recognizing the role of the laity assumed by the synod participants. Yet the

Lineamenta says that "the meaning and need of the laity's presence is not to be found so much in the growing conviction of their responsibility and participation in the Church's activity in the world, as in an awareness of the real nature of the Church's mission in the world" (no. 61).

Many of us who stayed at home are yet to discover "the Church's mission in the world." Yet the *Lineamenta* and the *Final List of 57 Propositions* of the synod are advocating a different approach. When the *Lineamenta* asked, "What can your Church do to improve the situation of human rights and promote democracy?" there were still members of the Catholic Church in Zimbabwe, religious and lay, who opposed the establishment of justice and peace commissions and condemned those that existed for meddling in politics. Guilds, SCCs, and other religious movements were still hesitant to address questions from the questionnaire such as

20. Describe the present state of affairs in your particular Church (diocese and country) as regards:
    a) Health, education and social structures?
    b) Human rights and democracy?
    c) Relations between different ethnic and religious groups.

If the bishops' conferences, priests, consecrated persons, religious institutes, Catholic universities, major seminaries, and catechists were as self-conscious and committed to reconciliation, justice, and peace as was assumed by the synod, there would be tremendous transformation of our church and society.

The majority of those who stayed at home never heard of the first African Synod held in 1994, yet the second synod was supposed to carry on the work of the first one. While some people talk about the apostolic exhortation of the first synod, *Ecclesia in Africa*, and praise it—and we have seen it referred to in magazines and journals—most people, including priests, women religious, and the lay faithful, have neither seen nor read it. In Zimbabwe it is yet to be simplified, translated, and popularized. In the meantime, the apostolic exhortation of the second African Synod is imminent.

The *Lineamenta* and the *Instumentum Laboris* for the second African Synod are available on the Internet. But how many of those who stayed at home had access to it? The documents were not translated into local languages and extensively distributed as recommended and assumed by the synod process. The synod bishops recognized in the *Final List of 57 Propositions* the gaps in the "organic, pastoral solidarity" of the Church-Family of God that could have facilitated wide discussion and conversation regarding the theme of the synod (Proposition 3). As a result they

encourage the Bishops in Africa to revive existing structures of ecclesial communion, especially COMSAM (The Confederation of the Conferences of Major Superiors of Africa and Madagascar) and promote others, such as:

—A continental council for the clergy;
—A continental council for the laity; and
—A continental council for Catholic women. (Proposition 4)

The gaps identified at the continental level are also evident at national, diocesan, and parish levels. Many commissions for justice and peace, where they have existed, have struggled with little success to encourage the people of God to establish relevant institutions capable of applying gospel values to social, political, and cultural issues. There is still ignorance—as well as fear and resistance—of this call to "contribute to setting up a more just secular order" (*Lineamenta*, no. 58). Generally, Catholics who enter into politics to fight for justice do not link their efforts to their faith or to the institutions of the church. Sometimes they actually engage in activities that undermine the values advocated by the church.

In fact, we still wonder, given our established ways of doing things, what it would mean to have extensive debate in the church on social issues. Our established traditions have tended to rule this out. What does it mean, and where and when can it be done? At mass there is no time and no space for such discussion, despite what Gregory F. Augustine Pierce has convincingly explained about the mass—"the Mass is never ended" and "the Dismissal Rite at the end of Mass is supposed to send the entire congregation out into the world."[3] In Zimbabwe, priests who have tried to preach the gospel and make it relevant to the social and political challenges of the country have been threatened with violence.

Our guilds and catechetical programs attract large numbers of Catholics, but rarely do they address social issues. The Guild of St. Joseph, probably the biggest lay association for Catholic men in Zimbabwe, has the capacity to bring together the major social, political, and economic leaders in the country. Yet the guild seems reluctant or unable to use its influence for political peace, national healing, or reconciliation. Saint Joseph, the husband of Mary the mother of Jesus, worked hard to protect his child, Jesus, from the cruel intentions of King Herod. Yet his contemporary followers fail to see that it is their duty, as people of faith, to do something about the political, social, and economic situations negatively affecting their own children today. The education, health care, and social services systems in Zimbabwe collapsed in the hands of our leaders, many of them members of the St. Joseph's Guild. The African Synod asked critical questions about the role of the laity in society, and the guild, together with others, failed to see this opportunity. To this extent, the synod was much poorer.

Joseph Healey's observations about SCCs that are more focused on Bible reading and accord little or no attention to issues of politics, economics, technology, and culture in Kenya also applies to Zimbabwe. Members of these communities are even fighting one another, while they are suffering from poverty, dying from treatable diseases, and their children are unable to go to school for want of school fees. At a time when the synod called on people to discuss how to bring reconciliation into their families, communities, and nations, our SCCs continued to be busy with baptisms, fundraising, Bible reading, funerals, weddings, and others tasks that did not seem relevant to the topic of the synod.

Church activities are legitimate activities for people of faith, but they need to be understood in their social and political contexts. They can be places for realizing reconciliation, justice, and peace. Unfortunately, many members of guilds and other Catholic movements are engaged in property grabbing at funerals and use weddings and payment of the *lobola* (bride price) as opportunities for self-enrichment and the exploitation of others.

The reluctance of Zimbabwe's Christians to engage in political issues is understandable in a country where such issues are dangerous and divisive. The Zimbabwe Catholic Bishops' Conference observed this when it wrote:

> In Zimbabwe today, there are Christians on all sides of the conflict; and there are many Christians sitting on the fence. Active members of our Parish and Pastoral Councils are prominent officials at all levels of the ruling party. Equally distinguished and committed office-bearers of the opposition parties actively support church activities in every parish and diocese. They all profess their loyalty to the same Church. They are all baptised, sit and pray and sing together in the same church, take part in the same celebration of the Eucharist and partake of the same Body and Blood of Christ. While the next day, outside the church, a few steps away, Christian State Agents, policemen and soldiers assault and beat peaceful, unarmed demonstrators and torture detainees.[4]

The synod assumed knowledge that did not actually exist in many structures of the church. Many Catholics never even heard of the synod. In my own parish, St. Canisius, in Marlborough, Harare, and in other urban parishes where there are socially conscious and literate Catholic professionals, I heard endless expressions of ignorance of the synod as I shared the AFCAST booklets prepared to help discussion of the synod topic.[5] Archbishop Lwanga of Uganda, speaking at the post-synodal meeting organized by the Symposium of Episcopal Conferences of Africa and Madagascar (SECAM) and Caritas Africa in Momemu, Maputo, recalled his conversation with a Catholic professional who expressed his ignorance of the synod.

Yet the African Synod presents an opportunity for social transformation. There are people in strategic positions in the church and society who continue to show commitment and courage in stimulating individuals, organizations, institutions, and processes toward creating a critical mass for the positive participation of Zimbabweans in processes that affect their lives. The social teaching of the church can help the faithful to link their prayerful activities to the realities of their lives. Resources and lessons from the African Synod can enhance the capacity of the church and society to respond to the challenges of today—healing, reconciliation, justice, and peace.

Relevance of the Synod's Theme to Africa

Did the theme of the African Synod resonate with and cover the urgent concerns in Zimbabwe? Wars, conflicts, genocides, poverty, disease, exploitation, and oppression have divided and polarized many people on the continent. The need for reconciliation on ethnic, racial, gender, class, age, and political-party levels cannot be overemphasized. In countries like Kenya and Zimbabwe, post-election violence had claimed many lives and left many maimed with properties destroyed and looted. Poverty has left many Africans traumatized, disgruntled, and angry. When the synod was announced, African Catholics were looking for healing, reconciliation, justice, and peace. The church was expected to take a lead, although it had failed in some instances. Aylward Shorter observes,

> In Africa the year 1994 will be forever remembered as the year of genocide, when between half a million and a million people were massacred in the tiny overpopulated African country of Rwanda. By any standards it was a country that was massively Christian. More than 60% of the population was Catholic, and Church authorities boasted of the high rates of church attendance and frequent reception of the sacraments.[6]

The church itself was under scrutiny. After the Rwandan genocide references to the church as "the salt of the earth" or "the light of the world" did not sound convincing. *Ecclesia in Africa* pointed to the need to address this weakness:

> The credibility of the church in Africa depended upon Bishops and priests who followed Christ's example and could give witness of an exemplary life; upon truly faithful men and women religious, authentic witness by their way of living the evangelical counsels; upon a dynamic laity, with deeply believing parents, educators conscious of their responsibilities and political leaders animated by a profound sense of morality. (no. 22)

While we cannot deny that the church in Africa has built up credibility over the years, particularly in the mid 1990s, its credibility was being challenged in the eyes of many people. This was even worse after the clergy sexual-abuse scandals in the United States and parts of Europe. In Africa itself we saw cases of priests and religious who failed to live exemplary lives; laity who not only failed to bear witness to Christ, but also perpetrated heinous crimes against the people of God; and political leadership that dramatically failed to show any sign of social responsibility or any sense of moral decency.

The situation, however, has not been entirely bleak. A number of people, lay and religious, Catholic and otherwise, who have heard of the synod have found it a great opportunity for translating its themes into the sociopolitical realm. Aylward Shorter, speaking in a different context, points out that Christian faith has inspired individuals to fight for their fellow humans. This point is confirmed by Elisée Rutagambwa, who writes in the context of the Rwandan genocide:

> Although the Church hierarchy has miserably failed to address the genocide, it is important to note that small numbers of individuals have shown admirable devotion to Christian morals and virtues. There were Christians—Catholic and Protestant, priests, nuns, and laity—who risked their lives for the sake of their fellow human beings. Some members betrayed the Church's mission, but others acted with true faith and commitment to the Gospel. It is in this small measure of true faith and commitment to Christian values and morals that we see evidence of hope for reconciliation. The faith and commitment of the heroes and heroines provides a foundation upon which to build and work toward the Church's renewal.[7]

Relevance of the African Synod for Zimbabwe

There is reason to believe that the synod can inspire the people of Zimbabwe. The reasons for the relevance of the synod can be attributed to the history of Zimbabwe itself. In the mid 1990s Zimbabwe was characterized by an economic downturn due to disruption of key economic sectors, unemployment, the erosion of a sense of the common good, and lack of international support.

Politically, Zimbabwe was not inspired by the common good. Many people lost any motivation to respect Zimbabwe's political institutions, organizations, and processes. They no longer associated with national symbols. Many left the country to look for jobs, education, health, or simply for space to experiment with new ideas and to say or write what they liked and to associate politically, culturally, and economically with others. At the time of the synod, Zimbabweans were deeply divided along political-party lines. Political institutions were weakened by deep divisions, which led a few people to monopolize them while many felt marginalized from the national institutions and processes.

Socially, most Zimbabweans felt alienated and stressed as basic commodities like fuel, food, water, electricity, shelter, jobs, education, and healthcare were either scarce or too expensive for ordinary people. They struggled to have a sense of belonging, a sense of pride.

Culturally, Zimbabweans suffered from a poverty of imagination. The dominant conception of Zimbabwe that informed their knowledge of and emotional response to their nation was very narrow. The history of Zimbabwe is that of a nation-state that, since 1890, has always been monopolized by a few elites. Since colonial times it has been a fort or *laager* protecting some against others. The lives of most Zimbabweans have been molded by institutions and experiences of war and violence, surveillance and suspicion. Zimbabweans perfected the language of hatred, strategies for destruction, and a culture of humiliating others.

The colonial humiliation of black people was very deep. There was clearly a need for many of the whites in Zimbabwe to shake off the ghetto mentality. They needed to begin seriously to develop a culture of human solidarity with fellow blacks in the country and abroad. As Pope Benedict XVI says in his 2005 encyclical, *Deus Caritas Est:*

> The First Letter of John shows that such love (love of neighbour) is explicitly demanded. The unbreakable bond between love of God and love of neighbour is emphasized. One is so closely connected to the other that to say that we love God becomes a lie if we are closed to our neighbour or hate him altogether. Saint John's words should rather be interpreted to mean that love of neighbour is a path that leads to the encounter with God, and that closing our eyes to our neighbour also blinds us to God. (no. 16)

The humiliation of blacks by colonialism was so deep that blacks internalized it and began a process of reproducing it among themselves. Culturally, Zimbabweans have never as a nation-state lived in comprehensive solidarity with one another. Their solidarity has always been limited and partisan. Their solidarity has always tended to be limited by racism, tribalism, and sexism. Since virtue is always learned through practice, as a nation we have never learned the virtues of comprehensive solidarity, of universal love, of genuine respect. Zimbabwe was in crisis at the time of the second African Synod. The challenge was to find ways of cultivating those virtues that Zimbabweans had denied themselves during their arduous history. The theme of the synod spoke directly to this challenge.

While the synod focused its attention on reconciliation, justice, and peace, there was also a need to emphasize national healing. Most Zimbabweans felt and still feel that they have been hurt and that there is need for healing. This is why on October 1, 2009, the Zimbabwe Catholic Bishops' Conference issued a pastoral letter on national healing and reconciliation, *God Can Heal the Wounds of the Afflicted*, in which they wrote:

We, Zimbabweans, have hurt each other in many different ways and over long periods of time. We are all guilty, for those who have been victims at one time have been aggressors at another and many more have done nothing in the face of atrocities perpetuated before their eyes. Today, we all need healing from these hurts and from our guilt. This healing will facilitate reconciliation within and among ourselves and also with our Creator. With healing and reconciliation, our nation will recover and set itself up for political, social, cultural and economic development.

This pastoral letter succinctly summarizes the various national historical wounds felt by many people and the great need for healing from them. Archbishop Robert Christopher Ndlovu of Harare, conscious of this burden and feeling of hurt experienced by most Zimbabweans, appealed to members of the church and people of goodwill just before he left for the synod: "I call on all our priests and deacons, men and women religious, the lay faithful and all people of goodwill to use their positions and create opportunities for the work of healing, reconciliation, justice and peace."[8]

At the time of the synod, truth was another virtue that most people in Zimbabwe felt had been lost. As the bishops prepared to meet in Rome, Zimbabweans relied on rumor for news. With the privatization of national institutions by the ZANU PF–led government, the press was highly polarized. Newspapers, radio stations, and mass media in general were either for or against the ZANU PF government. In this context, truth suffered, and people were largely in the dark with regard to events in the country. Perpetrators of violence were praised in the government press as liberators, and democrats were demonized. Hate language dominated political contestation and the church was implicated. As the Zimbabwe Catholic Bishops' Conference quite correctly observed in *God Hears the Cry of the Oppressed*:

> In Zimbabwe today, there are Christians on all sides of the conflict; and there are many Christians sitting on the fence. Active members of our Parish and Pastoral Councils are prominent officials at all levels of the ruling party. Equally distinguished and committed office-bearers of the opposition parties actively support church activities in every parish and diocese. They all profess their loyalty to the same Church.

As the synod process continued, members of the church in Zimbabwe were implicated in the nation's conflicts. Members of the church speculated that even the Bishops' Conference itself was divided. The faithful speculated on which bishop was on which side of the political divide. So, how could the church, through its most senior representatives, give truth to the Zimbabwean community? How could the faithful treat their bishops as credible conveyers of gospel truth and not participants in the deadly political-party games?

This must have weighed heavily on the Zimbabwean bishops when they received the invitation to collect views from their dioceses to feed into the synod processes. The politically poisoned air affected the church deeply. How could divided and polarized communities facilitate "extensive discussion on the synodal topic"? Given this situation, the discussions that were held in Zimbabwe as part of the synodal process were selective and controlled. They were held in the environments of pastoral councils and selected committees and commissions. This was the only way in which discussions could be held with a semblance of civility. Hence, they failed to capture and address the deep wounds and divisions of families, communities, and the nation. Yet the nature of the synodal topic required the church to create a free and open environment that encouraged individuals and communities to express their genuine thoughts and feelings and to engage members of the church, people of goodwill, the perpetrators of violence, the deeply hurt and traumatized, and also those described by the bishops as "sitting on the fence."

Synod Demands on the Church in Zimbabwe

If the synodal process required the different levels of the church in Zimbabwe to create an environment for raising issues of healing, reconciliation, justice, and peace, it meant that the church should have been able to receive the views and emotions that it evoked. Included in those reactions would be the apathy and social withdrawal that stemmed from feelings of mistrust and hatred cultivated from before 1890, when the area that is now Zimbabwe was colonized by Cecil John Rhodes on behalf of Britain. It seems clear that the church in Zimbabwe did not have the capacity to implement the synod processes fully. This capacity was supposed to have been institutional, implemented by skilled church personnel, with a clear values framework. We, the church in Zimbabwe, failed dismally on all accounts.

Institutional Capacity

The church in Zimbabwe needs institutions, structures, and organizations that work full time, not only to collect data relevant to the synodal theme, but also adequately to engage national, governmental, and civil society structures and processes to bring about healing, reconciliation, justice, and peace. While the church has established Catholic commissions, the weaknesses of these institutions were exposed during the visioning process, national elections, the process leading to the Global Political Agreement, and the process of drafting the national constitution.

The church has taken too long to develop its responses to critical national issues. It has sometimes used ad hoc committees with little capacity or sufficient life span to carry out their recommendations. The church needs to enhance its capacity to engage in research on national issues, to document its research, and to participate in policy-development processes. At present, what church structures or processes exist to engage the national presidency, parliament, judiciary, police, army, and other governmental structures on the theme of the synod? The church has experiences in education, health, and social development that can contribute to the process of reform. As Peter Kanyandago points out in his discussion in this volume of the church's mission with regard to the exploitation of Africa's natural resources, more sustained development and collaboration in church-related training institutions, universities, and research centers is needed. Otherwise, there is no reason to believe that enough information and insights about Zimbabwe's needs were carried to the synod. More important, given the present situation in Zimbabwe, there is no reason to believe that the apostolic exhortation will be implemented fully.

Personnel Capacity

Because the church in Zimbabwe has not trained personnel in areas other than philosophy and theology, it has not been able to make serious contributions to the process of shaping policies that affect the scientific and technological development of the nation. The church needs to provide leadership in areas that comprehensively enhance respect for the dignity of human beings and that of the environment. It should train and support personnel inspired by gospel values and principles who can serve as leaders in policy development.

Similarly, training and forming professional laypeople in the church's social teaching will help to transform the Zimbabwean church and society. As *Ecclesia in Africa* emphasizes, "Christians who occupy positions of responsibility are to be carefully prepared for political, economic and social tasks by means of a solid formation in the church's social doctrine, so that in their places they will be faithful witnesses to the Gospel" (no. 90). An important national need at the moment is the knowledge and expertise in how to encourage national healing, reconciliation, justice, and peace, and subsequently to reform our country's main institutions.

Ethical Framework

The Zimbabwean church needs more sustained and sophisticated discussions to develop values and principles that can form a framework for reflecting on our social reality. These values and principles are supposed to inform the chosen ideals of society and to serve as criteria for assessing or evaluating social institutions, processes, and practices. This entails reflection on how these values and principles can be transformed into policies and structures that bring more justice to the people. It is a given that Christians differ in how they read their history; they also have different political orientations and sensibilities. Notwithstanding, as Christians they are expected to transform the social sphere in the light of the gospel. Christians who are members of different political parties and social movements must help transform their respective organizations in line with the demands of reconciliation, justice, and peace. The role of the church in this task is critical.

Conclusion

The church and all Christians have a moral duty to contribute to the creation of social, economic, political, and cultural institutions, systems, structures, processes, and personalities that facilitate the integral growth and fulfillment of every human person. This is what was expected by the synod. On one hand, the call to contribute to the realization of the goals of the synod has exposed the weakness of the church in Zimbabwe. On the other hand, it has helped to clarify the church's mission and moral responsibility and to point out where Christians need to strengthen their resolve and make themselves relevant.

The preparatory questionnaire clarified that although it is important for the church to run schools, clinics, and social services, this is not sufficient if the institutional environment and the policies of government are not supportive. It points out the need for the church as a social and moral power to engage in a mature, sustained, constructive, and prophetic manner with political leaders, economic processes, and cultural institutions. This requires a transformed church. The event of the second African Synod and the ensuing process of implementing its proposals offer the church in Zimbabwe an opportunity to examine critically its capacities and its weaknesses and commit itself to doing better. The synod shows clearly that part of the church's mission is to respond to the joys, hurts, and anxieties of all Zimbabweans.

Notes

[1] Synod of Bishops, Second Special Assembly for Africa, *Lineamenta: The Church in Africa in Service to Reconciliation, Justice, and Peace* (Vatican City: Libreria Editrice, 2006), preface. Available on the vatican.va website.

[2] John W. O'Malley, Joseph A. Komonchak, Joseph Schloesser, and Stephen Neil J. Ormerod, *Vatican II: Did Anything Happen?* ed. David G. Schultenover (New York: Continuum, 2008).

[3] G. F. Pierce, *The Mass Is Never Ended: Rediscovering Our Mission to Transform the World* (Notre Dame, IN: Ave Maria Press, 2007), 11.

[4] Zimbabwe Catholic Bishops' Conference, *God Hears the Cry of the Oppressed*, pastoral letter on the current crisis in zimbabwe, Holy Thursday, April 5, 2007, 3–4. Available on the zimonline.co.za website.

[5] The African Forum for Catholic Social Teaching, a network of Catholics committed to promoting Catholic social teaching in the church and society in eastern

and southern Africa, held a special workshop in Kampala, Uganda, in December 2007, and published the proceedings of the workshop in a booklet entitled *The Church in Service to Reconciliation Justice and Peace: Preparing for the Second African Synod.*

[6] Aylward Shorter, *Christianity and the African Imagination: After the African Synod, Resources for Inculturation* (Nairobi: Paulines Publications, 1996), 11.

[7] Elisée Rutagambwa, "The Rwandan Church: The Challenge of Reconciliation," in *The Catholic Church and the Nation-State: Comparative Perspectives*, ed. Paul Christopher Manuel, Lawrence Christopher Reardon, and Clyde Wilcox (Washington DC: Georgetown University Press, 2006), 181.

[8] Archbishop Robert Christopher Ndlovu, "The Second African Synod: Letter on National Healing and Reconciliation," *Catholic Church News* 82 (October/November 2009): 21.

Part IV

Integrity of the Earth—
Ecology, Natural Resources, Poverty, and the Church

13

Theology, Ecology, and Africa

No Longer Strange Bedfellows

PETER KNOX

Theology in Africa is normally associated with issues of inculturation or justice, peace, and reconciliation, while ecological theology is frequently associated with churches of the more developed and industrialized countries. Shining examples of concern for African ecology, like Nobel Peace Prize Laureate Professor Wangari Maathai, who advocates the planting of indigenous trees, are not normally associated with theology. This chapter, however, discusses documents from the second African Synod that show that ecological concerns are definitely in the mainstream of the church's agenda and of theological reflection in Africa. The synod has brought ecology and theology in Africa together as never before.

Theology is the way in which people explore their faith in God and come to a deeper understanding of their faith relationship. Ecology is the study of organisms in relation to their physical environment. This chapter considers the way human beings share the physical space of Africa with its mineral resources and its living plants and animals. Offering such a reflection requires caution and humility. To begin with, *Africa* is not a univocal term; it means different things to different people. There is the land mass identified as continental Africa. But does it include the islands of Madagascar, the Canaries, Mauritius, the Seychelles, and so on, to name but a few? There is political Africa, referring to member states of the African Union, some of which are still in the process of being born, others that seem to have been stillborn, and others that appear to be dying a painful and protracted death. There is also an ethnic Africa. But is it everybody whose ancestors have come from Africa? Does it only include people who are "black?" Does it include "white" Africans (such as myself) who are committed to living in the continent? Does it include those whose lives have taken them to other continents in search of a better life or of survival and who entertain no hope of returning to the continent?

And there is Africa, the basket case of the world, and Africa, the "spiritual lung" of the humanity of today, to quote Pope Benedict XVI. There is Christian Africa, Muslim Africa, and traditional Africa; urban Africa and rural Africa; sub-Saharan Africa and Mediterranean Africa. However, admitting such multi-vocality should not intimidate the writer into silence. So I offer the following reflections in genuine humility, knowing that everything written here might be contested by a simple "But that's not the case in *my* Africa."

A Continent under Threat

Whatever else it is, Africa is a continent under threat. In terms of biodiversity, Africa is more than the picture postcards of gnu, gazelle, and giraffe. The continent is home to thousands of endemic species of plants and animals. Its deserts, forests, mountains, savannah, and wetlands provide unique biomes for species ranging from aardvarks to zebras. Some of these species are found nowhere else on the planet; they are so highly adapted to a particular environment that they can only survive in their particular niche. This wonder of creation is repeated all across the planet but perhaps nowhere more than in Africa. However, this reservoir of life is under threat from the sometimes uncontrolled, profit-driven extraction of mineral and biological reserves of the continent.

Vast swathes of the continent are being destroyed today, which is a great cause for concern. The Niger Delta region in Nigeria comes to mind: pollution from spillage from the oil pipelines threatens the livelihood and survival of many of the people of the Delta.[1] The inadequate and tardy response of those responsible for the spillage only exacerbates the extent of damages done to the sensitive estuarine ecosystem, not to mention the human suffering from pollution and lack of food and water.

Even the *orderly* extraction of minerals on the continent has brought unforeseen and widespread damage. One example is the aquifer of South Africa's gold fields, which has been poisoned by leaking acids, heavy metals, and toxic waste throughout a century of gold-mining activity.[2] Groundwater is now undrinkable for humans and cattle as well as unsuitable for the irrigation of crops. In an already water-stressed country, water has to be piped in from rivers hundreds of miles away to provide for the largest urban population in the country.

Many of the multinational companies that were responsible for the production of these poisons no longer exist, or they have merged or been bought out, to the point where it is no longer possible to isolate those who have profited from the extraction of the resources and require them to clean up the mess they have made. Those that still exist and can be held directly accountable for poisoning swathes of land are not above ducking their responsibility any way they can. Such is the example of asbestos mining in the Northern Cape Province of South Africa, where the British holding company responsible has deliberately disguised its corporate identity in order to evade paying the price of environmental cleanup and compensating poisoned civilians. This case has called attention to the reluctance of multinational companies to apply the same standard of occupational health and safety in developing countries as those that are enforced in the corporation's home country.[3]

In terms of the exploitation of *biological* reserves in the continent, there are the examples of the systematic depletion of the fishing reserves off the coast of pre-independent Namibia[4] and the wholesale destruction of the forests of tropical Africa, which are exported for hardwood to richer countries of the world. Flying over the continent at night (itself an ecologically unfriendly thing to do), one sees mile after mile of forest burning. These uncontrolled fires pump greenhouse gases into the atmosphere, further eroding the oxygen-producing lung of the planet and irretrievably destroying habitats of many species, some of which are not yet "known to science."

The consumption as "bushmeat" of many vertebrate species cannot continue unabated. Such consumption was sustainable when practiced on a village scale in traditional societies. But with the massive displacements of people from areas close to their food supply to the burgeoning population centers, the taste for bushmeat has grown to such an extent that there is fear for the survival of several species of animals. These species include the great apes, the nearest living relatives to *homo sapiens*.

Who cares? The church has the more pressing concerns of poverty in the continent, the threat of HIV/AIDS, the spread of Islam, food insecurity, refugees and forced migration, and the likelihood of further drought and desertification. Was it realistic to hope that the participants gathered for the second African Synod would spend time considering these more remote, long-term environmental concerns? Would they take the time to consult experts on life and climatic sciences? Would they include these considerations in any final list of propositions? Would they take a position of leadership on some of the global questions of the day? How could they afford not to, since these questions bear directly on the survival of Africa? With the churches as major landowners across the continent, we have responsibility for the best possible stewardship of our resources.

The First African Synod

The first thing to bear in mind is that a synod is not just a one-off meeting taking place in Rome with a definite start and end date. It is one part of a long process that builds on what has gone before. For example, the first African Synod convoked by Pope John Paul II in 1994 discussed many of the realities of the continent. These have not changed radically over the intervening fifteen years. Many of the environmental concerns of that time still pertain into the early twenty-first century.

The post-synodal exhortation of this first African Synod, *Ecclesia in Africa*, has only a single mention of the environment, and this is in the context of lauding the role Catholic universities, higher institutes, and cultural centers may play in society. John Paul II says that these centers constitute public forums that permit the church to make known Christian convictions about the environment, among other topics (no. 103). This is not a very promising expression of concern for the environment.

John Paul II's exhortation is, however, more expansive on the question of resources, both natural and human. It observes how the available scarce resources of the continent are being tragically mismanaged (no. 40). National resources and public funds are often diverted into foreign bank accounts to the profit of domestic or foreign private interests. John Paul II calls this plain theft, no matter what legal camouflage is used (no. 113). The post-synodal exhortation does not fail to deplore the way in which wars have decimated people and destroyed the natural and cultural resources of the continent for decades (no. 117).

The pope optimistically suggests that the cultural and spiritual resources of the people of the continent may be engaged to change the economic poverty that prevails despite such a wealth of natural resources (no. 42). He spells out how this may take place by reminding governments of their "binding duty to protect the *common patrimony* against all forms of waste and embezzlement by citizens lacking public spirit or by unscrupulous foreigners." They are to adopt appropriate policies to exploit and distribute "scarce natural resources in such a way as to provide for people's basic needs and to ensure an honest and equitable sharing of benefits and burdens" (no. 113).

Going beyond the question of resources on the African continent alone, John Paul II also considers why it is incumbent upon rich countries to support the efforts of their counterparts struggling to rise from poverty and misery. Citing the social teaching of the church, the pope reminds us that it is the right of all people in the world to have just access to the resources with which God has blessed the world (no. 114).[5] He addresses some dimensions of inequitable international relations to describe how this utopian vision might be achieved.

Global Context of the Second African Synod

Contextual theologies use the somewhat obvious insight that Christians and therefore theologians have at their disposal the tools of reflection and modes of thinking available to the people of a particular context. Tools such as social analysis, critical theory, and rhetorical analysis are applied to questions of the day in order to come to a theological understanding of situations of oppression, race, gender, violence, and so forth. Such contextual theologies might be called feminist theology, black theology, liberation theology, queer theology, or ecological theology, depending on the particular context that the theologians are trying to understand. This manner of doing theology distinguishes a church in touch with the concerns of the people of its age. Indeed, Vatican II's *Pastoral Constitution on the Church in the Modern World (Gaudium et Spes)* proclaims:

> The joys and the hopes, the griefs and the anxieties of the men of this age, especially those who are poor or in any way afflicted, these are the joys and hopes, the griefs and anxieties of the followers of Christ. Indeed, nothing genuinely human fails to raise an echo in their hearts. For theirs is a community composed of men. (no. 1)

A major anxiety of people of the late twentieth and early twenty-first centuries has been the threat to the natural environment from human activity. The people of Africa also share this global awareness. Many schoolchilden can now tell you that global warming is caused by greenhouse gases accumulating in the earth's atmosphere that trap the heat of the earth. These gases have been emitted in ever-increasing amounts since the West's Industrial Revolution. The slowly rising temperature of the earth affects climate and causes disastrous weather "events" across the world. Rainfall is particularly affected, causing droughts and flooding in unpredictable severity around the globe. The trapped heat also causes ice caps to melt, raising sea levels and threatening small island nations and large coastal cities with flooding. This is the picture in broad strokes. It is evident that there are too many variables to make exact predictions on a global scale of what lies ahead. People around the world are becoming familiar with terms like El Niño and La Niña; hurricane, flood, and drought as images of their effects are beamed around the global village.

As "secular" language has become available to express concern about the environment, Christians have been able to use this language to reflect on these concerns. In a 2002 historical overview of the concern of the Holy See for the environment, the Pontifical Council for Justice and Peace calls the environment an "all-embracing concern." The secretary of the council writes: "The teachings [of the Catholic Church concerning the environment] call for a radical change: for a conversion of the heart and mind so that all may have life, life in abundance. This implies living in harmony with all of creation. When this is so, the world will truly be at peace and all of creation will reflect the beauty of the Creator."[6]

This publication emphasizes how the popes have been concerned for the environment over the twenty-five years from the Stockholm Conference on Human Development to the Johannesburg Summit on Sustainable Development. It firmly locates ecological questions in the tradition of Catholic social teaching.

In 2004 the Pontifical Council for Justice and Peace published the magisterial *Compendium of Social Doctrine of the Catholic Church*. The entire tenth chapter of this compendium is dedicated to safeguarding the environment. Beginning (as is the methodology of the compendium) with the biblical aspects of the topic under consideration, and proceeding to discuss human beings and the universe of created things, the chapter devotes an entire section to the crisis in the relationship between humans and the environment. The compendium highlights the imperative to share the collective goods of creation for the benefit of all people, present and future, and states that this must imply a change in lifestyle and mentality to avert serious ecological problems. Given its comprehensive scope, this compendium was used as a resource for the bishops at the 2009 African Synod.

One might easily have the impression that ecological questions have received scant attention in magisterial teaching in Africa since *Ecclesia in Africa*. But the second African Synod has clearly been an opportune moment to revive and strengthen that strand of the church's teaching tradition. The synod was celebrated in October 2009, in the month following the UN Summit on Climate Change in New York on September 22, and some six weeks before the UN Conference on Climate Change in Copenhagen. Given the media attention on these two UN events, climate change and ecological questions could not fail to have been in the minds of the bishops and other participants assembled for the synod. A reading of the documents of the synod shows that they had more on their minds than the venal question of who will pay to mitigate the greenhouse gas output of the developing world.

Ecology, Resources, and Environmental Integrity in the Second African Synod

In its preparatory documents the synod process called attention to environmental issues under the overall title "The Church in Africa in Service to Reconciliation, Justice, and Peace." The *Lineamenta* for the synod recalled the crucial connection, made in *Ecclesia in Africa*, between the "savage" exploitation of Africa's resources and the arms trade (no. 117). Noting how the "resources of poor countries are systematically plundered to fuel the arms trade," the *Lineamenta* called for the force of arms to be replaced by the moral force of law (no. 78). This attention to Africa's resources raised hope that the issues of environmental justice and peace would receive prominence in synodal deliberations.

Three years later the *Instrumentum Laboris* for the synod took up this theme, calling attention to how industrialized countries seek access to Africa's mineral wealth at any cost. Thus the continent's wealth of mining reserves was understood to be a threat to peace as wars continue to be waged for access to these resources (no. 72). Indeed, the long-running battle over the resources in eastern Democratic Republic of Congo (DRC) has been dubbed

Africa's World War.[7] Both preparatory documents for the synod regard the wealth of the continent as something of a scandal—if not managed wisely, a potential stumbling block on the path of development.[8]

Final List of 57 Propositions

In a break with tradition, Pope Benedict XVI made available the final list of propositions at the end of the second African Synod before his anticipated publication of a post-synodal exhortation. Although the website of the Vatican's press office marks the list "unofficial and off-the-record," one can take this final list of propositions as an indicator of what was discussed during the synod.

Three of the fifty-seven propositions deal entirely with issues of environmental integrity, resources, and ecology. They are Proposition 22, "Environmental Protection and Reconciliation with Creation"; Proposition 29, "Natural Resources"; and Proposition 30, "Land and Water." These propositions indicate that some of the bishops and other participants at the synod have firsthand experience of the depredations suffered by the lands and water on which their people depend.

Proposition 22 begins with the theological statement that everything that God made is good (Gn 1) and that humans have been charged with the responsibility of stewardship of the earth (Gn 2:15). The synod participants deplore the fact that many people continue to destroy the world and abuse nature, which is supposed to be "our mother." They propose that particular churches promote environmental education and awareness, encourage people to plant trees, and respect the integrity of nature and the fact that it is a resource for the common good. They also propose that particular churches "persuade their local and national governments to adopt policies and binding legal regulations for the protection of the environment and promote alternative and renewable sources of energy." These proposals are very concrete, practical, quantifiable, and feasible. They are not so ethereal or idealistic as to be impossible to achieve. Thus they can empower the laity rather than leaving them feeling as though this is one more obligation that they can never fulfill.

Proposition 29 deals with the question of resources in a more global manner. Beginning with an expression of thanks to God for the abundant riches and natural resources that Africa has received, the synod decries how many African people have been victims of bad public management and exploitation by foreign powers. The bishops call for a culture of moderation to replace the wasteful global culture of consumerism that marginalizes Africa. They appeal for the international community to legislate ways in which local populations might benefit from the exploitation of their natural resources. Most of these proposals are on a macro level and need to be developed further so that the ordinary Christian can begin to achieve them at parish, diocesan, and national levels. On a practical scale, the bishops recommend that the church establish desks in various countries to monitor the management of natural resources.

Proposition 30 calls on national governments to ensure that citizens have security of land tenure and access to water. This proposal urges that

— the Church in Africa seek information and learn about land and
   water issues in order to educate the People of God and enable
   them to challenge unjust decisions in these matters;
— all negotiations on land deals be conducted in full transparency
   and with the participation of the local communities who may be
   affected;
— land alienation deals not be contracted out nor signed without
   the free, prior, and informed consent of the local communities
   concerned, nor should people forfeit their land without proper
   compensation;
— agricultural workers be guaranteed a fair wage in light of the
   fact that investments promote the creation of employment;
— governments promote the professional formation of youth in
   farming and the raising of animals as a way to stem the uncontrolled flight from the village to the cities;
— the models of agricultural production respect the environment
   and not contribute to climate change, soil depletion, and the
   exhaustion of drinkable water reserves;
— food production for export not endanger food security and sovereignty, or the needs of future generations;
— traditional land rights be respected and recognized by the law;
   and
— water not be exploited as a private economic commodity without due attention to people's interests.

These are steps larger than the ordinary Christian can undertake alone. However, with a small degree of local organization, they should become manageable.

Final Message

The natural environment receives only one mention in the *Final Message* of the second African Synod (no. 33), indicating the more pressing preoccupa- tions of the bishops gathered for the special assembly. Here, the context is a demand that multinational organizations stop their exploitation of Africa's resources, which is accompanied by the criminal devastation of the envi- ronment. We need only call to mind the forests of Gabon, the oilfields of

Nigeria, and the asbestos and gold mines of South Africa to be reminded that the rule has been "profits before environment."

The *Final Message* mentions twice the blessing that Africa's resources represent. In the first case (no. 34), the bishops acknowledge that God has blessed Africa with vast human and natural resources. They call for Africa to arise, to attain its full potential. The theme will no doubt be developed further by bishops calling on Africans themselves to become responsible agents in the stewardship of the continent's resources. But which Africa? The leaders, the politicians, the businesspeople, the disenfranchised and dispossessed?

The second mention of the blessings of Africa's mineral resources in the *Final Message* places them in a spiritual perspective, claiming that such mineral resources are less valuable a resource than Africa's being the "spiritual lung" of humanity today (no. 38). Here the message takes up the sentiment expressed by Pope Benedict during his homily at the synod's inaugural mass. This comparison appears incongruent. Are the two really commensurable: material and spiritual wealth?

It cannot be denied that there is a great spread of spiritualities across the continent and that their spiritual life enables many African people to cope with adversity that would otherwise be unbearable. This spiritual life may place African people in touch with the things of God more than any profit from its mineral resources might do. And this is a great gift from God. But it is important not to relativize or too quickly spiritualize the significance of the continent's mineral resources. They too are gifts from God to contribute to the wealth and contentment of the people of Africa. Properly utilized, their benefits can build appropriate educational, health, communication, agricultural, energy, and recreational infrastructures. It is difficult to imagine how this is not also part of God's will for the people of the continent.

Both these mentions of the blessings of the natural resources are significant and summarize many hours of reflection. However, as is the nature of such documents, the *Final Message* is thin on specifics. The challenge to the church is to bring this vision to reality in the local dioceses.

Consequences

We cannot wait for all of this to happen by itself. No benevolent uncle is graciously going to wave a magic wand or sprinkle billions of dollars, yen, euros, or yuan to achieve this vision on behalf of Africans. For responsible stewardship of our continent's resources, the peoples of Africa have to become agents of our own destiny.

We need to begin by making difficult choices, which may involve the changes of attitude called for by Bishop Crepaldi in 2002.[9] We will have to balance the immediate exploitation of natural resources, in the hope of lifting the masses out of poverty, against a longer-term, more cautious, and hopefully sustainable use of resources, taking due care of the environment in the process. We have to balance the legitimate aspiration to have all the modern conveniences of the industrialized, urbanized world against a resolution to avoid the many pitfalls of heavy industrialization and urbanization. We need to take a "gentler" path on the environment. We have to be reconciled to what might need to be sacrificed in the interest of a greater good, which may improve the lives of the greatest number of Africans.

We must recognize also that the extraction of the continent's wealth need not be done by "brute force." Our leaders have to distinguish between what is renewable and what is consumed once and for all. For example, the waters of the Congo River might be dammed to provide vast amounts of hydroelectric power. Combined with the wind, wave, and solar energy gracing the continent, the output would be sufficient to meet the current electricity needs of the population. Harnessing these renewable sources of energy would have ecological costs in terms of the flooding of the Congo basin and require setting aside vast areas for wind and solar farms. Will the electricity from such resources benefit the people on the ground, or will it go directly to the industrial centers? Can a "power-sharing" formula be reached, making it economically feasible to undertake such expensive projects? These are clearly nettles that the political leaders are not yet ready to grasp.

As agents of our own future, we should take initiatives in our local areas. These local initiatives have been practiced since humans first set foot on the continent. Traditional religions enshrine taboos that forbid the use of various plants and animals. These taboos are not capricious. They are the distillation of the wisdom of our ancestors, often concerned with the preservation of particularly vulnerable or useful natural resources. When taboos are broken, the consequences can be disastrous, such as the landslides in Uganda caused by the destruction of forests.

More down-to-earth local initiatives concern keeping our environment tidy. One cannot help but notice a contrast between the streets of South Africa and those of Rwanda. There is litter everywhere in South Africa: junk from the street vendors, packaging thrown aside, cigarette ends flicked away. In Rwanda, shopkeepers are obliged to keep the street outside their shop clean. On the last Saturday morning of every month, citizens must go outside and clean the streets. Seldom do you see a discarded soft-drink can or cardboard box lying around. The policy, which some people might find harsh, helps people to have a sense of ownership of their environment and to accord the environment a dignity to which every human person also is entitled.

Of course, it doesn't pay simply to sweep the litter into a pit at the back of the house—out of sight, out of mind. The blight of packaging is that so much of it is impossible to dispose of in an environmentally friendly manner. Metals, glass, paper, and many plastics can be recycled. But what about more complicated waste, like batteries and our obsolete electronic goods?

Do these end up in a dump somewhere, leaking poisons into the earth and eventually the food chain? Can our African governments and businesses rise to the challenge of finding suitable ways to dispose of the rubbish we generate every day? If we want to live in a modern, electronic, prepackaged society, we have to learn how to deal with its byproducts.

On the other side of the coin is the reality of poverty. Desperation often causes people to deplete the resources of the continent in a harmful and nonsustainable way. The need simply to survive drives people to exploit the forests for firewood and bushmeat. The need for level ground to cultivate crops and feed their animals drives people to remove natural vegetation, allowing tons of topsoil to be washed into the oceans every day—wealth lost irretrievably, exacerbating the reality of poverty.

Any discussion of poverty raises the question of population. Are we trying to support too many people, overstretching natural resources in the process? If the wealth of Africa is its people, might we not be wealthier in a different sense if we had slightly smaller families? The idea is often put forward that children are our security. But couldn't we live a more secure life if we weren't trying to support so many children? Whether or not to have more children is obviously a decision that parents must take very seriously. It is a very delicate ethical question, and Pope Paul VI in *Humanae Vitae* (1968) made it clear that Catholic Christians are to "recognize their own duties toward God, themselves, their families and human society . . . and are bound to ensure that what they do corresponds to the will of God the Creator." They are to exercise what he called "responsible parenthood" (no. 10).

Part VI of the *Final Message* of the second African Synod is entitled "Africa, Rise Up!" This is our clarion call as stewards of God's still abundant blessings. Christians must take the leadership in ecological sensitivity. We should be inspired by relevant points of the social teaching of our church. We should not permit political leaders or multinational corporations to destroy our precious planet. This is the only planet that God has given us, so we must reflect on the needs of our African environment in the light of our faith. Ecology, theology, and Africa are no longer strange bedfellows.

Notes

[1] Terisa E. Turner, "'The Land Is Dead': Women's Rights as Human Rights, The Case of the Ogbodo Shell Petroleum Spill in Rivers State, Nigeria," *Africa Policy E-Journal* (June 2001).

[2] H. Tutu, T. S. McCarthy, and E. Kukrowska, "The Chemical Characteristics of Acid Mine Drainage with Particular Reference to Sources, Distribution and Remediation: The Witwatersrand Basin, South Africa as a Case Study," *Applied Geochemistry* 23, no. 12 (2008): 3666–84.

[3] Jock McCulloch, "Asbestos Mining in Southern Africa, 1893–2002," *International Journal of Occupational and Environmental Health* 9, no. 3 (September 2003): 230–35.

⁴ Steve Murray, *Namibia's Fishing industry: SEEN Environmental Learning Sheet*, no. 11 (Okahandja: National Institution for Educational Development, 2005), 4. Available on the nied.edu.na website.

⁵ The pope is citing *Populorum Progressio, Sollicitudo Rei Socialis,* and *Centesimus Annus.*

⁶ Giampaolo Crepaldi, "Presentation," in *From Stockholm to Johannesburg,* ed. Marjorie Keenan (Vatican City: Pontifical Council for Justice and Peace, 2002), 10.

⁷ Gérard Prunier, *Africa's World War: Congo, the Rwandan Genocide, and the Making of a Continental Catastrophe* (Oxford: Oxford University Press, 2008).

⁸ It may be more appropriate to discard the "resource curse" theory in the DRC and identify it rather as a curse of bad management.

⁹ Crepaldi, "Presentation," 10.

14

"Let Us First Feed the Children" (Mark 7:27)

The Church's Response to the Inequitable Extraction of Resources and Related Violence

PETER KANYANDAGO

The Second African Synod chose the theme "The Church in Africa in Service to Reconciliation, Justice, and Peace." The rationale behind this choice is clarified by the synod's *Lineamenta*, which points out that in addition to the obstacles to evangelization, there are "situations of poverty, injustice, sickness, exploitation, a lack of dialogue, division, intolerance, violence, terrorism and war" (no. 7).[1] This essay examines the injustices and violence related to the extraction of natural resources in Africa. However, material poverty and violence must be linked to the anthropological poverty they produce.

According to the late Cameroonian theologian Engelbert Mveng, anthropological poverty means the tainting, traumatizing, and impoverishing of the human condition in its deepest sense. This is what happens when "in our homes, the human condition is marked by dependence, insecurity, and precariousness. . . . There is no greater deprivation than that of one who has lost their soul."[2] Anthropological poverty is usually caused by conditions of material deprivation. In order to develop fully their dignity and identity, human beings must have and enjoy a minimum of material resources. A spirituality or a theology that fails to concede this point risks reinforcing anthropological poverty. It is this situation of anthropological and material poverty and violence that calls for an adequate response from the church in Africa and elsewhere. I maintain that the church in Africa has a special mission in this regard. In order to develop an adequate response to problems related to Africa's wealth in resources, the church in Africa must

171

take a very clear analytical approach to the root causes of the poverty and violence on the continent.

Violence and poverty on the continent are not essentially due to a lack of resources. Ironically, they are caused by the abundance of African resources. The slave trade that devastated and depopulated Africa for over four hundred years was linked to the continent's ability to "supply" strong and resilient human beings. Colonization, which followed or sometimes accompanied the slave trade, was also closely linked to Africa's immense human and material resources. While *resource* refers both to human and material resources, this essay is limited to the discussion of natural resources.

Understanding the Root Causes of Africa's Poverty

It can be argued that the external impetus that triggered the reckless exploitation of Africa's resources was essentially caused by a lack of resources in Arab and Western countries. However, in addition to the slave trade and colonialism as root causes, one should add many other factors, including the betrayal of the continent by its past and present leaders. Foreign agents of exploitation, whether states or multinational companies, have usually found accomplices among Africans themselves.

Other factors to be noted include the ill-adapted education systems in Africa, which contribute to poverty because through them African governments, parents, and students often invest in practices and ideologies that promote the exploitation of the continent. It should also be mentioned that misguided evangelization and theology have sometimes contributed to Africa's impoverishment by denigrating the African and reinforcing racism.

As has been demonstrated by proponents of liberation theology, an analysis of the root causes of poverty can serve as a spring board for Christian reflection and practice that will not only emphasize prophetically the doctrine of the church (orthodoxy), but also promote prophetic Christian practice (orthopraxis). Such prophetic commitment must denounce oppressive and negative forces and structures, and be accompanied by a credible witness.

In addition to the lack of resources that pushed Western Europe and Arab states to search for resources outside their borders, the plundering of Africa's resources often was justified by an ethico-anthropological belief that non-Westerners were not human or fully human. This belief was used to exploit and plunder these people's human and natural resources.

The official side of the Catholic Church issued at least three bulls to justify the slave trade and the taking of the land of non-Westerners. On June 18, 1452, Pope Nicholas V issued the papal bull *Dum Diversas*, which authorized Alfonso V of Portugal to reduce any "Saracens (Muslims) and pagans and any other unbelievers" to perpetual slavery. This facilitated the Portuguese slave trade from West Africa. The same pope wrote the bull

Romanus Pontifex on January 5, 1455, to the same Alfonso V, extending to Catholic nations of Europe dominion over discovered lands during the Age of Discovery.[3]

This document resulted in the seizure of non-Christian lands and the enslavement of native, non-Christian peoples in Africa and the New World. On May 4, 1493, Pope Alexander VI issued the bull *Inter Caetera,* which stated that one Christian nation did not have the right to establish dominion over lands previously dominated by another Christian nation.[4] It is not a coincidence that this was issued after 1492 when Christopher Columbus mistakenly went to the West, thinking he was in India. However, other popes, including Gregory XVI and Leo XIII, strongly condemned the slave trade. The official documents encouraging the slave trade, nonetheless, were more effective than those that condemned it.

The Right to Use Resources and Negation of the African

Natural resources in Africa and elsewhere must first benefit those who own them; if others are to benefit from them, the terms of such sharing must be determined by the owners. The biblical text in the title of this essay, "Let us first feed the children" (Mk 7:27, GNB), from the encounter between the Phoenician woman and Jesus, is meant to emphasize this point. Without delving into a technical exegesis of the text and the problems it raises (especially when it adds, "It isn't right to take the children's food and throw it to the dogs"), it appears that Jesus is telling the Phoenician woman that the Jews are the first beneficiaries of Jesus' ministry and proclamation. This statement does not negate the claim that Jesus' mission extends beyond the Jewish people, as Jesus himself points out in other parts of the gospel.

It would seem that the principle of a people enjoying their own resources is not questioned in other countries, although it usually becomes controversial when it comes to Africa's resources. In 1927 Albert Muller advanced a "Christian" and "theological" principle to justify colonialism by stating that superior races have the right to appropriate the resources of inferior races. Using the principle of the providential destination of the goods of this earth, he wrote that "retarded people are not in a position to put to good use their portion of the goods concealed in the territory which they occupy, and left to themselves can only let these resources lie fallow to the detriment of the general prosperity."[5]

Assertions like Muller's have been used, albeit in more subtle forms of argumentation, as a reason to deprive Africans of their right to enjoy fully the benefits of African resources. The debate about who rightfully owns what is not the issue if we agree with the principle that is also stipulated in the UN-initiated Convention on Biological Diversity, which was concluded on June 5, 1992. Article 8(j) states, "Each Contracting Party shall . . . encourage the equitable sharing of the benefits arising from the utilization of such knowledge, innovations and practices." What is said about biological diversity can be applied to other natural resources. By extension, the article means that equity must be considered, even in cases where there have been legal transactions. There are instances, however, where governments (African or foreign), companies, or people overlook or deny this principle of equity and proceed to exploit resources, usually resulting, whether directly or indirectly, in violence.

The import of Muller's text should not be dismissed on the grounds that it was written in the 1920s. It represents a mentality grounded in the ethico-anthropological assumption cited above, which is still prevalent today. Nearer to us are similar views, such as that expressed by John O'Donohue, who suggests that the "major cause of Africa's present [melancholy story] situation is her people's, quite understandable, failure to adapt to the modern situation the intellectual and moral categories inherited from the traditional situation."[6]

For O'Donohue, the "modern situation," or the Western situation, would seem to have a universal value to which all people must adapt. The author equates modernity with the values of the West, which for him include efficiency, creativity, patience, rational endeavor, concern for non-kin, and a willingness to take risks. O'Donohue maintains that these do not exist in Africa, where people have no confidence in themselves, are not responsible, are lazy and fatalistic, take the past as the model, believe in instant solutions, do not use their creative faculties and do not experiment, do not work hard "when they know that in the end all will be determined by spirits."[7] It is evident that while Africa is to be held responsible for some of its problems, as I have already pointed out, O'Donohue's solution reinforces a belief that a negative ethico-anthropological mentality exacerbates Africa's anthropological poverty.

This mentality was also evident in President Nicolas Sarkozy's speech in July 2007, when he visited Senegal prior to his election to the French presidency, ostensibly to reaffirm his commitment to work with Africa to find solutions to the problems of the continent. His talk at the Cheikh Anta Diop University, Dakar, mainly targeting the youth of Africa, evoked and echoed colonialist discourse characteristic of the era associated with the scramble for Africa. Paternalistic at best and condescending at worst, his delivery was overtly racist and indicative of how some Europeans still fail to recognize that Africans or non-Westerners are fully human beings. He claims that some negative influences from the West are not worth emulating. Yet there are positive aspects such as liberty, freedom, and justice, as well as an emphasis on the use of reason and global consciousness. The tragedy of Africa's history is to have been bypassed by these principles. In the African mentality, time is a perpetual wheel that turns without allowing room for human adventure or innovation. It is an endless repetitive cycle, and this is Africa's problem. The challenge confronting Africa is for the continent to embrace the history of progress exemplified by Europe and generate its own energy for progress. Sarkozy is saying that even if Europe did violence to Africa, it is acceptable because it helped Africans to share in the virtues of the West. His position is not far from that of O'Donohue. Sarkozy goes on to deny that Africa has sufficiently entered into history and states that Africa is incapable of changing by itself. These ideas were not written in the Middle Ages but in 2007.

Such a negating ethico-anthropological justification has been and is still being used to deny Africans their right to benefit fully from who they are and what they have.[8] While it is true that Africans bear a heavy responsibility for the continent's woes, at the same time one cannot deny that what happened in the past affected Africa negatively and in some cases is still occurring today.

What the African Synod Says about Africa's Resources

A close reading of the documents of the two African Synods should provide useful material for evaluating and elaborating on the church's response to the exploitation of natural resources in Africa. The post-synodal Apostolic Exhortation *Ecclesia in Africa* of John Paul II, published after the first African Synod, refers only indirectly to Africa's natural resources when referring to the continent's positive values (no. 33). The exhortation states laconically that "although Africa is very rich in natural resources, it remains economically poor" (no. 42).

The question of natural resources receives more attention in the *Lineamenta* of the second African Synod. This preparatory document states that "Africa's resources are in direct contrast to the misery of its poor. The situation becomes even more scandalous if consideration is given to the wealth amassed in the hands of a privileged few" (no. 15). What is more interesting is the *Lineamenta*'s attempt to identify the root causes of Africa's poverty. After having recognized that Africa has the labor, land, and capital that are necessary for development, the document suggests possible causes of the problems of Africa (no. 19), including cultural practices, a lack of competitive spirit or enthusiasm for work, unproductive land use, and desperately low prices for Africa's agricultural products.

The *Instrumentum Laboris* of the second African Synod takes a closer look at the extraction of Africa's natural resources:

Outside forces . . . back those in power, irrespective of human rights and democratic principles, so as to guarantee economic benefit (the exploitation of natural resources, the acquisition of important markets, etc.). They threaten to destabilize entire nations and to eliminate persons who wish to free themselves from their oppression. (no. 12)

For the first time, this document develops the link between the plundering of Africa's resources and the role of outside forces. It refers to the multinationals that continue to invade the continent in search of natural resources in complicity with African leaders (no. 28). The synod notes that the plundering of resources usually has an adverse effect on the environment. It condemns groups that exploit and deplete natural resources (no. 57) and industrialized nations that pursue their present course of seeking access to the greatest mining reserves of the world. The *Instrumentum Laboris* notes the abundance of natural resources on the African continent that continues to pose a threat to peace, justice, and reconciliation (no. 72).

Finally, the document acknowledges the contribution of women toward the management of natural resources (no. 140). It is noteworthy that the document recognizes the role women play in properly managing resources. This gender element should never be neglected by the church.

These important observations call for a concerted effort for Christian churches to work together to denounce these injustices in and outside Africa and to put pressure on companies—both in the West and in Africa—to be just and equitable in their use of the continent's natural resources. There is an equal need for the church itself to be just in its structures and practices so that it can be credible. The church in Africa needs to lobby sister churches in North America and Europe so that together they can find means to promote justice and equity in developing African resources. Initiatives like those that have been taken by the churches in Chad and the Democratic Republic of Congo (DRC) to ensure that benefits accruing from the exploitation of resources are equitably shared are commendable and offer a credible model for other countries.[9]

The second African Synod revisited the link between the abundance of resources on the African continent and poverty and violence. During the opening mass for the synod, Pope Benedict XVI referred to the "abundant riches of the territory [of Africa] which have unfortunately become and continue to be a cause of exploitation, conflict and corruption." In his appropriately entitled book *Resource Wars*, Michael T. Clare presents multiple examples to illustrate how minerals, oil, timber, and water are causes or sources of conflict.[10]

The *Final Message* of the synod includes several references to the use of resources. In sections 4 and 5, the *Final Message* says that in these tragic situations, "Africa is the most hit. Rich in human and natural resources, many of our people are still left to wallow in poverty and misery, wars and conflicts, crisis and chaos." As an answer to these problems, it calls for the establishment of a new world order in light of Benedict XVI's encyclical *Caritas in Veritate* and emphatically states: "Multinationals have to stop their criminal devastation of the environment in their greedy exploitation of natural resources. It is short-sighted policy to foment wars in order to make fast gains from chaos, at the cost of human lives and blood" (no. 33).

Furthermore, under the title "Africa Rise Up!" the *Final Message* repeats the belief that the cradle of the humanity lies somewhere in Africa: "[Our] continent has a long history of great empires and illustrious civilizations. . . . God has blessed us with vast natural and human resources. . . . Now Africa must face the challenge of giving her children a dignified level of living conditions" (no. 34). The church in Africa must explicate the implications of this statement.

By referring to the great civilizations that existed on the continent and the historical injustices committed against Africa, the synodal message makes a strong statement that Africa's problems are not genetic and not only cultural, as some people have suggested.[11] It also implies that teaching on creation should include reference to the origin of humanity as being in Africa, even when it raises questions about the interpretation of the scriptures on creation.

In the area of liturgy Africa has much to celebrate. For centuries racist doctrines have belittled and denigrated physical features and attributes of the black person, thus reinforcing the anthropological poverty of Africa. The features of the African body, especially its blackness, should be valorized in the symbols used in the liturgy. Christian art should also use images that celebrate and bring out more positively the attributes of the African person. Such an approach would contribute toward rehabilitating Africans in their culture and appearance.

The *Final List of 57 Propositions* of the synod also refer to the resources of Africa. In the whole of Proposition 22, the synod addresses themes of environmental protection and reconciliation with creation that touch upon the use of resources. The synod states:

> To make the earth habitable beyond the present generation and to guarantee sustainable and responsible care of the earth, we call upon the particular Churches to:
> — promote environmental education and awareness;
> — persuade their local and national governments to adopt policies and binding legal regulations for the protection of the environment and promote alternative and renewable sources of energy; and
> — encourage all to plant trees and treat nature and its resources, respecting the common good and the integrity of nature, with transparency and respect for human dignity. (Proposition 22)

In sum, without a clear knowledge of the importance of these resources for Africa and the world economy, the church cannot adequately respond to the plundering of Africa's resources. It is also important to have solid information about the extent of Africa's resources in order to understand why they are often a source of problems.[12]

What Will Be an Adequate Response?

If the church in Africa is to give an adequate answer to the unjust exploitation of the resources with its attendant violence, it needs to know where the
resources are located, the amount available, and have a clear understanding
of their uses. The houses of formation and Catholic universities with courses
in theology, spirituality, and other disciplines must include material on the
importance of Africa's resources so that church workers are equipped to be
prophetic promoters of justice. Similarly, appropriate church celebrations
should be devised to thank God for Africa's natural endowments. Both approaches will help Africans appreciate and defend what God has given them.

However, the church must do more; knowing what resources Africa has
and where they are found is not enough. The church in Africa must do all it
can to ensure that these resources are processed and converted to useful
products. Again, Catholic universities in Africa can play a major role by
collaborating with universities in Europe and the United States that have
the required technology. The episcopal conferences in Africa have a role to
play as lobbyists and advocates in appropriate government structures, both
locally and nationally; they can also draw on the expertise of episcopal
conferences, governments, and multinational companies in the North.

The church must undertake both diachronic and synchronic analysis to
understand why Africa's wealth leads to its poverty. Such analysis requires
an interdisciplinary approach, integrating theological, pastoral, economic,
and sociopolitical analyses. While these should be undertaken in institutions of higher learning, appropriate adjustments should be made so that
they are understood and appropriated by Christians at all levels. It is important that all sectors of the church and society be involved to ensure the
participation of all people in the just use of Africa's resources.

Finally, in its prophetic commitment to foster justice, the church must be
credible and just in its structures and in the way it manages resources at its
disposal. Serious concerns have been raised about how the church in Africa
uses aid and manages projects, and accusations of corruption have been
leveled against it. Sometimes the lifestyle of some members of the church
raises questions. The Synod of Bishops' *Justice in the World* gave very clear
direction on how the church should use material possessions: "In regard to
temporal possessions, whatever be their use, it must never happen that the
evangelical witness which the Church is required to give becomes ambiguous. The preservation of certain positions of privilege must constantly be
submitted to the test of this principle."[13] These words should be supple-
mented by what John Paul II says in his 1988 encyclical letter *Sollicitudo
Rei Socialis*:

Thus, part of the *teaching* and most ancient *practice* of the Church is
her conviction that she is obliged by her vocation—she herself, her

ministers and each of her members—to relieve the misery of the suffering, both far and near, not only out of her "abundance" but also
out of her "necessities." Faced by cases of need, one cannot ignore
them in favour of superfluous church ornaments and costly furnish-
ings for divine worship; on the contrary it could be obligatory to sell
these goods in order to provide food, drink, clothing and shelter for
those who lack these things. (no. 31)

Such texts underline the importance of a credible witness as a prerequisite
for promoting and defending justice and human dignity.

Conclusion

The foregoing discussion has described how Africa's material and anthropological poverty are closely linked to Africa's abundant human and material
resources. The focus has been primarily on the material resources in order
to show that their unjust exploitation is linked to the negation of the dignity and cultures of the African person. The different types of documents
related to the second African Synod and the social teaching of the church
demonstrate that church leaders are aware of what is at stake and have in
some cases suggested concrete means for themselves and other about how
to use Africa's resources equitably to improve the lives of Africa's people.
The root causes of Africa's poverty can be traced to historical and present
practices and ideologies perpetuated by Africans themselves as well as out-
siders, albeit the latter have historically played a preponderant role. Today
the church in Africa needs to take the lead in being prophetic and just in
determining that Africa's resources are fully understood and properly used.

Notes

¹ The texts of all the church documents of the second African Synod—as well as
encyclicals, exhortations, and so forth—are available on the vatican.va website.
² Engelbert Mveng, "*Eglise et solidarité pour les pauvres en Afrique,*" paper
presented to the First Meeting of the African and European Theologians at Yaoundé,
April 4–11, 1984, 14.
³ For the texts of the bulls, see the romancatholicism.org website.
⁴ For the text of the bull, see the nativeweb.org website.
⁵ Albert Muller, *Principes chrétiens et colonisation* (Brussels: Editions de la Cité
Chrétienne, 1927), 16.
⁶ John O'Donohue, "The Problem of Africa," *The African Mind* 1 (1989): 136.
⁷ Ibid.
⁸ An example of negative and prejudicial discourse can be found in Martin
Meredith, *The Fate of Africa: From the Hopes of Freedom to the Great of Despair,
A History of Fifty Years of Independence* (New York: Public Affairs, 2006).
⁹ On Chad, see Antoine Bérilengar, "Advocacy for Just Distribution of Oil Rev-
enues: The Case of Chad," in *Peace Weavers: Methodologies of Peace Building in*

Africa, ed. Elias Omondi Opongo (Nairobi: Paulines Publications Africa, 2008), 86–94. On the contribution of the Congolese National Episcopal Conference to the making of just mining contracts in the DRC, see Ferdinand Muhigirwa, "Review and Evaluation Process of Mining Contracts in the Democratic Republic of Congo," also in Opongo, *Peace Weavers*, 95–102.

[10] Michael T. Klare, *Resource Wars: The New Landscape of Global Conflict* (New York: Henry Holt, 2001).

[11] One of the most explicit publications I have come across that puts black people at the bottom of humanity is Richard J. Herrnstein and Charles Murray, *The Bell Curve: Intelligence and Class Structure in American Life* (New York: Free Press, 1996).

[12] For an approach outlining how natural resources are important and linked to conflict, see Klare, *Resource Wars;* and Jeremy Lind and Kathryn Sturman, eds., *Scarcity and Surfeit: The Ecology of Africa's Conflicts* (Pretoria: The Institute for Security Studies, 2002). For figures and statistics of Africa's share of some of the world's natural resources, see the British Geological Survey, 2001–2005; for bauxite, copper, iron ore and uranium, see "Africa in World Mining Geography"; for cashew nuts and cocoa, see Peter Jaeger, "Global Markets for Cocoa, Cashew and Specialty Coffee and Africa's Position in these Markets," and "Cocoa Atlas on Regional Integration in West Africa"; for chromium see Mineral Information Institute; for coltan, see Helen Vesperini, "Congo's Coltan Rush"; for manganese, see "Manganese Alloy Production." These documents are all available online.

[13] See Synod of Bishops, *Justice in the World* (1971). Available on the osjspm.org website.

15

The Enduring Scourge
of Poverty and Evangelization
in Africa

Nathanaël Yaovi Soédé

In his homily for the opening mass of the second African Synod, Pope Benedict XVI likened Africa to "an immense spiritual 'lung' for a humanity that seems to be in crisis of faith and hope." His poignant remark aroused a feeling of pride in some people and doubt in others. For the former, the pope's words honored Africa, because he acknowledged the continent's importance and the crucial role it plays in the reconstruction of a new humanity. For the latter, the pope's flattering appellation belies the real condition of the continent. These contrasting reactions suggest a need to reconsider Pope Benedict's words—to analyze their socio-ethical and pastoral implications.

Perhaps an exploration of the meaning of this expression, "a spiritual lung for humanity," will help us make a critical diagnosis of the diseases that assail Africa. A church that speaks of Africa as the spiritual lung of humanity cannot avoid taking into account the problem of poverty on the continent. Theological reflection on the relationship between evangelization and human development may reveal challenges that the church should assume in response to the scourge of poverty in Africa.

In order to fulfill its vocation, the church must imitate the model par excellence of mission, Jesus Christ. The image of Bartimaeus used by Pope Benedict in his concluding homily at the second African Synod invites the church to a renewed commitment to its vocation in the world by rising up to walk with Christ.

This study draws on Pope Benedict's homilies for the opening and closing of the second African Synod as well as the *Lineamenta* and the *Instrumentum Laboris*. My aim is to reread these documents in the African context while considering the church's responses to the challenge of the scourge of poverty in Africa.

The Context and Meaning of Pope Benedict's Thought

Benedict XVI presented Africa as a spiritual lung for humanity at the opening mass of the second African Synod on October 4, 2009. The pope's remarks were addressed to all the participants, inviting them to undertake an in-depth study of the synod's theme: "The Church in Africa in Service to Reconciliation, Justice and Peace: "You Are the Salt of the Earth. . . . You Are the Light of the World (Mt 5:13, 14)." Beyond the synod participants, he envisaged a larger audience composed of the church of Africa and the universal church.

Beginning with scripture that affirms "the primacy of God, Creator and Lord," Bendict XVI applied this core belief to Africa. He declared that "recognition of the absolute lordship of God is certainly one of the salient and unifying features of the African culture" and pointed out that in Africa, God is "the Creator and the source of life" and people have a "profound sense of God."

Benedict lamented the attitude of some people who consider Africa's natural resources as its principal treasures, which unfortunately have become "causes of exploitation, conflict and corruption." The pope declared forcefully: "The Word of God, instead, makes us look at another patrimony: the spiritual and cultural heritage, which humanity needs even more than raw materials." For justification of this position, Benedict turned to scripture: "For what does it profit a man," Jesus said, "to gain the whole world and forfeit his life?" (Mk 8: 36). It is in this context that Benedict declared that Africa constitutes "an immense spiritual 'lung'" for a humanity that appears to be "in a crisis of faith and hope." He noted that this lung can also fall sick and that, indeed, it is already sick.

At the closing mass of the synod the pope appealed to another biblical image—that of Bartimaeus (Mk 10:46–52). He invited the church in Africa to a new evangelization, lasting peacebuilding, and "interventions in favor of the promotion of humanity."

The expression that Africa is the spiritual lung of humanity is not simple flattery to be received idealistically and passively. What does it mean for Africa to be a spiritual lung for humanity? If Africa is the spiritual lung for humanity in crisis, why then does the continent appear ill like this humanity instead of being its revivifying spirit? Is the recognition of God's absolute primacy sufficient, then, for Africa to constitute the spiritual lung of humanity?

Spiritual Lung of Humanity, an Infected Lung

Biologically, the lung is one of the vital organs of the human body. Located in the thorax, its primary function as a respiratory organ is to maintain the flow of air to the heart in order to keep the body alive. The lungs oxygenate the blood and expel carbon dioxide from it, assuring the balance of the body. Blood is vital, but it needs the lungs to send it oxygen.

When Benedict speaks of a spiritual lung, he uses the lung as an analogy; the spiritual lung is for humanity what the biological lung is for the body. Accordingly the African continent is vitally important for humanity; it supplies "oxygen" that vivifies, regenerates, and assures the balance, health, and wholeness of humanity.

Spiritual oxygen evokes a set of spiritual values (freedom, life, and peace) that Paul juxtaposes to "the flesh" (Rom 8:1–17). With these spiritual values and fidelity to the fundamental principles of the gospel, Africa will be, in the world, a factor of balance, rejuvenation, and witness to enduring cultural, religious, and ethical values. This inestimable resource unites humanity in love, rendering it capable of overcoming all kind of sins and social crises.

When the lung is unhealthy, it can no longer function as the regulator of the body's metabolism. Such a sickness can be fatal. According to the pope, the spiritual lung of humanity is affected by two viruses: "practical materialism, combined with the relativist and nihilist thought" and "religious fundamentalism." The first virus is from the West and the second from political and economic interests of a minority of African leaders supported by the powers of the global North.

Following the logic of the pope's argument, the West bears great responsibility for Africa's present problems, even if it cannot be denied that Africans themselves also have their part to play. Benedict argued: "It is nevertheless indisputable that the so-called 'first' world has sometimes exported and is exporting toxic spiritual refuse which contaminates the peoples of other continents, including in particular the population of Africa." The *Lineamenta* notes that "Africa is deliberately left out, being only remembered when its miseries need to be displayed or exploited" (no. 8). The pope avoids this colonialist interpretation of Africa's predicament. He admires the continent's knowledge of God's sovereignty and that it does not confess the "practical materialism associated with the relativistic and nihilist thought."

A Critical Approach to Africa's Diseases

Pope Benedict asserts that humanity is sick due to a crisis of faith and hope. Since Africa acknowledges the primacy of God the Creator, the humanity in question is Western. The West, claims the pope, exports "toxic spiritual refuse" to the other continents. If so, this virus of practical materialism would be part of the illnesses of Africans who are subjected to the pernicious effects of Western culture. However, it is an exaggeration to claim that the main source of the illness from which Africa generally suffers comes from this virus.

In Africa, people who suffer from practical materialism constitute a small minority of the well off, devoted to the interest of the West, who profit from the continent's riches. Among these people are the elite and political leaders. For reasons that are generally practical or material, they adopt Western currents of agnosticism, relativism, and nihilism in contradiction of the primacy of God the Creator revealed in religions, especially the Judeo-Christian religion.

Statistics show that the vast majority of Africans live below the poverty line; as such, they are not captive to the lures of practical materialism. It is this group that acknowledges God's primacy. Yet, given their condition, it would not be surprising if some of them were vulnerable to the second virus mentioned by the pope, that of religious fundamentalism. The sources of this illness come from a political and economic order that impoverishes African populations. By extension this virus underlies and provokes religious violence, opposing Christians and Muslims in African countries.

A practical embodiment and example of religious fundamentalism is particularly evident in evangelical Christianity in Africa. Certain types of this form of Christianity consider the word of God primarily as a tool or means for delivering people from the clutches of poverty and guaranteeing instant prosperity. Such religious fundamentalism fosters practical materialism. Therefore, it appears that, generally, problems of poverty lie at the root of religious fundamentalism manifested in some traditions of Christianity in Africa.

The manifestations of practical materialism, relativism, and nihilism that Benedict addresses are also visible in African religions. Acute poverty leads some people in Africa to doubt God's existence. Cameroonian theologian and Dominican cleric Eloi Messi Metogo has demonstrated convincingly the tenuousness of the popular and widely held view that all Africans are essentially religious. According to Metogo, faced with the miseries of life, Africans from traditional societies become irreligious and are only concerned with finding practical solutions for their problems.[1]

The problem of poverty in Africa is intricately linked to the viruses that, according to Benedict, affect the spiritual lung of humanity. Cameroonian historian and political scientist Achille Mbembe has analyzed the reactions of impoverished Africans who are victims of various forms of exploitations engineered by corrupt and despotic leaders. Mbembe's analysis shows how much poverty in Africa provokes several moral, spiritual, and social crises.[2] This drama of poverty explains the recurrence of acts of violence, the impotence of African states before the rich countries, neocolonialism, and difficulties related to the emergence of an African Christianity with its own rituals, theological and pastoral traditions, canon law, and so on.

In effect, the causes of Africa's illnesses extend beyond the diagnosis made by Benedict XVI. The West is not all to blame. Beyond a theological pronouncement delivered by a pontiff, what is needed is a wider analysis of the generalized poverty of African nations and churches. As Peter Kanyandago points out in his contribution to this volume, Africa's poverty is, according to Engelbert Mveng, an "anthropological poverty."[3] Mveng contends that this "anthropological poverty" encroaches into all domains of life in African countries and churches. The synod's *Instrumentum Laboris* recognized that "the Churches in Africa . . . bear in them the fragility of the present situation of African countries at the institutional, financial, theological cultural and juridical levels" (no. 21). In today's globalized world, Africa remains largely marginalized and prone to stereotypical depictions on account of widely publicized acts of inhumanity and misery that occur on the continent and because of its dependence on other countries. The speech of French President Nicolas Sarkozy in Dakar, Senegal, is an expression of this attitude of condescension, as Kanyandago also argues.[4]

In reality, in church and in society, Africa cannot be respected internationally or universally as long as the continent fails to respond to its vital and existential needs, and until it ceases being dependent perpetually on Western support. Worse still, a perpetually dependent continent cannot claim to be humanity's spiritual lung.

In this vein Pope Benedict's labeling of the West as exporters of toxic spiritual refuse and viruses should not lead Africans to consider themselves only hapless victims. Africans also bear responsibility for their continent's anthropological poverty. As human beings, they are the first to be responsible for their life and societies. As several authors in this volume have pointed out, many social practices in Africa paralyze the development of African countries. Though not limited to the continent, examples of such paralyzing practices abound: lack of democracy, bad governance, corruption, religious fatalism, economic parasitism, and blind imitation of everything Western. Generally, Africa suffers from these behaviors that are the antithesis of integral development.[5] Unfortunately, in this sociopolitical context, African churches are not always credible witnesses of the gospel of Jesus Christ. Hence, the viruses that provoke the sickness of Africa come more from Africa than the West.

To present Africa as a spiritual lung need not imply that the West is fundamentally secular and atheist. In my opinion, Benedict's imagery is a direct challenge to the church in Africa to assume its responsibility and bring to the rest of the world its own cultural and religious values so that this church and continent can become a spiritual lung for humanity.

The remedy is clear: Africa needs to be healthy, viable, and self-dependent in order to resist external *and* internal viruses so that the "lung" can fulfill its function in the world church and global society. But exactly how can the church in Africa respond to this challenge?

Evangelization and Human Promotion: From Theory to Practice

For a healthy Africa, the church has to promote *in practice* the link between evangelization and human promotion. Africa will not be, *in fact*, "an immense spiritual 'lung' for a humanity that seems to be in a crisis of faith and hope" as long as theologies and pastoral practices do not enable Christians to incarnate their faith in historical and contextual realities.

The issues of reconciliation, justice, and peace that led to the second African Synod and determined the choice of its theme are related to the scourge of poverty through human actions and social irresponsibility. According to the *Lineamenta*, we must find "solutions in order to emerge from the crisis faced by Africa" (no. 1). The *Instrumentum Laboris* talks about "the fight against every sort of human poverty" (no. 19) and of the action to be taken so that "Africa emerges from poverty and marginalization in a general movement of globalization" (no. 8). Referring to issues that have "a great impact on the Christian conscience" (*Lineamenta*, no. 21), the *Instrumentum Laboris* notes that on the economic plane and "in the business world . . . people are displaying a determination to create wealth so as to reduce poverty and misery and to improve the health of populations" (no. 24). It thus considers that baptized Christians who work for development out of their faith are "forces in life [that] ought to grow stronger, because their transforming effects will help check the advance of poverty and misery" (no. 140).

For this to happen, the church must renew the evangelization of Africa. Some pastors must leave behind theologies and pastoral practices that provoke not only a rupture between the gospel and culture, but also between gospel of Jesus Christ and the fight against poverty and misery.

The greatest drama in contemporary Africa south of the Sahara is the rupture between the good news of the kingdom of God and integral human development. Though the church affirms an inseparable link between the two and promotes education, health, Christian social witness, and so on, the poorest countries of the world are still located in sub-Saharan Africa. The tangible signs of the actuality of the kingdom of God proclaimed by the church remain largely invisible for the majority of Africans. On the contrary, what people experience on the continent are myriad situations of misery, conflicts, injustice, and violence, as attested by the synod's *Lineamenta* (nos. 8–23) and the *Instrumentum Laboris* (nos. 21–33). Africa, humanity's spiritual lung, rooted in a firm belief in the absolute primacy of God, vegetates in poverty, awakened from its stupor, as the *Lineamenta* claims, "when its miseries need to be displayed or exploited" (no. 8).

As Gabriel Mmassi and others have argued in this volume, it is important and urgent that we break with African practices that still maintain a theology of "pie in the sky when you die" and excuse baptized Christians from a radical commitment to further just economic, political, and cultural activities in the society. Faithful Christians must reject any teaching that does not enable the baptized to consider action against every sort of spiritual or historical poverty as a duty.

The *Lineamenta* recalls John Paul II's appeal to African people: "Young people . . . take in hand the development of your countries, . . . love the culture of your people, and . . . work for its renewal with fidelity to your cultural heritage, through a sharpening of your scientific and technical expertise, and above all through the witness of your Christian faith" (no. 23). Faith in the mystery of God's incarnation should encourage pastors and the faithful to consider these responsibilities as sacred duties. In our African context, with its paradox of poverty in the midst of abundant natural resources, the church should avoid hastily separating the spiritual from the material, while vigorously proclaiming the gospel of salvation in Jesus Christ.

Learning from the Teachings and Practices of Jesus

The God revealed in the person of Jesus Christ is not indifferent to human suffering. In his closing homily Pope Benedict XVI quoted Exodus 3:7–8 to remind the people of Africa that God sees the misery of God's people. Aware of the hunger faced by the crowd, Jesus, the bread of eternal life (Jn 6:35), halted his preaching to take care of the hungry people (Lk 9:19–17; Jn 6:1–15). He affirmed through his acts and words that God is not insensitive to the misery that strikes the people of God (Lk 9:13; Jn 6:5–6).

In the above examples, Jesus made a movement of three steps. First, he took time to stop, to see, and to consider the problem of people's hunger (Mt 14:14; Lk 9:13; Jn 6:2–5). Then he listened and corrected the ideas of the twelve disciples[6] about the needs of the hungry crowd (Mt 14:15–16; Mk 6:35–37; Lk 9:12–13; Jn 6:5–7). Thus Jesus committed the disciples to take action and respond to the needs of the crowd. He received the pieces of bread they brought to him (Mt 14:17–18; Mk 6:41; Jn 6:9, 11), asked them to have the crowd sit down (Jn 6:10; Mt 14:19; Mk 6:39–40; Lk 9:14), and nourished all of them (Mt 14:19–21; Mk 6:40–42; Lk 9:17; Jn 6:11–13). Finally, he invited the poor, now filled, to look not only for the bread that comes from the earth, but also and especially for the bread of eternal life.

What conclusions can we draw from this praxis of Jesus? The *Instrumentum Laboris* declared that the problems of Africa are serious, requiring an urgent commitment from the church (no. 48). Bishops and leaders in Africa need to listen to the Master of the mission, who tells them, "Give them to eat" (Mt 14:16; Mk 6:37; Lk 9:13). As the *Instrumentum Laboris* notes, "Christ's disciples are called upon to collaborate in the coming of this Kingdom by attending to the hungry, the sick, the stranger, the humiliated (who are naked) and the prisoner; for the Lord has said 'Truly, I say to you, as you did it to one of the least of these *my brethren*, you did it to me' (Mt)" (no. 35).

According to Ugandan theologian John Lukwata:

Today the social teaching of the Church emphasizes the preferential option for the poor and the voiceless in carrying out the Christian obligations. This is because Christ who is worshipped and adored

identified Himself with the hungry and the needy (Mt 25: 40). . . .
The command, "Do this in memory of me" (Lk 22:18) goes hand in
hand with "Give them something to eat yourselves" (Mt 14:16), to
feed the hungry, to show compassion to the rejected, to heal the sick,
to bring about reconciliation and salvation to all.[7]

Like their model, Jesus, and in response to his command, pastors and the
faithful in Africa should pause and focus on analyzing in depth the problems of development on the continent. They should look for lasting solutions
so that Africa will no longer simply listen to God's message while anthropological poverty makes its people incapable of playing their role as
humanity's spiritual lung. As church we must be able to help the continent
resolve its problems related to hunger so that people can welcome the message of the Bread of eternal life—the one who feeds them and empowers
them to transform from within the socioeconomic and political conditions
of the continent.

In Africa's social context the commitment of the church should include a
critical assessment of what it has done for the integral development of the
people (education, health, economy, culture, and so forth). The issue should
be how to develop people and not just structures. Structures are useful only
when they support the building up of the people and are not motivated by
ostentatious and extravagant intentions. The challenge for the church to
"stop" preaching, following the model of Jesus, in order to feed the starving also means ceasing practices that do not provide a means to build and
empower people and to promote scientific, technical, and spiritual development in Africa.

The issues raised at the second African Synod—coinciding with the fifti-
eth anniversary of the independence of several countries on the
continent—show that the time has come *(kairos)* to undertake such reflections and to find concrete and lasting solutions to the problems of Africa.
Leaders and members of African churches need to be involved in these actions by convening forums at diocesan, national, regional, and continental
levels to study the problems of the scourge of poverty and dependence and
evangelization in Africa. Such initiatives should include an African council
(not a synod) to discuss issues shaping the meaning and relevance of Christianity in Africa. These efforts should result in the establishment of
sustainable development projects.

Like Bartimaeus, Africa Rise Up!
Ending Poverty and Dependence,
and Promoting an African Christianity

One cause of the poverty of the church of Africa and its people is its dependence on the West.[8] This poverty helps to maintain and nurture the

domination of the West over Africa. As the *Instrumentum Laboris* points out, at present it is not possible for Africa to resolve its problems without Africans themselves struggling against the scourge of poverty and without taking into consideration the involvement of the churches and socioeconomic institutions of rich countries (no. 13). To realize this task, it would help—as Jean-Marc Ela has stated—if the universal church, especially the Roman Catholic Church, took the church of Africa seriously, without fear that it would one day opt for separation or become unfaithful. Ela adds that African bishops also need to take the risk of freedom, the freedom that they require to accomplish their vocation in the universal church in communion with Peter's successor.[9]

The first African Synod (1994) might not have encouraged enough African church leaders to take the risk of freedom. By comparing the continent to the traveler who fell into the hands of brigands on the road to Jericho, "lying there and waiting for others to help him," the first African synod might even have contributed in part to the failure of the church in Africa to take charge of its own destiny (*Ecclesia in Africa*, no. 41). The image of Bartimaeus that Benedict pressed into action at the closing mass of the second African Synod seems more apt. Blind Bartimaeus was a person who defied people who wanted to keep him in his miserable condition of blindness and dependence on relief assistance. He took courage and went to Jesus. He discovered true healing and freedom and followed Jesus, completely renewed.

Humanity's spiritual lung has to imitate Bartimaeus. The pope presented Bartimaeus as witness of light and courage and invited Africa to get up. The church in Africa needs a healthy body to get up and testify to God's primacy. But first and foremost it needs the freedom that comes from Christ in order to be aware that it must rise on its own and be capable of doing so to find healing from God and to accomplish its mission. This image of Bartimaeus is appealing: it promotes a Christian life and a new evangelization founded on internal renewal, spiritual regeneration, self-commitment, courage, and action to get up, walk, and follow Jesus without fear. It invites pastors, priests, and the faithful to affirm their freedom, a "freedom in truth," in order to be faithful to the present demands of evangelization and human promotion on the continent. Through this freedom, the church of Africa will no longer be a church under tutelage but a sister church to other churches, together forming the universal church in unity and difference.

The pope declared at the closing mass that the church of Africa can count on the help of other churches in the challenging mission of evangelization after the second African Synod. But will "the prayer and the active solidarity of the entire Catholic Church," from which the church in Africa can benefit, be sufficient? Will it encourage the African church to fulfill its mission as humanity's spiritual lung? Will the churches of Europe, North America, and the church of Rome provide the church of Africa with the support of "prayer and active solidarity" it needs to be free from dependence on external cultural, theological, liturgical, pastoral, canonical, and financial aid?

Paradoxically, the "lung" that should regenerate and renew the West is still dependent on the West. Only a truly self-reliant church in Africa can serve as humanity's spiritual lung and, in the words of Benedict XVI at the closing mass, become "a blessing for the universal Church, making its own qualified contribution to building a more just and fraternal world."

Conclusion

The papal homily at the closing of the second African Synod ended with an appeal for reconciliation: "The urgent action of evangelization . . . involves an urgent appeal for reconciliation, an indispensable condition for instilling in Africa justice among men and building a fair and lasting peace that respects each individual and people." True reconciliation should take place within the African church itself, with others, and with God. According to Benedict XVI, such reconciliation comes from the Holy Spirit, who renews and transforms the heart of the church in Africa and its theological reflections and pastoral practices.

In the past, in Egypt, Africa saved Jesus' life from the persecution of Herod. The church has to continue welcoming Christ in the poor and oppressed people of Africa. Herod, from whom these human beings are to be saved, is symptomatic of personal sin, structural sin, ecclesial sin, and the scourge of poverty and dependence. These sins paralyze the African church and impede the healthy functioning of humanity's spiritual lung and the witness to the good news of the primacy of God over the world.

Notes

[1] Eloi Messi Metogo, *Dieu peut-il mourir en Afrique? Essai sur l'indifférence religieuse et l'incroyance en Afrique noire* (Paris: Karthala-Ucac, 1997).

[2] Achille Mbembe, *Afriques indociles: Christianisme, pouvoir et Etat en société post-coloniale* (Paris: Karthala, 1988).

[3] Engelbert Mveng, *L'Afrique dans l'Eglise: Parole d'un croyant* (Paris: L'Harmattan, 1985).

[4] Collectif, *L'Afrique répond à Sarkozy: Contre le discours de Dakar* (Paris: Edition Poche, 2008).

[5] Ibid.

[6] Luke's Gospel mentions the twelve, while Mathew, Mark, and John write of the disciples.

[7] John Lukwata, *Integrated African Liturgy* (Eldoret, Kenya: AMECEA Gaba Publications, 2003), 187–88.

[8] See, for example, Meinrad Hebga, *Emancipation d'Eglises sous tutelle: Essai sur l'ère post-missionnaire* (Paris: Présence Africaine, 1976).

[9] Jean-Marc Ela, *Repenser la théologie africaine: Le Dieu qui libère* (Paris: Karthala, 2003), 382.

Part V

Theological and Ethical Issues and HIV/AIDS

16

The Second African Synod and AIDS in Africa

Michael Czerny

When I found out that I was going to serve at the second African Synod (2009) as an *adiutor* (assistant), it first struck me that HIV/AIDS does not obviously, directly, or explicitly connect with the synod's theme, "Service to Reconciliation, Justice, and Peace." Yet in the course of the synod I discovered how deeply connected the two are. Socioeconomic factors are included in the church's work for greater justice, while addressing moral-cultural failures and sin belongs to the work of reconciliation. Combating AIDS in these two ways contributes to that *shalom*-peace or fuller life that everyone desires and that Jesus came to bring. Thus the synod fortifies and nourishes the church's holistic approach and response to the challenges posed by the HIV/AIDS pandemic.

For about ten years after the first African Synod (1994), concern began to grow about the spread and impact of HIV and AIDS in Africa. International commitments seemed strong, and resources were steadily increasing to combat it. Yet today international interest in AIDS and the issues clustered around it is on the wane. This problem is treated with less urgency by international governmental and nongovernmental agencies (NGOs) and even by governments and NGOs at the African level, and thus receives less public attention.

The recent provision of anti-retroviral treatment (ARVs) in African countries has surely had a beneficial impact. Many people live more positively with HIV, and fewer are dying of AIDS-related illnesses. However, widespread ignorance, prejudice, poverty, injustice, and conflict mean that access to treatment remains a distant dream for many. Those who obtain access to ARVs represent less than half of those who need them, especially among the poorest and those outside major urban centers. In addition, many of those on ARVs cannot afford the nutritious food necessary to obtain the maximum benefits and to tolerate their side effects. The number of orphans and abused, vulnerable, and infected children continues to grow exponentially. Worse still, stigma remains a powerful enemy.

193

The Second Synod Tackles AIDS

The church now knows firsthand the real impact of HIV and of AIDS upon the sons and daughters of Africa. Accordingly the second African Synod showed undiminished concern for this complex reality. Here is the synod's understanding of HIV and AIDS:

> *AIDS is a pandemic, together with malaria and tuberculosis, which is decimating African populations and severely damaging their economic and social life. It is not to be looked at as either a medical-pharmaceutical problem or solely as an issue of a change in human behaviour. It is truly an issue of integral development and justice, which requires a holistic approach and response by the Church.*[1]

Without exaggerating it as the only or the most important issue, the synod handled HIV and AIDS sensitively, maturely, and with due proportion.

The identification of AIDS in Africa as *an issue of integral development and justice* in all its complexity does not come from international agencies or media. Rather, it is a deep truth learned from our experience as a people of God. For the second synod, AIDS is neither finished nor negligible. The pandemic takes its proper place amid the great challenges and the long-term and interrelated problems facing Africa and engaged by the church as a servant of reconciliation, justice, and peace.

Moreover, given the nature of a synod of bishops as a kind of council, its conclusions "reflect a pastoral urgency, offer practical suggestions and programs, make references to doctrine which is particularly timely, and provide suggestions for pastoral activity."[2] In other words, its conclusions are pastoral, practical, and programmatic, and that is how we should read them. The African Synod encourages the church in Africa to approach HIV and AIDS, not from one or two angles, but in a holistic and pastoral manner.

To approach HIV and AIDS holistically means to treat people as whole persons. There are many forces in the world that diminish or reduce human beings to something less, just a fraction, an example being to reduce human sexuality to simply "having fun." It is from Christ that we learn what it means to be a whole human being. To approach the pandemic pastorally means "to bring to [our] brothers and sisters affected by AIDS all possible material, moral and spiritual comfort" (*Ecclesia in Africa,* no. 116).

Accompaniment and Care

Anecdotal evidence suggests that half of all AIDS-related services in Africa are provided by Catholic organizations; the proportion is even higher in remote rural areas. Many Africans, whether Christians or not, appreciate how the Roman Catholic Church is responding to the pandemic in all corners of the continent.

Those who are infected or affected readily attest that the worst thing is not the infection and its medical consequences but the stigma and discrimination attached to the infection. Here is eloquent testimony from a synod participant:

> The stigma associated with AIDS is too heavy for people as individuals or as communities to carry alone. I have seen fear and despair in the eyes of our people. They should find courage and hope from us. They hear from religious leaders and their families that in one way or another, words or actions, they are responsible for their illness. They have sinned and are now paying for it. The stigma comes from us, not from those who suffer it. We are the ones who mark them as sinners even after God himself has forgiven them.
>
> We need to help our people to know that HIV-AIDS is a sickness and that it is wrong to blame themselves or others for it. They may have overstepped some moral issues, but illness calls us to have compassion.
>
> We have seen where families send away their children or in-laws (especially their daughter-in-law) because of their sickness. Family rejection of their children is an abomination. It is a grave sin in the eyes of God. It is a distortion of the gospel message of Jesus which is forgiveness, reconciliation and the return to the community: the return to the family of God. The lepers after they were healed by Jesus were told to go to the priest and return to the community. We do great work with those who are sick. We continue to mark them by not standing with them as Jesus did with the lepers (Luke 17:11–19).[3]

The synod characterizes pastoral care—for the infected and the affected—as offering people *a life without stigma and discrimination*. This represents a restoration of their human dignity, a recovery of their place in family and society. Quite a few who live with AIDS call this profound reconciliation their own "resurrection from the dead." Stigma and discrimination were "killing" them—and now Christian pastoral care has brought them back to life. The synod spells out the necessary components of care for the infected and the affected:

> —*a pastoral care which offers those living with HIV and AIDS access to medication, food, counselling for a change in behaviour, and a life without stigma*
> —*a pastoral care which offers orphaned children, widows and widowers a genuine hope of a life without stigma and discrimination.*

The care should include medical care, nutrition, psycho-spiritual support and, above all, reconciliation with others—*a life without stigma and discrimination*—so that, rather than feeling cast out and condemned to die, a person living with HIV can feel whole and hopeful and "live positively" once again.

Avoidance and Prevention

Besides the care that leads to positive living, the church also works hard so that people avoid giving or getting HIV in the first place.[4] Unfortunately, serious factors continue to leave Africans very vulnerable to the HIV infection and make AIDS difficult to treat effectively. The synod deals with many of these factors, which can be divided into two groups: moral-cultural and socioeconomic.

First, the synod addresses the moral-cultural conditions that favor the spread of the infection: *the breakdown of family life, marital unfaithfulness, alcohol, drugs, promiscuity and a life style which is devoid of human values and Gospel virtues.*[5]

Fifteen years ago, *Ecclesia in Africa*, the apostolic exhortation issued by Pope John Paul II after the first African Synod, identified "irresponsible sexual behavior" as playing a significant role in spreading HIV (no. 116). Now the second African Synod *vehemently condemns all deliberate attempts on the part of individuals or groups to spread the virus . . . by their personal lifestyle.*

> *This Synod, with the Holy Father, Pope Benedict XVI, seriously warns that the problem cannot be overcome by the distribution of prophylactics. We appeal to all who are genuinely interested in arresting the sexual transmission of HIV to recognise the success already obtained by programmes that propose abstinence among those not yet married, and fidelity among the married. Such a course of action not only offers the best protection against the spread of this disease but is also in harmony with Christian morality.*

Second, the synod proposes that those socioeconomic conditions that help to spread the infection be avoided or overcome. They include the following:

1. Violence: "AIDS has ravaged the foundations of [African] society. It has the potential to be used as a weapon of war and conflict. How do you forgive one who deliberately infects you with the killer virus?"[6] So the church *vehemently condemns all deliberate attempts on the part of individuals or groups to spread the virus as a weapon of war.*

2. Injustice: *Those who are sick with AIDS in Africa are victims of injustice, because they often do not receive the same quality of treatment as in other places . . . as in Europe.* Even within Africa, "treatment is available for citizens but unfortunately not for refugees and foreigners living in the country."[7]

3. Corruption: *The Church asks that funds destined for those with AIDS be actually used for this purpose.*

4. Poverty and abuse: "In many situations, sex-workers or prostitutes, of whom 80% are infected by the HIV/AIDS virus, are forced to this life-style by poverty and are sexually abused by well-salaried people."[8]

In these four areas and in related areas (such as human rights and the environment), the church's ministry has long been struggling for justice, peace, and integral development, and thereby resisting HIV and AIDS.

Promoting Abstinence among Youth

The dominant globalized culture, including advertising, media, and entertainment, has a seductive message for unmarried young people that suggests that the sex drive is so powerful that it cannot and should not be controlled. By contrast, the church's message of true human dignity and fulfillment is counter-cultural and addressed appropriately to every boy and girl, man and woman, at each stage of life.

Because young unmarried people who willingly practice sexual abstinence are often the target of campaigns to "normalize" sexuality as recreation without commitment, they need the church's consistent pastoral and public support. They need the church to say, in effect, "You believe in your future, and we wholeheartedly support you." These young people need to keep hearing that such abstinence does not represent a deficiency but something very positive. It means being faithful to their future spouse and their future lifelong commitment, with hope of authentic human development and that of their (future) family.

With its pastoral teaching,[9] the Roman Catholic Church supports behavior maintenance for the abstinent and encourages those who have made mistakes to change their behavior and return to abstinence until they make their lifetime commitment. *We address ourselves particularly to you, the youth. Let no one deceive you into thinking that you cannot control yourselves. Yes you can, with the grace of God.*

Priests, sisters, catechists, chaplains, teachers, and pastoral workers need to learn how to form and support these youth, including Catholics and other Christians, Muslims and other believers, and youth of good will. They surely constitute the majority of young Africans, and we cannot let them down by silence, weak or ambiguous messages, or reluctance to preach the full gospel.

Promoting Fidelity in Marriage

When it comes to marriage and family life, the African Synod warmly congratulated Catholic families "for doggedly remaining true to the ideals of the Christian family and retaining the best values of our African family."[10] But the synod also expressed deep concern about "the destruction of an authentic idea of marriage and the notion of a sound family"[11] and warned about "virulent ideological poisons from abroad"[12] that undermine the foundational values of marriage and family.

Promoting fidelity in marriage therefore includes methods like "partner reduction" or "zero grazing" that reduce the risk of giving or receiving HIV, but it goes much further. "Abstinence and fidelity are not only the best way to avoid becoming infected by HIV or infecting others, but even more are they the best way of ensuring progress towards lifelong happiness and true fulfillment."[13] In addition, the church encourages any who may have failed to remain faithful to reconcile with God and with their spouses. Such teaching and support for the married can extend beyond the church's own to many couples who, belonging to other religions or none, want to be faithful for life.

Pope Benedict XVI explains that HIV prevention must be placed within the much fuller context and meaning of marriage:

The Church's contribution to the goal of eradicating AIDS from society cannot but draw its inspiration from the Christian conception of human love and sexuality. The understanding of marriage as the total, reciprocal and exclusive communion of love between a man and a woman not only accords with the plan of the Creator; it prompts the most effective behaviours for preventing the sexual transmission of disease: namely, abstinence before marriage and fidelity within marriage. It is for this reason that the Church dedicates no less energy to education and catechesis than she does to health care and corporal works of mercy.[14]

Assisting Discordant Couples

The HIV pandemic has given rise to the important categories of "discordant" and "doubly infected" couples, namely, those couples where one or both members are HIV positive. In a discordant couple, the HIV-positive one is quite likely to infect the other. In a doubly-infected couple, each is in danger of exacerbating the other's infection in the event that one transmits a different strain of the virus to the other.

Two cases of conscience can typically arise: one is the couple's legitimate desire to express their marital love through intercourse, and the other is their longing to have children. In such cases the role of the pastoral agent is to accompany the couple, helping them to inform themselves fully of the facts and form their consciences for the greatest possible freedom from self-deception and selfishness in making their choices.

Developing a well-informed and well-formed adult conscience is the great task of Christian growing up and initiation. Paul Béré underlines the critical importance of the conscience in his chapter in this volume on the word of God. *Informed* means having the facts (in this case, about HIV and AIDS); *formed* means having wholesome values. For example, the bishops of Chad recognize the role of conscience as the "ultimate moral rule" and leave to the formed-and-informed couple the final decision on how best to prevent the spread of HIV from one spouse to the other. They echo the Southern African bishops: "Decisions of such an intimate nature should be made by both husband and wife as equal and loving partners."[15] The church teaches and guides in this delicate area through counseling by pastors and other means that must always be sensitive to the multiple challenges that couples face and respectful of their privacy.

Thus the synod calls for *pastoral support that helps couples living with an infected spouse to inform and form their consciences so that they might choose what is right, with full responsibility for the greater good of each other, their union, and their family*. Notice that the subject of the verb "to choose" is not the bishop, the parish priest, or the counselor, but the couple who, with well-formed and fully informed consciences, make the decision for the greater good under difficult circumstances.

The synod also recognizes that discordant couples are entitled to the church's advice and guidance at a personal level, not a merely impersonal and generalized discourse. Rather than repeating abstractions, church teaching and practice are meant to respond to the concrete challenges of Christian living in the age of AIDS. Thus we see the Catholic Church, as Pope John XXIII so happily saw it, as *mater et magistra*—the pastoral mother and the teaching master. How this is further explained, how this is applied, and perhaps most important, how this is properly imparted to the church's pastoral agents is the subject of much further work.

Solidarity and Research

Given all the challenges associated with HIV and AIDS, the African Synod pleads *for sustained support to meet the needs of many for assistance*.[16] Sustaining such support may not be easy for agencies and donors when international concern about AIDS in Africa seems to be waning, and other issues like global warming have caught the media's attention.

International agencies are also asked *to acknowledge church institutions and movements and support them in respecting their specificity*. Here the intention is to countervail the noxious ideological bias of many agencies and institutions against Catholic Church–related AIDS efforts. Echoing the eloquent plea of Pope John Paul II in *Ecclesia in Africa* (no. 116), "I too urgently ask the world's scientists and political leaders, moved by the love and respect due to every human person, to use every means available in order to put an end to this scourge." The synod *urgently recommends that current research into treatments be expanded so as to eradicate this severe affliction.* Furthermore, the synod asks SECAM to

> develop an HIV/AIDS pastoral manual for all those involved in the Church's AIDS ministry (priests, religious, doctors, nurses, counsellors, catechists, teachers) applying the Church's moral and social doctrine in the different situations, where the People of God in Africa are facing the various challenges of the pandemic.

Such a manual will present many aspects of HIV/AIDS handled by the African Synod (as well as earlier church documents) and noted in this article.

Conclusion

While the focus of this chapter is the discussion of HIV and AIDS at the second African Synod, readers' questions will naturally range more broadly and perhaps include the following: How is it going with AIDS overall?

It is right to decry the prevalence of HIV and AIDS, whatever the rates of infection and illness, wherever they occur. It is natural, then, to be especially concerned about the exceptionally high rates in Africa generally and among particular groups there and elsewhere. Why are the rates higher here than there, among these more than those? What data and analysis can help us to shape our responses? These are questions for multifaceted research in many domains (including the physiological, socioeconomic, educational, and even political and ideological). The church does not aspire to be the leader in such research, but it insists on seeing the problems holistically and it persists in serving where service is most needed.

The African Jesuit AIDS Network (AJAN) illustrates such a response by the church to the widespread and multifaceted nature of AIDS in Africa and its devastating effects. Thus, as part of a broad and vigorous response from the church, AJAN helps Jesuits and others to respond to all facets of the problem, from prevention through treatment to caring for the sick, the dying, those who mourn, and those who suffer from the effects of stigma.

Through its efforts existing initiatives have grown and many new ones have begun. Some examples include homes and schools for orphans; home-based care programs; youth groups combating AIDS through education and performing-arts activities and mutual support; information exchange on best practices; research, theological reflection, and publications; and fundraising. These activities are constrained by having far fewer resources than elsewhere to address the scourge, even for basics such as testing. Here, again, is proof of HIV and AIDS as a question of justice. The Roman Catholic Church has often addressed global inequalities in its social teaching. It often appears that the wider world prefers to debate the use of condoms rather than work toward the integral human justice that Pope Benedict XVI elaborates in *Caritas in Veritate*.

The Church is second to none in the fight against HIV/AIDS and the care of people infected and affected by it in Africa. Compassionate and generous church service has been the lived African experience practically from the onset of the AIDS pandemic. Those afflicted have usually found acceptance, solace, and assistance from the church whether they are members or not. Unfortunately, there have been instances where church representatives, especially in earlier years, inadvertently contributed to stigmatizing and discrimination; in addition, flamboyant rhetoric about "divine wrath" and clumsy associations of AIDS with sin are much to be regretted and have been roundly repudiated.

The Synod thanks all those who are generously involved in this difficult apostolate of love and care, and offers encouragement to all Church institutions and movements who work in the field of health and especially of AIDS. A church that tirelessly serves those in need is also credible in the teaching and formation that it offers.

As indicated in the opening paragraph of this chapter, the church in Africa and elsewhere cannot serve reconciliation, justice, and peace without seriously addressing the issue of HIV and AIDS. We cannot be completely at peace and reconciled with ourselves and others while this challenge cruelly assaults us in our families, our communities, and our societies. Here there is much more to explore, pray about, and discuss during the coming years of implementing the second African Synod.

"Africa, arise, take up your pallet, and walk!"[17] until AIDS is no more.

Notes

[1] There are two synod texts about AIDS: no. 31 of the official *Message to the People of God of the Second Special Assembly for Africa of the Synod of Bishops* and no. 51 of the unofficial *Propositiones* given by the synod to the Holy Father for his future Post-Synodal Exhortation. In this chapter all citations from no. 31 and no. 51 are in *italics*; other citations are in "quotation marks" with a reference. These two—and all documents of the second African Synod—are available on the vatican.va website.

[2] *Vademecum Synodi Episcoporum* (Vatican City: E Civitate Vaticana, 2009), no. 61.

[3] Archbishop Boniface Lele (Mombassa), *Intervention* 110, 9th General Congregation, October 13, 2009. A summary of the interventions can be found in the *Synodus Episcoporum Bulletin*, available on the vatican.va website.

[4] The contribution of Paterne-Auxence Mombé, "Moving beyond the Condom Debate," in this collection, elaborates on several issue raised in this chapter.

⁵ Here, alcohol and drugs have been added from Proposition 53.

⁶ Bishop Frank Nubuasah, SVD (Francistown), *Intervention* 94, originally referring to Botswana, 8th General Congregation, October 9, 2009.

⁷ Ibid., referring to Botswana.

⁸ Archbishop Liborius Nashenda, OMI (Windhoek), *Intervention* 179, 13th General Congregation, October 13, 2009.

⁹ Many basic elements of Roman Catholic Church's teaching on AIDS and sexuality are presented in a straightforward manner by Robert J. Vitillo in *Pastoral Training for Responding to HIV-AIDS* (Nairobi: Paulines Publications, 2007). Further debate on these issues may be found in Jon D. Fuller and James F. Keenan, "Condoms, Catholics and HIV/AIDS Prevention," in *The Furrow* 32, no. 9 (September 2001). For an extensive presentation of the Roman Catholic Church's teaching in Africa, see Catholic Bishops of Africa and Madagascar, *Speak Out on HIV and AIDS*, 2nd ed. (Nairobi: Paulines Publications, 2006).

¹⁰ *Message to the People of God*, no. 24.

¹¹ *Instrumentum Laboris* (2009), no. 31.

¹² *Message to the People of God,* no. 24.

¹³ SECAM (Symposium of Ecclesiastical Conferences of Africa and Madagascar), *The Church in Africa in Face of the HIV/AIDS Pandemic*, 2003. Catholic Bishops of Africa and Madagascar, *Speak Out on HIV & AIDS*, 109.

¹⁴ Pope Benedict XVI, Address to the New Ambassador of Namibia to the Holy See, December 13, 2007.

¹⁵ Bishops of Chad, *Statement on AIDS*, October 2002; and *A Message of Hope from the Catholic Bishops to the People of God in South Africa, Botswana, and Swaziland,* July 30, 2001. See also Catholic Bishops, *Speak Out on HIV and AIDS*, 92–95, 82–84.

¹⁶ See also *Ecclesia in Africa:* "Countless human beings . . . are in dire need of Good Samaritans who will come to their aid" (no. 41).

¹⁷ *Message to the People of God* (no. 43), citing John 5:8.

17

Moving beyond the Condom Debate

PATERNE-AUXENCE MOMBÉ

Raising the issue of the condom in the context of the second African Synod dedicated to themes of reconciliation, justice, and peace may seem inappropriate or irrelevant. Yet one can easily recall that in March 2009, on a flight to Cameroon for an apostolic visit, Pope Benedict XVI gave an interview that reignited the debate on the ethics of HIV prevention. His observation on the use of condoms in response to a question on the realism and effectiveness of the Catholic Church's approach to the fight against HIV/AIDS raised a storm of negative media condemnation.

The virulent reaction shows that the position of the Catholic Church on condom use in the fight against AIDS remains a burning issue, often stirring a passionate debate within the church itself. Thus it was expected that a synod on social challenges faced by the church in Africa should have something to say about this devastating disease. In the words of the founding director of the African Jesuit AIDS Network (AJAN) and special assistant at the synod Michael Czerny, "The Church in Africa cannot work for reconciliation, justice and peace without seriously addressing the issue of HIV and AIDS. We cannot be completely in peace and reconciled with ourselves and others while this challenge is cruelly assaulting us in our families, our communities, our societies."[1]

The polarizing effect of the condom debate pits the church against the secular world. My aim here is to engage in this debate and suggest ways forward for HIV-prevention in Africa in light of the African Synod documents, which point to wider factors related to the fight against HIV/AIDS within the African population. Thus this essay highlights the AIDS scenario in Africa, revisits key elements of the condom debate, and proposes ways forward to combat the plague of HIV.

The Extent of the AIDS Pandemic in Africa

As Jonathan Mann, the first director of the World Health Organization (WHO), stated, "How society defines a problem determines the manner by which we confront it."[2] How does the church in Africa perceive AIDS in Africa?

The Catholic Church considers AIDS to be one of the most tragic situations facing the African people. Building on the Apostolic Exhortation that followed the first African Synod, *Ecclesia in Africa*, the *Lineamenta* of the second African Synod underlines the major concerns that need to be addressed in Africa:

> the widespread deterioration in the standard of living, insufficient means for educating the young, the lack of elementary health and social services with the resulting persistence of endemic diseases, the spread of the terrible scourge of AIDS, the heavy and often unbearable burden of the international debt, the horror of fratricidal wars fomented by unscrupulous arms trafficking, and the shameful, pitiable spectacle of refugees and displaced persons. (no. 114)

Twelve years after the Apostolic Exhortation, AIDS continues to be a thorn in the flesh of Africa in its checkered march toward integral development. In fact, Africa remains by far the hardest-hit region in the world. The latest report on the global AIDS epidemic, published just a couple of months after the African Synod, shows that the rate of HIV infection remains very high. According to the report, in 2008 1.9 million people in sub-Saharan Africa became newly infected with HIV, bringing to 22.4 million the number of people living with HIV. Meanwhile, 1.4 million people have died from AIDS.[3]

Fifteen million Africans have died prematurely of AIDS, leaving behind more than twelve million orphans.[4] HIV prevalence among the adult population in sub-Saharan Africa remains high (5.2 percent in 2008), and women, disproportionately at risk, represent close to 60 percent of those infected in the region. Young people are also vulnerable. Although access to antiretroviral treatment (ARVs) has drastically improved the lives of people with HIV and AIDS and reduced the overall death toll, less than half of those in need of ARVs in Africa were receiving them at the end of 2008.

Going beyond these alarming statistics, the AIDS pandemic represents immense suffering in Africa, affecting households, schools, workplaces, and economies. Its impact on human development has led to a drastic decrease in life expectancy in many countries; reduced economic growth; resulted in a loss of agricultural and qualified manpower, including teachers and medical staff; and increased poverty. It seems clear that its impact will remain severe for years to come.

The root causes of the spread of AIDS range from individual behavior to social and structural factors that determine behavior. One of the most prominent factors is the rampant poverty in which the vast majority of African people (especially women) live: "Poverty facilitates the transmission of HIV, makes adequate treatment unaffordable, accelerates death from HIV-related illness, and multiplies the social impact of the epidemic."[5] Beside poverty, which stems from an "exploitative global economic system,"[6] among other factors, the spread of HIV is fuelled by extensive human rights violations, including HIV-related stigma and discrimination, gender imbalance, rape and violence against women, restricted or denied access to adequate care, treatment, or even to decent education that could reduce vulnerability to HIV infection.

Between the first and the second African Synods, a significant shift is discernable in the church's perception of HIV/AIDS and the root causes of its spread. *Ecclesia in Africa* presents irresponsible sexual behavior as a major cause and proposes Christian marriage as an appropriate response that must be taught to Christians, especially the young (no. 116). Proposition 51 of the second African Synod maintains that AIDS "is not to be looked at as either a medical-pharmaceutical problem or solely as an issue of a change in human behaviour. It is truly an issue of integral development and justice, which requires a holistic approach and response by the Church."

The *Lineamenta* of the synod invites the African church to reflect on "what must be done to give a glimmer of hope to the barrier which looms in Africa's socio-economic horizon" (no. 8). In this context the question of how to prevent HIV infection and reverse the trend of AIDS in Africa deserves closer attention.

The Condom Debate

To many, the worldwide wave of reaction against Pope Benedict XVI over his comment on condoms may seem surprising and disproportionate. In fact, the pope merely reaffirmed the main lines of the already-known church position regarding condoms and effectives means of preventing HIV infection. For Benedict XVI,

> this problem of AIDS cannot be overcome with advertising slogans. If the soul is lacking, if Africans do not help one another, the scourge cannot be resolved by distributing condoms; quite the contrary, we risk worsening the problem. The solution can only come through a twofold commitment: firstly, the humanization of sexuality, in other words a spiritual and human renewal bringing a new way of behaving towards one another; and secondly, true friendship, above all with those who are suffering, a readiness—even through personal sacrifice—to be present with those who suffer. And these are the factors that help and bring visible progress.[7]

The media firestorm that greeted the pope's comments reveals that controversies surrounding the condom debate continue to rage. This debate takes place at two levels: the secular world versus the Catholic Church, on the one hand, and within the Catholic Church, on the other.

The Secular World vs. the Catholic Church

For many secular institutions the condom-based approach constitutes the most effective way to slow down the spread of HIV/AIDS. For the proponents of this position, who include doctors, scientists, and international agencies and institutions, the only efficient and realistic means to reduce sexual transmission of HIV available at the moment is the use of condoms. And they will remain the key prophylactic tool for years to come. According to WHO, "consistent and correct" condom use (safe or safer sex) reduces the risk of infection by 90 percent.[8] Although HIV/AIDS practitioners and activists of various ideological persuasions acknowledge the value of abstinence from sex and fidelity in stopping the spread of the deadly disease, they maintain that people fail to apply these values because they are too difficult to implement. They believe it is utopian, idealistic, or merely unrealistic to depend entirely on these approaches to combat the sexual transmission of HIV.

The Catholic Church has no officially articulated position on condom use in relation to HIV/AIDS. However, many officials in the Catholic Church, including Pope John Paul II, cardinals, and bishops who are members of pontifical councils or episcopal conferences, insist that responsible HIV-prevention is to be achieved through "education about respect for the sacred value of life and formation about the correct practice of sexuality, which presupposes chastity and fidelity."[9] A significant statement against condom use from the Catholic hierarchy, echoed by many, is that of the Catholic bishops of South Africa, who stated in a declaration in July 2001 that "condoms do not guarantee protection against HIV/AIDS. Condoms may even be one of the main reasons for the spread of HIV/AIDS. Apart from the possibility of condoms being faulty or wrongly used they contribute to the breaking down of self-control and mutual respect."[10] In their pastoral letters or reflections on HIV-prevention, Catholic bishops refuse to endorse condom use as part of the Catholic Church's strategy and instead propose education in personal and family values.[11] Refusing to endorse condom use, the late president of the Pontifical Council for the Family, Cardinal Alfonso Lopez Trujillo, argued about condom permeability by stating that

> the U.S. Food and Drug Administration requires manufacturers to use a water test to examine samples from each batch of condoms for leakage. If the test detects a defect rate of more than 4 per 1,000, the entire lot is discarded. . . . If four leaking condoms are allowed in every batch of 1,000, there could be hundreds of thousands or even

millions of leaking condoms circulating all over the world, either sold or distributed for free, and most probably contributing to the spread of HIV/AIDS and STDs.[12]

Cardinal Lopez Trujillo called for labels to carry the warning on condom packaging that condoms do not guarantee total protection in order to inform the public of the risks to which they may expose themselves. For Monsignor Robert Vitillo, special adviser on HIV and AIDS for Caritas Internationalis, sexual abstinence outside marriage and lifelong mutual fidelity within marriage are scientifically valid and have proved to be effective in preventing the spread of HIV.[13] He denounces the fact that many scientists and AIDS activists are so fixed on condom promotion that they do not give due attention to the risk avoidance that may be achieved through abstinence or fidelity.

The view of church leaders maintaining that condoms may fuel the spread of HIV has been corroborated by some studies and AIDS prevention experts. The director of the AIDS Prevention Research Project at the Harvard Center for Population and Development Studies, Dr. Edward C. Green, claims that the best evidence at our disposal today confirms that the pope is right to say that condom distribution may exacerbate the problem of AIDS. And, according to Anthony McCarty,

> the best evidence we have shows that condoms do not work as an intervention intended to reduce HIV infection rates in Africa. . . . What we see in fact is an association between greater condom use and higher infection rates. . . . We are seeing HIV decline in at least 8 or 9 countries in Africa. In every case the proportion of men and women reporting multiple sexual partners has decreased a few years before we see the decline.[14]

Debate within the Catholic Church

Within the Catholic Church some bishops, priests, religious sisters, and pastoral or moral theologians question the refusal to endorse condom use amid the ravaging AIDS pandemic in Africa. For instance, Sr. Alison Munro, OP, writes:

> Ultimately, condom issues are secondary to practices of compassion, justice and inclusion. Education about condoms is not condom promotion. My plea really is about putting the condom in its rightful place as one among other means of HIV prevention rather than forever drawing undue attention to its efficacy and usefulness, or lack thereof, and to its place within a hierarchy of what the Church teaches.[15]

Some Catholic thinkers propose an approach that includes those who cannot conform to the requirements of chastity and fidelity. Advocating the use of condoms for those for whom abstinence is not an option, they invite the church to take into account the circumstances in which people live, which may determine their choices and way of living, a position consistent with Pope Benedict XVI's recent declaration on condom use.

Ann Smith from the Catholic Agency for Overseas Development highlights contextual factors that place people in risky situations, including "the economic deprivation of many families (and women in particular), cultural attitudes to women, pressures to conform to certain stereotypes, social and cultural attitudes towards sexuality and illness and exploitative employers." In such cases, she argues, it would be "idealistic and pastorally naïve" to expect behavior change and conformity to church teaching.[16] Thus, condoms may be the best option to reduce risk, especially for certain social groups such as sex workers.

An increasing number of church leaders and some theologians believe that the Catholic Church should revisit its position on condoms, especially when a spouse is unfaithful or in the case of discordant couples (when one spouse is HIV-positive). Using a condom in these cases may be understood as protecting one's health or life and not as a contraceptive method.[17] Jon Fuller and James Keenan maintain that in the case of a married couple in which the husband is HIV-positive and the wife is post-menopausal, "Condom use . . . would not be for contraceptive purposes, but rather to prevent a fatal infection from being transmitted from husband to wife."[18] In the case of a discordant couple where the wife is not yet at the menopausal stage, they show that there are two effects at stake—prevention of HIV transmission (intended effect)—and avoidance of pregnancy (unintended effect), and conclude that "this is a classic application of the Catholic moral principle of 'double effect.'"[19]

Moral theologians, taking into account various circumstances, have proposed other moral principles to justify condom use. These include the principle of lesser evil, which implies preventing another evil (sex with the risk of infecting the other) from being added to the moral wrongfulness of an action (extramarital sex), and the principle of cooperation, which supposes that one is involved in the wrongdoing of another although one does not approve this wrongdoing (as in the case of a Catholic institution providing public health information on condoms in order to reduce risk).

Another criterion within the Catholic Church that supports condom use evokes the principle of life, claiming that condom use is an essential element in protecting life. This principle of life, especially within the African cultural context, is crucial. Writing from an African perspective, Agbonkhianmeghe Orobator states that "life constitutes the principle against which the value of individual actions, behavior and choices are measured. Their value is determined or evaluated by the measure in which they enhance or diminish the 'power' or 'force' of life."[20]

Moving the Condom Debate
Further Along

At this point, it is important to return to the documents of the second African Synod to see how they can shape a response to the pandemic that continues to threaten the life of millions of Africans. My assumption is that there is the need to shift from what Keenan calls "first generation issues," such as condom use, to second-generation issues, which imply social justice. The African Synod documents *(Final List of 57 Propositions* and *Message to the People of God of the Second Special Assembly for Africa of the Synod of Bishops)* suggest such a shift, proposing a useful framework for facing HIV/AIDS in the African context. This, I believe, will help to move beyond the endless debate on condom use and focus on what is truly essential to curb the AIDS pandemic.

Lisa Cahill writes that "AIDS is a justice issue, not primarily a sex issue. AIDS as a justice issue concerns the social relationships that help spread HIV and fail to alleviate AIDS, relationships of power and vulnerability that violate Catholic norms of justice and the common good."[21] Cahill calls attention to social conditions that fuel the spread of HIV/AIDS rather than focusing on individual behavior and seeking solutions solely at this level. In other words, combating AIDS efficiently requires consideration of the social and structural root causes of its spread.

It is in this same line of thought that participants at the second African Synod invite us to view the challenge of HIV/AIDS. Proposition 51 states: "AIDS is . . . not to be looked at as either a medical-pharmaceutical problem or solely as an issue of a change in human behavior. It is truly an issue of integral development and justice." The bishops indicate that the widespread expansion of AIDS in Africa results from global injustice that prevents African populations from accessing the most effective treatment and care.

Documented and verified positive results in containing HIV prevalence in the developed world stem largely from the availability of antiretroviral drugs of quality for those who need them. For the African Synod, fighting AIDS in Africa requires fighting poverty and social conditions that lead to the breakdown of family life, marital unfaithfulness, promiscuity, and so forth.

Conceptual Framework
for Fighting AIDS in Africa

In its *Message to the People of God* the synod participants lay down a fundamental conceptual framework for identifying and evaluating interventions to tackle HIV/AIDS that are healthy for the African people and deserving of further development.

African Values of Family and Human Life

In the *Message to the People of God* the synod participants denounce the inclination to neglect values that are essential to African populations and to substitute anti-values or foreign categories that impoverish Africans anthropologically or dis-empower them (no. 30). They suggest that any intervention for or service offered to African populations should respect the sense of family and human life that characterizes Africa. This means that the value of interventions aimed at curbing the AIDS pandemic should be evaluated in the light of this respect (or lack of it). Beyond these key values, they also suggest a value-based approach to HIV prevention rooted in the values of abstinence, fidelity, and self-control.

Respect and Dignity

Denouncing the economic marginalization of Africa and the fact that African interests are secondary to the interests of the developed world, the synod participants invite the world powers to "treat Africa with respect and dignity." This call is relevant in the context of HIV where other interests sometimes seem to prevail over the good of the African people. Limited access to quality treatment clearly indicates a lack of consideration for the value of their lives.

The solutions sometimes imposed on Africa, regardless of its world view, values, or real needs, are another sign of a lack of respect. For instance, in reaction to the comments of Pope Benedict XVI, Spain's left-wing government announced that it would send one million condoms to Africa. Such political posturing falls short of respect for and acknowledgment of the profound sense of the dignity of the African people. Recognizing the dignity of Africa and the African people must be the foundation of ethical cooperation with the international community if the fight against AIDS in Africa is to be successful.

Concluding Remarks

Three observations are helpful in shifting the focus on HIV/AIDS beyond the condom debate.

The first is *the relativity of condoms*. The popular perception of condoms is often that they offer 100 percent protection, obscuring the fact that the 90 percent effectiveness rate attested to by WHO presumes certain conditions that are not always assured, specifically in African contexts. In a working group on HIV prevention strategy in Burundi attended by the author, some medical doctors insisted strongly on the need to stress clearly that condoms do not offer complete protection. One doctor explained his position by sharing a personal experience: a friend of his approached him and said angrily: "You misled me. I have been buying and using best quality condoms following your advice. How come I am now infected?"

Risk and vulnerability are key factors that must be taken into account in HIV prevention. HIV risk is the likelihood that an individual gets infected. Vulnerability refers to a range of external factors that weaken the ability of a person to avoid risk, exposing him or her to HIV infection. Condoms may definitely reduce the risk of HIV transmission when used consistently. Yet they increase vulnerability to HIV infection, especially when promoted among younger and less educated populations, because their availability may influence them to adopt increasingly risky behaviors. The strategy of promoting condoms as the best means to prevent HIV infection may have led to risk compensation, that is, a decreased risk perception that leads to consequent increases in risky behavior.[22] Given the context of prevailing HIV infection in Africa, particularly among youth, society as a whole and public health institutions in particular must move beyond ideologies and acknowledge the primacy of risk avoidance methods over risk reduction methods.

A second observation is the *incompatibility of condom use with the principle of life*. A client once came to my office to share her story. HIV-positive since 1998, she met a man, HIV-negative, who chose to be with her despite her sero-status. They approached a medical doctor, who advised them to use condoms. They strictly followed this advice, and the husband went periodically for testing. One day the woman came to say that her husband had tested positive and was completely depressed. I had to work hard to help him accept his status and to continue to live positively. Such cases take place more often than are documented. They raise the following question: How would a pastor account for such a situation if he or she happened to be the one who recommended condoms to a discordant couple?

The situation of discordant couples is one of the most challenging pastoral situations facing the church today. The temptation is rife to propose condoms as a solution to their condition. However, it is wise to realize that such an approach may turn out to be delaying rather than avoiding infection in the safe partner. As Michael Czerny suggests in his contribution to this volume, as Christians we have the task to offer compassionate attention and to develop a well-informed (knowledge) and well-formed (values) adult conscience that may help discordant couples make good decisions for themselves and their family. In any case, given that the effectiveness of condoms is relative, the argument of protecting life through condom use should be questioned.

Third, there should be a stronger *focus on second-generation issues*. The spread of AIDS is fuelled by poverty, and good treatment is a key factor in fostering prevention. It is established that the spread of HIV can be stemmed by the use of antiretroviral drugs, medications that interact with the life cycle of HIV and keep the amount of the virus in the body at a very low level. As a result, the likelihood of an infected person passing the virus on to another person is reduced.

Ultimately, the fight against HIV/AIDS in Africa would be more effective if those governments from the developed world that showed concern for Africa because of the so-called controversial statement by Pope Benedict XVI committed themselves to reducing poverty in Africa and to ensuring access to antiretroviral drugs for 75 percent of those in dire need of them. Such a commitment would reverse the devastating trend of Africa's AIDS.

Notes

[1] Interview with Michael Czerny, October 4, 2009, Rome, no. 2. Available on the contemplativesinaction.blogspot.com website.

[2] Jonathan M. Mann, "Human Rights and AIDS: The Future of the Pandemic," in *Health and Human Rights*, ed. Jonathan M. Mann et al. (New York: Routledge, 1999), 216.

[3] Joint United Nations Programme on HIV/AIDS and World Health Organization, "AIDS Epidemic Update" (Geneva: UNAIDS, 2009), 21. Available on the data.unaids.org website.

[4] See AVERT, "The Impact of HIV and AIDS in Africa." Available on the avert.org website.

[5] Symposium of Episcopal Conferences of Africa and Madagascar, "The Church in Africa in Face of the HIV/AIDS Pandemic: 'Our Prayer Is Always Full of Hope,'" in *Speak Out on HIV and AIDS: Our Prayer Is Always Full of Hope*, ed. Catholic Bishops of Africa and Madagascar (Nairobi: Paulines Publications, 2004), 106.

[6] Lisa S. Cahill, "AIDS, Justice, and the Common Good," in *Catholic Ethicists on HIV/AIDS Prevention*, ed. James F. Keenan and Jon Fuller (New York and London: Continuum, 2002), 282.

[7] Pope Benedict XVI's interview, reported in John-Henry Westen, "Harvard AIDS Expert: Pope Correct on Condom Distribution." Available on the catholic.org website.

[8] According to some other studies, condoms have an effectiveness of 85 percent as a contraceptive method and 69 percent as a prophylactic tool.

[9] This statement, first mentioned in the Message of the Pontifical Council for Health Care Workers for World AIDS Day 2004, has been presented by the press, including the *Washington Post* in January 2005, as part of the address of Pope John Paul II to the Netherlands' new ambassador to the Vatican, just days after Bishop Juan Antonio Martinez Camino, spokesman for the Spanish Bishops' Conference, said "condoms have a place in the global prevention of AIDS" (see Daniel Williams, "Pope Rejects Condoms as a Counter to AIDS: Church Doctrine on Abstinence Affirmed," *Washington Post*, Sunday, January 23, 2005. Available on the washingtonpost.com website.

[10] Southern African Bishops' Conference, "A Message of Hope," issued during the plenary session of the Southern African Bishops' Conference at St. Peter's Seminary, Pretoria, July 30, 2001. Available on the oikoumene.org website.

[11] On this issue we can mention Cardinal Theodore McCarrick, who published a pastoral letter entitled "Fullness of Life" in 2003, available on the cabsa.org website;

and Cardinal Alfonso Lopez Trujillo, who wrote a paper entitled "Family Values versus Safe Sex" (December 1, 2003), available on the vatican.va website.

[12] Lopez Trujillo, "Family Values versus Safe Sex."

[13] Karna Swanson, "Beyond Condoms to Truth in the AIDS Debate," Interview with Monsignor Robert Vitillo, February 2008. Available on the catholic.org website.

[14] Anthony McCarthy, "(The Pope, Condoms, and HIV:) Why the Pope May Be Right," *British Medical Journal* 338 (April 14, 2009): 1498. Available on the bmj.com website.

[15] Alison Munro, "Responsibility: The Prevention of HIV/AIDS," in *Responsibility in a Time of AIDS: A Pastoral Response by Catholic Theologians and AIDS Activists in Southern Africa*, ed. Stuart Bate (Pietermaritzburg: Cluster Publications, 2003), 40.

[16] Ann Smith, quoted in John Kleinsman and Michael McCabe, "AIDS and Condoms: An Ongoing Debate," *The Nathaniel Report* 18 (2006). Available on the nathaniel.org.nz website.

[17] Ibid.

[18] Jon D. Fuller and James F. Keenan, "Condoms, Catholics and HIV/AIDS Prevention," *The Furrow* 32, no. 9 (September 2001): 461.

[19] Ibid., 463.

[20] Agbonkhianmeghe E. Orobator, "Ethics of HIV/AIDS Prevention: Paradigms of a New Discourse from an African Perspective," in *Applied Ethics in a World Church: The Padua Conference*, ed. Linda Hogan (Maryknoll, NY: Orbis Books, 2008), 149.

[21] Cahill, "AIDS, Justice, and the Common Good," 282.

[22] See Michael M. Cassell, Daniel Halperin, and James Shelton, "Risk Compensation: The Achilles' Heel of Innovations in HIV Prevention?" *British Medical Journal* 332, no. 7541 (March 2006): 605–7. Available on the bmj.com website.

18

Africa and the Challenge of Foreign Religious/Ethical Ideologies, Viruses, and Pathologies

Paulinus I. Odozor

In his homily at the opening mass of the Second Special Assembly of the Synod of Bishops for Africa on October 4, 2009, Pope Benedict XVI reminded his audience that "the absolute Lordship of God is one of the salient and unifying features of the African culture." This deep sense of God makes Africa "the repository of an inestimable treasure for the whole world" and "an enormous spiritual 'lung' for a humanity that appears to be in crisis of faith and hope." However, the pope was concerned that the "lung" was under attack from certain dangerous pathologies, some with their origins in other parts of the world, notably the Northern Hemisphere, and already widespread within those societies. He observed that the "spiritual toxic waste" from these countries was now contaminating other parts of the world, especially Africa, with such "viruses" as practical materialism, moral relativism, nihilist thinking, and religious fundamentalism, mixed with political and economic interests.

He further noted two other sources of attacks on Africa: first, religious fundamentalists who mix religion "with political and economic interests"; and, second, an assortment of external religious groups spreading throughout the continent of Africa "in God's name, but [that] follow a logic that is opposed to divine logic, that is, teaching and practicing not love and respect for freedom, but intolerance and violence." In this sense, said the pontiff, "colonialism which is over at the political level has never really entirely come to an end."

Several participants at the synod also expressed concern at the growing negative foreign influence on Africa. Two synodal interventions offer examples: the first from Archbishop Robert Sarah,[1] and the second from the *Message to the People of God of the Second Special Assembly for Africa of the Synod of Bishops.* Archbishop Sarah was particularly concerned about a particular type of gender theory ("la théorie du genre") being spread throughout Africa by certain UN agencies, organizations of the African Union, and even some church institutions like Caritas Africa. This theory, according to the archbishop, is a "Western socializing ideology" that is in part trying to undermine traditional truths concerning the spousal identity and complementary nature of the relationship between man and woman in marriage, the issue of maternity and paternity in the human family, and procreation.[2]

Sarah noted that such gender theory also denies the sexual classification into male and female as intrinsic to human biological identity while positing, on the contrary, that the identification of male and female is only a social construct with no intrinsic worth except as an oppressive cultural imposition that does not allow the individual to choose his or her sexual orientation. Furthermore, such a belief argues that the relationship between men and women in society is marked by a struggle for power between the sexes, to the advantage of men, and that there is a need, therefore, to deconstruct the prevailing relationship between the sexes in order to allow women equal social power with men and to allow individuals the freedom to choose their own sexual orientation, including homosexuality. Since human nature by this view is indeterminate, it is society that models masculine and feminine gender according to the changing choices of the individual. Thus homosexuality becomes a culturally acceptable choice within this theory of gender.

Sarah's concern is that such a gender ideology is being imposed on Africans through the exploitation of the legislative process in a number of African countries and also by the manipulation of the mass media by which information on homosexuality, abortion, and contraception is spread, ostensibly in the name of "reproductive health" for women and in the name of civil rights for homosexual persons. He believes that the gender ideology being peddled by these foreign agencies is contrary to African culture and the gospel and is undermining the view of family and married life that Africans have nurtured and preserved intact until the present time, thus destabilizing African societies.[3]

The *Message to the People of God* expresses similar concerns about the role of foreign entities influencing aspects of African cultures and values. It states that even though it believes that the work of various UN agencies in Africa is commendable in some aspects, it views with concern "all surreptitious attempts to destroy and undermine the precious African values of family and human life." There is a need for vigilance, therefore, over the services of these agencies, and other nongovernmental agencies working in Africa, to ensure that "the services being offered to our people . . . are good for us" (no. 30).

It is necessary at this point to clarify the meaning of some of the terms used in this essay in order to better appreciate the issues at stake. Three words are of particular interest: *foreign, virus,* and *pathology.* Implicit in all of these terms, drawn mostly from medicine and applied to the African situation, is the understanding that Africa as a living entity is under attack from non-native forces that are infesting it with corrupt influences, abnormalities, and nefarious consequences to further their foreign interests on the continent. Included in these pathologies are secularism; materialism; a pro-abortion and pro-contraceptive ethos; an extreme form of feminism that conceives of the relationship between the sexes in terms of warfare; and a pro-homosexuality lobby that not only advocates nondiscrimination against persons based on their sexual orientation, but also recognition of same-sex unions as a civil right in Africa. The assumption then seems to be that left unchecked, these ideologies could cause much spiritual and social damage in Africa.

It is important to question the validity of these assertions. Is Africa really under moral and ethical assault? Are these attacks, if they exist, really coming from outside, or are they homegrown, and to what extent? To address these concerns I concentrate on four of the issues mentioned by various voices at the synod: religion and violence, contraception, abortion, and homosexuality.

Religion and Violence in Africa

There is great irony in Pope Benedict's remarks about religion in Africa. The widespread sense of God among Africans is quickly becoming a source of pain for the continent. Apparently, according to the pope, this development is an invitation to a new colonization of Africa, this time a religious one. Agreeing with Benedict, it must be acknowledged that currently there is indeed a new scramble for Africa under way. Although this new scramble for Africa is mainly a religious affair, it is by no means less serious than the one that foisted colonialism on Africa in the wake of the Berlin conference of European powers in 1885, which partitioned Africa into spheres of influence. In fact, the religious scramble for Africa is in some ways as violent as and perhaps no less disruptive of the social fabric in Africa as the earlier scramble for Africa. As in the first scramble, the various religions vying for the African soul are striving to outdo one another in terms of material resources, ideologies, and even violence.

Africa has been home for African indigenous religionists, Christians, and Muslims for many centuries. Africa has a population of about 900 million today. About 100 million Africans identify themselves as African indigenous religionists. There were an estimated 391 million Christians in Africa in 2000, about 45 percent of the population, with Muslims representing about 40 percent of the African population.[4] By some accounts Islam is the fastest-growing religion on the continent. By other accounts this honor belongs to evangelical and charismatic Christianity, which numbered a few hundred people in Africa at the beginning of last century but now has several million adherents and counting on the continent.

The older Christian communities continue to be prominent and growing. Africa has the largest Anglican Communion anywhere in the world, while the growth of the Catholic community, estimated at about 3.5 to 4 percent of the total population, is the fastest growing in the Catholic world. Of the 390 million who are estimated to be Christians, close to 130 million are estimated to be Catholics.[5] "By 2025 the number of Catholics will increase to more than 228 million. The future of the Catholic Church in Africa is the future of the universal Church in significant measure."[6]

Other religious communities, both Christian and non-Christian, project very optimistic numbers and a future full of growth. All agree that aside from increases that happen through birth, much of this growth will happen through conversions that will come about through active and sometimes aggressive proselytization. In other words, the three main religions of Africa—African Religion, Islam, and Christianity—are experiencing tremendous growth all over the continent. This fact brings with it many challenges in need of urgent solutions.

The challenges that the growth of the various African religions pose for life on the continent can be grouped into four categories: (1) historical, (2) theological, (3) political, and (4) social. From a historical perspective all of these religions harbor memories of wrongs they believe to have been perpetrated against them by other religions in Africa and elsewhere.[7] Theologically, the search for new converts is putting the religions on a collision course as never before. Politically, rival and often incommensurate conceptions of the nature and organization of the common good means that often politics—to borrow a phrase from Alasdair Macintyre—becomes civil war by other means and that the control of the instruments of state can become a deadly affair. And from the point of view of society, the lack of agreement on the nature of the common good has often led to total breakdowns that make dialogue in any form extremely difficult, if not impossible.

Thus, when the pope states that violence and intolerance are being visited on Africa "in God's name," he is stating an obvious truth. The rest of this section examines some of the causes of this tension, using Nigeria as a test case, under the three main headings of politics, economics, and law.

Nigeria as a Test Case

Nigeria has become a hot bed of conflicts between Christians and Muslims. Because this has not always been the case, it is important to ask what has changed in the relationship between the religions. Four factors seem to account for this changing scenario. First, religious conflicts in Nigeria coincide with what Nigerian scholar Iheanyi Enwerem refers to as the politicization of religion.[8] As Nigeria struggles to democratize and as politicians struggle to convince people of their suitability for public office, one of the cards available to them is that of religious identity.

A country of 140 million people, 250 ethnic groups, and many religious affiliations is bound to have tensions and fault lines. In Nigeria's history the earliest and easiest fault line to exploit was that of ethnicity. Although ethnicity is still a potent issue, it is no longer as effective a means of winning votes as is religion. In Nigeria and in other parts of Africa today politicians who care less about religion and may live rather irreligiously suddenly turn themselves into champions for the rights of particular religious groups at election time and in this way exacerbate existing areas of tension in the polity.

Another reason for the rise in religious tensions in Nigeria is economic. A cruel irony in Nigeria is that as the country discovers more and more oil fields, a sizeable proportion of the population sinks more deeply into poverty. The concomitant decline of investment in the education and economic well-being of people, especially the young, makes the latter easy prey for religious fanatics or lunatics who promise them something greater than themselves, whether in this world or in the next.

Marriage Law as a Source of Tension

Another area of constant tension and conflict among the various religions of Africa is marriage law. Between Christianity and African Religion, for example, legal issues surrounding marriage have been much challenged and discussed. Such issues range from the meaning of marriage itself to conditions for its validity and for its continued existence. In much of Africa marriages are communal affairs that are carried out in carefully thought-out sequences meant to emphasize various human and spiritual values. This understanding is very similar to Christian traditions on marriage and often expands and enriches those traditions.

African Religion, however, allows two practices that are contrary to Christian theology and law on marriage. These are polygamy and divorce followed by remarriage. The dialogue between Christianity and African Religion on these two aspects of marriage has continued since the two religions encountered each other. The solution accepted in most parts of Africa is to allow three types of laws to govern marriage. First is *customary law*, which grows from African Religion and governs aspects of marriage for all African marriages or all of the marriages of those who are total adherents of African Religion. *Civil law*, the law of the state, is usually similar to the laws of the country that was the colonizing power of the country in question. These laws have been fashioned as well out of elements of African Religion. The third type of law is *canon law*, which governs the marriages of Catholics and forbids polygamy and divorce with remarriage. Fortunately, there is a fairly happy consensus in Africa that respects the force of these laws on the individual members of the various communities in question. It is pertinent to add that in places with predominant Muslim populations, Muslim laws on marriage also serve as basic law for Muslims in that area.

Sharia *as a Source of Tension*

Perhaps the greatest bone of contention in modern Africa with regard to Muslim-Christian coexistence comes from the drive to make *Sharia* or the Islamic penal code the basic law, if not for everyone, at least for Muslims in some countries of Africa. In Nigeria, where Christianity, Islam, and African Religion have large followings, wrangling over the imposition of *Sharia* has generated considerable violence in recent years. Protagonists of *Sharia* argue that it is an expression of the Islamic way of life meant to govern all aspects of the life of a believer and that strict adherence to and enforcement of *Sharia* are important and effective ways to check social vices.

One of the arguments against making *Sharia* the law of the land is that, as Archbishop John Onaiyekan of Abuja has put it, to accept *Sharia* is "to accept the Islamic way of life, and practically become a Muslim," a situation that cannot be acceptable to Christians who cannot accept both Christ and Mohammed at the same time.[9] As Onaiyekan points out, there are some important principles of *Sharia* that Christians must accept and endorse because they coincide with Christian principles. These include the sovereignty of God and the supremacy of God's law over all other laws and the idea that a believer has both a religious duty and an inalienable right to order his or life in accordance with the law of God in all aspects of life— social, personal, political, and economic. Christians, like their Muslim compatriots, have an equal duty and desire to build a society that respects God's holy will. Also, Christians, Muslims, and Jews have a basic moral tenet that is founded on or at least inspired by the Ten Commandments.[10] All three religions recognize a version of the Golden Rule.

Therefore, when Christians object to *Sharia*, they must not be seen as objecting to people doing the will of God or to efforts to reform morals in society. Aside from objecting to *Sharia* on the ground that it enshrines a particular understanding of the will of God that may not be shared by Christians, Christians object to *Sharia* as an imposition of the will of God by force of civil sanction. This amounts to a violation of people's right to freedom of conscience and God's will, as Christians understand it.[11] Religious freedom is a fundamental human right. As Vatican II teaches in *Dignitatis Humanae*, "all human beings, because they are persons, that is, beings endowed with reason and free will and therefore bearing personal responsibility, are both impelled by their nature and bound by a moral obligation to seek truth, especially religious truth" (no. 2). The obligation to seek truth can be carried out only in freedom since it is a moral duty. Catholic moral theology teaches that knowledge and freedom are necessary to make an act a human and thus a moral act. We must know what we are doing, and we must do it freely. Any serious absence of either freedom or knowledge prevents an act from being a human act.

The same is true for faith. Faith that is forced is not faith; it is faith only when it proceeds from free human volition. The right to seek religious truth leads to the norm to live by that truth when it is found.[12] A person who grasps the nature of faith and freely refuses it, condemns himself or herself. Those who do not grasp the nature of faith do not reject it as such, and their ignorance may not be culpable.

Although Christians are convinced that God has spoken the final word to humankind through Jesus and that they have a responsibility to make God's word known to everyone, they also believe that the spread of the good news "must be done by preaching and persuasion." It is wrong to "force anyone to accept our perception, no matter how convinced of its truth and excellence," for to do so is "to encroach on the rights of the person to identify for himself or herself what is God's will."[13] One should be able to disagree or agree with the tenets of any faith (even one's own) without incurring *state* sanction. This is not possible under *Sharia* as state law. Thus, the divergent understanding of how to read, understand, or respond to what God is ordering is a continued source of tension between Muslims and Christians in Africa, as in other parts of the world.

Globalization as a Source of Tension

Another reason for the apparent rise in interreligious tensions in many parts of Africa is globalization. Ideologically driven religious occurrences halfway around the world can result in devastating consequences for local populations. Thus, an incident in Denmark with regard to the depiction of the Prophet Mohammed spurred some Muslims in Nigeria to rampage and slaughter those they considered infidels and to burn and loot the property of those who appeared non-Muslim to them.

Christians, on the other hand, can demonstrate an alarming sense of triumphalism and total insensitivity to issues of interreligious coexistence. This lack of sensitivity is apparent in some Christian circles in Africa today as evangelical Christianity secures more and more footholds on the continent. While the older Christian churches have had their struggles with African Religion and with Islam, these struggles in many parts have resulted in a respectful relationship that normally takes the other seriously and respects what they are about, even though it does not preclude conversions.

This "equilibrium" is being upset today by reckless and insensitive actions and utterances by some evangelical Christians who consider tolerance as toleration and acquiescence and who think that there is nothing good in either Islam or African Religion and that the only way forward is massive conversions of Africans. They enlist "crusaders" from America or Europe in the battle to claim these Muslim or "pagan" souls for Christ and upturn cherished cultures and customs that are in no way inimical to the gospel.

Members of the mainline churches are as much the victims of their insensitivity and shallow and triumphalist theologies as are Muslims.

Three Other Ethical Challenges

Three other areas open to foreign manipulation in Africa are in some ways related to the ethics of human sexuality: contraception, abortion, and homosexuality. The constraint of space allows only a brief treatment here.

Contraception has long been an issue of controversy in the Catholic Church and in many other communities as well. This issue has been a source of concern for much of the world since the nineteenth century, when Thomas Malthus offered his theory of population. He argued that the world's population was increasing at an exponential rate and would soon expand to the point where there would be neither enough food nor adequate space for the numbers of human beings who would call earth their home. The solution was to do whatever possible to cut the growth of the world's population.

The response to the Malthusian theory of population was swift. In the scientific community it spurred a great deal of research into a means of contraception that would be both cheap and effective. Since the mid-twentieth century such research has led to the discovery of hundreds of new forms of contraceptive devices, including the discovery of the birth-control pill and the latex condom. In the religious sphere the fear of overpopulation led to a breakdown in consensus among the various Christian churches against contraceptives. This was first expressed at the Lambeth Conference of 1930 and then later in the 1959 endorsement of its moral legitimacy by all other Christian churches (except the Roman Catholic Church and the Eastern Orthodox Church) at the World Council of Churches meeting in Geneva.

Politically, the theory of Malthus led to the founding of Malthusian leagues, which later metamorphosed into Planned Parenthood, founded by Margaret Sanger. Today, in the name of women's reproductive rights, Planned Parenthood is active in all of Africa as well as other places in the world.

This brief history of contraception in modern times is important in order to put the issue in perspective. In Africa the politics and ideological divisions over contraception have become more pronounced in recent years due to the pressing need to address issues such as the eradication of diseases like HIV/AIDS; the need to find legitimate ways to empower women and provide adequate healthcare for them; and the need to end bad governance, continued colonial interests in Africa's resources, and ignorance. The myriad problems besetting Africa render the continent vulnerable to ideologically driven developmental aid. In some parts of Africa today Planned Parenthood has established its presence, first by registering locally as an NGO

devoted to women's health issues and subsequently by partnering with local entities to further their agendas.[14] Planned Parenthood and its local
affiliates can justly take credit for promoting the good of women, albeit
under the aegis of a pro-abortion and pro-contraception agenda.

The criticisms aimed at the teaching of the Catholic Church on contraception overlook the fact that it is the largest single nongovernmental
provider of healthcare services on the continent. As Paterne Mombé argues
in his essay on HIV/AIDS, the crux of Pope Benedict's statement en route to
Cameroon is clear: the ready availability of condoms as a solution to the
AIDS crisis gives people a false sense of security and promotes promiscuity,
which in turn leads to the spread of HIV. As the pope's later statement on
condoms suggests, what is needed more than anything else is education in
virtue, including the encouragement of abstinence, sexual responsibility
between partners, the reform of certain cultural practices in Africa that
foster the AIDS pandemic, and intense government efforts to eradicate poverty in African societies.

A second area where foreign influence in Africa is most palpable is the
issue of abortion. A recent National Public Radio Program broadcast in the
United States reported that the United States government has stepped up its
efforts to provide assistance overseas, especially in Africa, for what Secretary of State Hillary Clinton called "reproductive health services" and for
the provision of contraceptives for young people.[15] It was reported in the
same news broadcast that the Obama administration had restored funding
for the United Nations Population and Development Fund (UNPDF) and
that the president had "lifted an executive order that existed in the Reagan
and Bush administration that prohibited U.S.-funded programs from providing information about abortion services."[16] Certainly, the greatest
"beneficiaries" of this great "act of kindness" would be African countries.

A third area where foreign influence is becoming more and more evident
lies in the challenge posed by homosexuality and homosexual unions. Although African societies, like all societies everywhere, have known the
phenomenon of homosexuality, these societies generally have considered
the heterosexual lifestyle and marriages as normative. In recent years in the
West, homosexuality has become a very hotly debated issue, and many
people, especially from outside Africa, are bringing enormous pressure on
African governments to enact laws that would not only assure that homosexual persons are treated fairly in society but that would also allow same-sex
marriages and unions.[17]

Many traditional African societies experience this trend as a novelty. In
the first place, an open discussion of homosexuality as an acceptable and
credible lifestyle would be considered suspect. Second, the suggestion that
homosexual unions should be given equal recognition as alternatives to
marriages between men and women would be considered abominable. The
issue of homosexuality has been keenly debated around the world and in
various parts of Africa. What started as a debate in Western societies now

appears equally urgent in many countries of Africa.[18] There is an assumption that whatever is a moral question in contemporary Western societies must also be so in Africa, and with equal vigor. Anyone who dares suggest that the issue is of little concern to Africans is accused of being dishonest. There is also the perception of inferiority or lack of critical acumen if African societies are not seen to be feuding over the same problems as those that are at issue in the West at a particular time. Thus, if Western societies are worrying about the recognition of same-sex unions, then that must be the case in Africa too. Failure to be so concerned is an indication of backwardness.[19] Worse still, should African societies take a different approach to the matter, this too is a sign of moral inferiority or at best of moral underdevelopment, which is tantamount to a colonial mentality. Experience has shown us that technological superiority is not equal to moral superiority. This fact is implicit in the pope's homily already referred to at the beginning of this chapter.

Conclusion

This essay has presented some of the enormous pressures that confront African societies today. Some of these pressures for change are internally generated, while others are a result of external pressures and globalization. The phenomenon whereby the whole world becomes in some ways a single place allows what happens in one part of the world to become instant news in other parts of the world. And what is acceptable or fashionable in one place makes its way into other parts of the world, wanted or unwanted. For Africa, the crucial question is about the way the continent is drawn to or contributes to the emerging new world order. Will Africa continue to be the passive recipient of other people's "toxic" ideas, or will it have what it takes to do what is morally right and good for itself?

I contend that because of the weak structure of the African continent, African societies have remained largely passive recipients of ideas and ideals hatched and tested in other lands that make their way into Africa through an imperialistic fiat made possible by the beggar status of African countries. Africa is the continent most in need of foreign assistance, the services of international agencies, UN peacekeeping operations, and all other forms of relief services. This dependency comes at an enormous price to the stability of African societies and nations.

Ultimately, however, the answer to the question posed at the beginning of this chapter—whether Africa's values and moral environment are under "assault" from foreign influences and trends—is more complex than it seems at first glance. On the one hand, some of Africa's current moral dilemmas are definitively homegrown, while others are not, as I have tried to show in this essay. Whatever the case, the age of African innocence is now gone. Africans must be made to account for what they are doing to themselves and for how they have succeeded or failed to establish a right moral order on the continent. In this regard African theology must be much more critical of Africa's past and present than is currently the case, even as it remains critical of the impact of other people's ideas on Africans.

One of the crucial tasks of the church is to assist Africans in building communities that do not depend on outside help to solve their problems, while keeping in mind that the interconnectedness of the world's peoples and societies through globalization is a feature of modern life. Furthermore, the church's role includes contributing to the proper religious and moral education of African Christians and maintaining vigilance. There is no substitute for a mature religiously and morally educated laity. Only such a group is able to stand at the gate and identify and challenge effectively any religious or ethical viruses that threaten the health of African societies and peoples.

Notes

[1] Archbishop Sarah is the emeritus archbishop of Conakry Guinea and now secretary of the Congregation for the Evangelization of Peoples in Rome.

[2] See the synodal intervention of Archbishop Sarah: "L'église et la théorie du genre en Afrique."

[3] The archbishop insists that African societies, to the contrary, deserve the peace and justice that comes from proper relation between the sexes, for without peace there is no justice or stability in family life and "without cooperation between the man and the woman there is no father and mother. In the name of non-discrimination, this ideology creates grave injustices and compromises peace."

[4] See David Barrett et al., *World Christian Encyclopedia: A Comparative Survey of Churches and Religions in the Modern World* (New York: Oxford University Press, 2001), esp. 13–15. Barrett gives the following estimates on the growth of Africa's three main religions: African Traditional Religion: 96,805,405 (12.3%); Christianity: 360,232,182 (45.9%); and Islam: 317,374,423 (40.5%).

[5] John Ricard, "The Further Dimensions of Solidarity with Africa," *Origins* 33, no. 18 (October 9, 2003): 291.

[6] Ibid.

[7] See Bradford Hinze, *Practices of Dialogue in the Roman Catholic Church: Aims and Obstacles, Lessons and Laments* (New York: Continuum Press, 2006), 236.

[8] Iheanyi M. Enwerem, *A Dangerous Awakening: The Politicization of Religion in Nigeria* (Ibadan: IFRA, 1995).

[9] John Onaiyekan, "The *Sharia* in Nigeria: A Christian View," *Bulletin on Islam and Christian-Muslim Relations in Africa* 5, no. 3 (July 1987): 3–4.

[10] Ibid., 4–5.

[11] Ibid., 5.

[12] See Paulinus Ikechukwu Odozor, *Moral Theology in an Age of Renewal: A Study of the Catholic Tradition since Vatican II* (Notre Dame, IN: University of Notre Dame Press, 2003), 37.

[13] Onaiyekan, "The *Sharia* in Nigeria," 6.

[14] In Nigeria, for example, Planned Parenthood is in the country under the guise of an NGO known as the Society for Family Health.

[15] Here is how Renee Montagne, co-host of NPR's *Morning Edition,* introduced this news item on February 2, 2010: "During the Bush administration, conservatives opposed even the use of the term 'reproductive health services.' U.S. support for family planning abroad declined significantly. Now Secretary of State Hillary Clinton says that under the Obama administration, millions of women worldwide will have greater access to family planning, contraception and HIV counseling and treatment." Available on the npr.org website.

[16] Ibid.

[17] See, for example, the Maputo Protocol, chap. 14.

[18] The recent situation in Uganda, where a law has been proposed against homosexuality, is a case in point.

[19] This is evident in the case of the ordination of openly gay men to the episcopacy in the Anglican Communion. Anglican Archbishop Akinola of Abuja has been vilified for daring to stand up for what the Anglican Church has taught for years based on its understanding of scripture and human experience. It has been suggested that he has caused a schism in the Anglican Communion. David van Biema, writing in *Time* magazine, had this to say about Akinola: "If the Anglican communion, the 400–plus-year-old, 78 million fellowships that the British empire seeded around the globe, falls apart, Peter Akinola, the Archbishop of Nigeria, will have been a catalyst" (David van Biema, "The Time 100: Leaders and Revolutionaries" [May 3, 2007]). Available on the time.com website.

19

The Scourge of Corruption

The Need for Transparency
and Accountability

GABRIEL MMASSI

The second African Synod chose reconciliation as one of the constituent elements of its overarching theme. Although this choice reflects the immediate needs of both the church community and society (*Lineamenta,* nos. 7–13), it also indicates the need to promote values that nurture long-term stability for the continent of Africa (no. 9). For this reason this assembly seems to borrow from a solid church tradition in order to respond to a need that is as old as the foundation of this community itself. This choice is informed by two existential challenges: the stark reality of the events evident in contemporary African societies, on the one hand, and the need for a better, lasting response to them, on the other.

This process is reminiscent of the effort that the church once relied upon in grounding the sacrament of reconciliation. There are three stages of this process: first, a struggle with the issue of perfection or holiness evident in 1 Corinthians 5:1–12 and 11:29–33; second, Paul's admonition for holiness in his letter to the Ephesians in 5:25–27; and, third, a proposal of a practical solution or conclusion as indicated in Matthew 18:15–18. The similarities between contemporary African realities and the implied path taken in establishing this sacrament appear to proceed from the first African Synod. That synod raised several issues concerning the church as a community coming of age, but it was also aware of its shortfall and limitations.[1] The immediate concern, therefore, lies in the need for a pragmatic way to address the realities that threaten the very existence of this community. This challenge, though one, is multifaceted in its causes as well as in its possible solutions.

A close look at two documents generated by the second African Synod, namely, the *Instrumentum Laboris* and the *Final List of 57 Propositions,*[2] reveals an interesting approach to corruption, one aspect of reconciliation that informs this essay. The *Instrumentum Laboris* makes explicit mention of the term nine times (nos. 11, 31, 37, 56, 57, 76, 102, 136, and 138), while the *Final List of 57 Propositions* refers to it only once (no. 25). Equally enlightening is the treatment of corruption in these two documents. The document *Final Propositions* condenses it into one spot but does not undermine its gravity, for it is clearly shown that corruption is a source of such destabilizing effects as coups d'état, violent conflicts, and wars. The *Instrumentum Laboris* deals with it more extensively, showing that corruption is the root cause of suffering in African societies as well as one of the obstacles to a just society. This document also underlines various ways of curbing its spread. Provisionally, the first possible conclusion is that freedom from corruption is a *conditio sine qua non* for a reconciled, just, and peaceful church and society.

There is abundant literature on corruption in Africa and elsewhere.[3] The primary intent of this essay is not to analyze this literature but to approach the question of corruption from the perspective of the need for transparency and accountability. Although the notion of corruption is slippery, I argue that any attempted definition should include the following elements: "unfairness, greed, bribery, fraud, embezzlement of public funds, misuse of authority and power, rigging of elections, tax evasion, and nepotism in employment."[4] Singly or collectively these terms evoke a breach of social and religious contracts and necessarily call for some form of reconciliation.

The central argument of this essay is that transparency and accountability, though diametrically opposed to corruption, are, in fact, a means to a reconciled, just, and peaceful church and society. These two concepts embody a pragmatic sense and translated into a community can render its members, as *Instrumtum Laboris* states in its preface, the "salt of the earth and light of the world" in social, cultural, and religious spheres. However, this can happen only if they are contextualized in a concrete milieu, such as in the socio-religious elements of a given person or community. Finally, I endeavor, by way of conclusion, to link several elements in this study to show how they can gainfully influence one another. In other words, I intend to demonstrate that the post-synodal project of reconciliation should seriously consider the subject of corruption. Since current efforts in addressing this problem have not met with great success, it is time to try another approach, and the approach I am suggesting is to consider more seriously the influence of African Religion.

Reality on the Ground

As I write, the coalition government in Kenya, namely, the arrangement put in place to avert a societal breakdown brought about by the post-election violence, lurches from one crisis to another.[5] At issue is the disappearance of billions of shillings, funds that were allocated to two ministries for the service of the people.[6] This direct consequence of corruption threatens to damage the government seriously and destabilize all Kenyan society.[7] While admitting that there are other factors at play in this crisis, it is perhaps the lack of transparency and accountability that best captures this reality. The current arrangement in Kenya seems built on personalities rather than institutions; it is a situation more likely to succumb to corruption than to rectify it. Sadly, tales like these are common in many parts of the continent.[8]

By way of a brief excursus, after apartheid in South Africa, reconciliation was seen as the first priority for any meaningful healing of the community, and truth telling was naturally thrust into prominence (*Gaudium et Spes*, no. 78). It was evident that unless there was a willingness to own up to one's role in the conflicted history of South Africa, not much would happen to redress the situation.

However, it also became clear that truth was not something that is "out there" and available for everyone; instead, it was part of a process that had to be teased out from confused realities. The mechanism developed for this purpose, the Truth and Reconciliation Commission, was thus creatively conceived and established.[9] Under such circumstances, transparency and accountability were not optional but fundamental to the whole exercise.

As the process of seeking truth unfolded, it became clear that the problem in the apartheid system was not simple racist prejudice but rather systemic economic inequality. As it was cogently argued, "Racial antagonism and racial policies were at the surface, rather than at the depths of the problem. Redressing injustice and bringing about social transformation was therefore the first step to real reconciliation."[10] At stake, therefore, was the first level of truth, namely, an informed, objective analysis that was required to bring the issues to the fore.

In the context described above, reconciliation was an aspiration that was not imposed from outside but that welled up from the inner self of the human person,[11] and from there it spread centrifugally and exponentially to influence the world of that person. In this current reflection a second level of truth involves those who are seeking to face themselves both in their dark and bright sides as they are known to them alone.

Vatican II is helpful to this analysis when it speaks of four important levels from which imbalances in our societies should be redressed: world, family, race, and social class. We should add the individual human person (*Gaudium et Spes*, nos. 8, 9). However, these levels should, in turn, always be informed by the two levels of truth mentioned above (an informed, objective analysis and personal recognition and acceptance). These levels seem a good place to begin, and I propose to adapt these elements *mutatis mutandis* to our African reality. If the battle against corruption is to be won and if reconciled, just, and peaceful church and societies are to be created on this continent, transparency and accountability should be at the center of all we do.

Let me now flesh out my understanding of the position of Vatican II in regard to transparency and accountability.

Social Systems

Social systems, most particularly the family, have great potential in attempting to develop transparency and accountability in Africa. Although both nuclear and extended families are instrumental, it is the extended family, with its several latent groups of solidarity for mutual support, that is decisive.[12] However, it is important to distinguish between nuclear and extended families, as they might vary according to the social systems that are operative and the values that are attached to them.

Aquiline Tarimo claims that family solidarity should not be taken lightly, but he is very critical of such solidarity when it does not bear a sense of responsibility.[13] He believes that a lack of responsibility runs the risk of straining limited resources at the disposal of a nuclear family, thus placing an excessive burden on the productive members of the family. In my opinion, Chinua Achebe sheds light on the case in his book *No Longer at Ease*, using the words of an old man at a meeting of the Umuofia Progressive Union, Lagos Branch:

"Thanks to the Man Above," he continued, "we now have one of our sons in the senior service. We are not going to ask him to bring his salary to share among us. It is in little things like this that he can help us. It is our fault if we do not approach him. Shall we kill a snake and carry it in our hand when we have our bag for putting long things in?" He took his seat.[14]

Clearly, a heavy burden is placed on Obi Okonkwo, the hero of this novel, by his extended family and beyond, to include also the clan. Achebe portrays him as an honest man who is bent on acting responsibly, but various pressures exerted on him eventually trigger his downfall.[15] Okonkwo is unable to maintain his personal commitment to transparency and accountability when he must function within different social structures.

African Beliefs, Religion, and Customs

An African understanding of transparency and accountability is also affected by the African world view. In most African societies religion influences human life in various ways.[16] As Laurenti Magesa notes, no one will dispute that, in Africa, religion is the source of abundant life; however, differences exist in the manner in which this abundance is attained in different social settings.[17] He further asserts that religion informs peoples' "perception of the Holy that demands and enforces their emotional and behavioral commitment and so gives direction to their lives."[18] It also opens the door to "the mind and heart of Africa and truly appreciates the controlling motivations of her values and her people's attitudes."[19] Religion unites the living with the living-dead, and it is also used as a source of order among the living.

Furthermore, religion provides a neatly tailored hierarchy that ordinarily guides any serious decision-making process in a given African society. Reward or punishment is viewed through the lens of such a religious understanding. George Ayittey brings this point home forcefully by citing Kojo Yelpaala's enumeration of "four levels of authority or sources of control" involved in making choices:

> First, there is the authority of the living exercised by such personalities as the king, the chief, and the lineage heads. Second, there is the authority of the ancestral spirits over the living. The authority of the living, particularly that of the lineage heads, is monitored and subordinate to that of the ancestors. Third, there is the authority of other supernatural forces whose cosmic norms and authority take precedence over those of the ancestors and the living. Finally, there is the authority of the supreme omnipotent being, who rewards or punishes the dead according to the quality of their lives on earth.[20]

Based on this way of perceiving reality, Ayittey continues, "The average African must consult four standards before initiating any action on his own and resolve any resultant conflicts and contradictions."[21]

Closely connected to this hierarchical perception of reality in the African world view is the order portrayed in the created universe. Thus, in Magesa's terms, "to callously disturb created order by abusing it disrespectfully means nothing else, ultimately, than to tamper dangerously with human life. . . . If the world is disturbed, God, the spirits and the ancestors . . . are likewise unsettled."[22]

In order to observe the order implied in the created universe, society operates within a moral code that is imparted on the African through various mechanisms in place for such a purpose. Strangely, this moral code is enforceable even when the perpetrators are unaware of straying from it, so long as it is part of the society to which they belong. Incest offers a good example for this situation: whenever such an act occurs, even if the individuals involved are unaware of their relationship, even unknowing incest can still bring about misfortunes on both the individuals directly involved as well as their community. Referring to incestuous marriage among the Gikuyu, Magesa affirms that even if the individuals involved were unaware of it, they would still be "considered to be guilty of the incest taboo."[23]

It follows that religion, or the notion of morality, greatly influences—or so it is believed—the African world view. If that is the case, then one can naturally conclude that it permeates the rest of a person's life; again, the notion of wholeness is supreme in this world view. In other words, it is expected that the way the African person discharges his or her duties is reflective of his or her world view. Thus, religion or morality pushes a person to act rightly, even if religion alone does not make one upright.

This understanding is seen in the concept of shame. Although shame is a widespread notion, it does, however, carry a special weight in Africa.[24] A good example lies in the release of a list of the alleged perpetrators of the post-election violence in Kenya. The resulting uproar can be interpreted in two ways: first, as a cause for concern if one was proven guilty; and second, and perhaps more important, because it brought shame on the persons alleged to have engineered the violence. Actually, the list of the names in the envelopes given to the prosecutor at the Special Court in The Hague is popularly known as the "list of shame," indeed, a most appropriate appellation.[25]

The Concept of Wealth Accumulation

The understanding of wealth accumulation in Africa bears a certain degree of sophistication that debunks foreign misconceptions on the issue of wealth in traditional Africa. Such beliefs include, among others, ownership, acquisition, responsibility, access, benefit, and the obligation of wealth.[26] Africa generally has two caveats dealing with wealth that are operative in many ethnic groups and that are reflected in how wealth is acquired and managed by African elites. The first deals with the need of the rich to assist the needy, although this admonition is at the discretion of the group.

The second caveat, however, stipulates that the pursuit of wealth should take place within certain "boundaries prescribed either by religion (Islam) or social norms." The Somali approach, described by Ayittey, summarizes it best in its warning against "the potential conflict between the desire for personal gain and the responsibilities of clanship."[27] It appears that the process of accumulating wealth has been neatly defined by the different functions of traditional society.

The African Legal System and the Moral System

In Africa these two systems are inseparably linked together. It is important to note here that in Africa, as elsewhere, the objective of litigation is to redress a committed wrong, thus restoring a broken relationship between two or more parties. Examples abound in many African traditional settings in which this practice is upheld as the norm. In most cases elaborate procedures provide the framework for such a practice to be fruitful. Although this process generally follows an agreed-upon legal system, one distinctively African element should not go unheeded. In dealing with a breach of law, a distinction is made between a tort or a delict and a crime. A delict or tort refer to "wrongs against norms and customs" and "the punishment of these wrongdoers involves compensation, to be determined by those structures in society that may, in this sense, be called 'courts.'" A crime, by contrast, is a "violation of a formal legislation of the state."[28] A further distinction is made between "adjudication" and "law." Magesa explains this point:

> Gluckman is correct, therefore, in calling this a "process of adjudica-tion, rather than law." As he explains, "This is the process by which . . . judges take and assess the evidence, examine what they regard as facts, and come to a decision in favour of one party rather than an-other." But the meaning and point of "judgment" is usually to obtain concurrence on the judgment by both parties, rather than to force a decision on one of the parties. . . . A successful judgment is one that brings about concurrence and reconciliation between the litigants. Sometimes judges make the decision to "postpone a ruling in the hope that the parties will reach accord on their own."[29]

It is clear, then, that this process is normally geared toward reestablish-ing a broken relationship between parties that have wronged each other. In other words, incrimination of the culprit and restoration of the incurred wrong are not necessarily viewed as the central outcomes of this process. An understanding of these distinctions may clarify some outcomes of the African judicial systems that may otherwise seem puzzling.

Leadership

The nature of political leadership necessarily implies a religious, moral, or ethical system. As Magesa again asserts, "In traditional Africa there is gen-erally no specific 'political' structure that is distinct from the social and religious structures of society."[30] It has been common for the same person to occupy a position of power in both structures at the same time and hold-ing a ritual or religious office actually enhanced the person's authority. One cannot take such an arrangement lightly, for it draws on both human and ancestral pools. Showing a lack of authority or a lack of veracity toward such a person negatively affects not only the individual but also the com-munity of the living and of the living-dead.

Traditionally, a person entrusted with authority looked after political, religious or moral, and economic happenings—the three elements that guided a community. Magesa affirms that "any person in authority is invested *ipso facto* with the power and the responsibility to guard and allocate justly the community of goods." Given that a leader is invested with such immense "powers," it is significant, as Magesa indicates, that both the ability to lead and the validity of any leadership depend greatly on whether or not the leader is fair and just." Magesa adds, "Favoritism is a vice frowned upon by God and the ancestors."[31]

It is interesting to note that the concept of leadership in African Religion refers not only to elected leaders, but also to others, including parents, who are leaders of their respective families. As leaders, they are expected to relinquish their leadership roles if they have failed in their parental responsibilities. Such failures are seen as both social and moral.[32] Understood more poignantly, the notion of leadership is much wider, and so are its implications. Thus:

> Failing to provide food to one's people in times of famine diminishes the life of the community, a very serious wrong indeed. However, even neglecting to properly entertain one's age mates from time to time with food and beer can indicate moral culpability in that it also diminishes life. . . . It is accepted that resources are to be used to effect communion through complementarity and mutuality. Leaders must see to the wise use of all resources to avoid an affront or offence against the ancestors and God.[33]

Linked to this understanding is the recognition that human wrongdoing against the ancestors and God is sometimes capable of bringing hard times and suffering to the family, clan, or community. A leadership position in this setting makes enormous demands on the person or persons who are leaders; failure to deliver could lead to near-catastrophic consequences that might put both individuals and the community at risk.[34]

Application

Corruption is not something new to humanity; it is actually as old as humanity itself. Although the first African Synod did not have corruption central to its agenda, it is featured there even so. In "The Church in Africa Today," Archbishop Michael Kpakala Francis places it at the top of a list of challenges facing the church.[35] He then raises issues that are critical if the problem is to be tackled pragmatically. He enumerates, for example, such aspects as the appreciation of human rights, the correct understanding of political authority, promotion of a sound philosophy of law, and the rule of law. As tools he proposes, among others, the social teaching of the Magisterium.[36]

Later the archbishop makes a slightly different observation. He argues that the first African Synod, aware that the church in Africa was still missionary in nature as well as in mission, entrusted to this church the mission of making it more viable and responsible for an Africa for Christ.[37] While I could not agree more with him on these points, there is one question that refuses to go away: Why, after so many attempts and with the use of various tools available to the African church, is this church unable to address effectively the challenge of corruption with its lack of transparency and accountability?

I suggest using a different approach—that of addressing the need for transparency and accountability by turning to five themes from African Religion: Africa's social systems and beliefs, and an African approach to wealth, legal and moral systems, and leadership. Traditional Africa boasts clear theories and practices in these areas that not only produce rightful observations, but are also able to deal with aberrations.

These themes and the traditional practices drawn from them can affect issues of transparency and accountability either favorably or adversely. On the level of beliefs, such as taboos, for example, the impact is favorable, because no one in his or her right mind would willingly or easily violate these taboos. To go against the values of the society would be to risk severe punishment. On the other hand, the value of the extended family is likely to have a negative influence on the matter of transparency and accountability because of the pressure it may exert on a highly placed member of the extended family.

In the end, if the acquired values have not been fully absorbed, either through religious settings or their social counterparts, they may not be as successful in enforcing the desired behavior in a given situation. In matters of litigation, for example, judgment and adjudication, although distinctly different in nature, can both serve justice, but with different implications.

At stake here is the world view in which one operates and whose repercussions may or may not influence a given society beneficially. Kä Mana would equate such a view with an African metaphysical system and add that such a system should be at the center of the world of an African.[38]

In a similar vein, a current debate in Kenya raises another important issue. At the center of the debate on whether the sitting chairman of the Truth and Reconciliation Commission, Ambassador Bethuel Kiplagat, should resign from this post is the system of values. As I follow the arguments for and against, my question is this: After the dust has settled on this case and the man is either exonerated or condemned, what will have been acquired? Will it be reconciliation, meaning the restoration of a broken relationship, or will it be a judgment that will create more problems than it solves?[39]

Although it has a different focus, a study on economic and social indicators by the 1998 Nobel Laureate for Economics, Amartya Sen, is intriguing. Sen's research on marginal economic issues that addressed problems related to individual rights, justice and equity, majority rule, and the availability of information about individual conditions inspired other researchers to turn their attention to issues of basic welfare.[40] It seems to me that Sen argues for the significance of the context in any serious study. Similarly, issues of transparency and accountability must be put in their context and, for what concerns Africa, religion is key. On matters of morality, it is religion that speaks most profoundly to the African.

Conclusion

In addressing the issue of corruption in connection with the second African Synod, I have focused my attention on two important concepts closely linked to corruption: transparency and accountability. I maintain that accurately addressing these two aspects could bring about a serious change in the levels of corruption in Africa. A successful treatment of this subject should probe deeply into the internal factors that are influential in the human psyche. Given the African world view, one needs to study the religious and moral aspects; these are the foundation for all other factors. Whether it is the church community or society in general, reconciliation with oneself in these two contexts is key to creating a reconciled, just, and peaceful church and society.

Notes

[1] Maurice Cheza, ed., *Le Synode Africain: Histoires et texts* (Paris: Karthala, 1996), 357–64.

[2] The synod documents, as well as other church documents, are available on the vatican.va website.

[3] See Michela Wrong, *It's Our Turn to Eat: The Story of a Kenyan Whistleblower* (London: Fourth Estate, 2009); Kimberly Ann Elliott, ed., *Corruption and the Global Economy* (Washington DC: Institute for International Economics, 1997); Susan Rose-Ackerman, *Corruption and Government: Causes, Consequences, and Reform* (London: Cambridge University Press, 1999); Arnold J. Heidenheimer and Michael Johnston, eds., *Political Corruption: Concepts and Contexts*, 3rd ed. (Piscataway, NJ: Transaction Publishers, 2002); Aquiline Tarimo, *Applied Ethics and Africa's Social Reconstruction* (Nairobi: Acton Publishers, 2005), 95–97; George B. N. Ayittey, *Africa Betrayed* (New York: St. Martin's Press, 1992) and *Africa in Chaos* (New York: St. Martin's Press, 1998), esp. 47–83; Pius K. Kidombo, *The Faces of Corruption in Kenya* (Nairobi: Sino Printers and Publishers, 2004); Kivutha Kibwana, Smokin Wanjala, and Okech-Owiti, eds., *The Anatomy of Corruption in Kenya: Legal, Political, and Socio-Economic Perspectives* (Nairobi: Clarion, 1996); Ludeki Chweya et al., *Control of Corruption in Kenya: Legal-Political Dimensions 2001–2004* (Nairobi: Claripress, 2005); and Evêques de la RD Congo, "La restauration de la Nation par la lutte contre la corruption," *Congo-Afrique* 437 (September 2009): 487–95; and Ignatius Edet, "The Church and Corruption," *AFER* 51 and 52 (December 2009 and March 2010): 625–55.

[4] Kidombo, *The Faces of Corruption in Kenya*, 3.

[5] The December 2007 polls, spilling into 2008, in Kenya gave rise to a bitter contest between the rival parties, leaving thirteen hundred Kenyans dead, thousands displaced, and properties worth billions of shillings destroyed (see Agbonkhianmeghe E. Orobator, "A Tale of Two Elephants: Overcoming the Postelection Crisis in Kenya," *America* [March 10, 2008]: 14–16).

[6] For more on the ministries of Agriculture and Education, which are accused of corruption deals costing the people of Kenyan billions of shillings, see "Kenyan

Coalition Will Not Collapse, Says Raila" (nation.co.ke); see also "How Kibaki, Raila Row Started" (www.nation.co.ke); and "No Kenya Crisis, Says President Mwai Kibaki" (news.bbc.co.uk).

[7] Many of the failed states in Africa and elsewhere have begun in a similar way, for example, Somalia.

[8] Niger, which has been dogged with prolonged crises, is likely to be plunged into another impasse that seems to be brewing, currently brought about by a constitutional crisis (see "Niger Leader 'Held' by Soldiers" [news.bbc.co.uk]).

[9] See Aquiline Tarimo and Paulin Manwelo, *African Peacemaking and Governance* (Nairobi: Acton, 2007), 52–57. Interestingly, an effort to establish a similar commission in Kenya has been dogged by interminable wrangling on its composition; see, for example, Editorial Team, "Moment of Truth for Kiplagat and Team," *The Sunday Nation* [Kenya] (February 21, 2010); and "Kiplagat Faces MPs as Tutu Backs Quit Calls," *Daily Nation* [Kenya] (February 26, 2010).

[10] James Cochrane et al., eds., *Facing the Truth: South African Faith Communities and the Truth and Reconciliation Commission* (Cape Town: David; Athens: Ohio University Press, 1999), 58–59.

[11] This logic tallies well with what *Gaudium et Spes* brings out in its argument that life in its fullness offers that which human persons pursue (no. 9).

[12] George B. N. Ayittey, *Indigenous African Institutions* (New York: Transnational, 1991), 1–9; see also Tarimo, *Applied Ethics and Africa's Social Reconstruction*, 162–86.

[13] Tarimo, *Applied Ethics and Africa's Social Reconstruction*, 173–74; see also an observation by Barack Obama in *The Audacity of Hope: Thoughts on Reclaiming the American Dream* (New York: Crown, 2006), 54.

[14] Chinua Achebe, *No Longer at Ease* (New York: Random House, 1960), 91.

[15] On John Githongo, the Kenyan anti-corruption czar turned whistleblower, see Wrong, *It's Our Turn to Eat*, esp. chap. 7, "The Call of the Tribe."

[16] Ayittey, *Indigenous African Institutions*, 10–22.

[17] I am adapting Laurenti Magesa's description of religion; see his *African Religion: The Moral Traditions of Abundant Life* (Maryknoll, NY: Orbis Books, 1997), 2.

[18] Ibid., 3.

[19] Ibid., 3–4.

[20] Ayittey, *Indigenous African Institutions*, 21. See also Kojo Yelpaala, "Circular Arguments and Self-Fufilling Definitions: 'Statelessness' and the Dagaaba," *History in Africa* 10 (1983): 375.

[21] Ibid.

[22] Magesa, *African Religion*, 61.

[23] Ibid., 167.

[24] Ibid., 46.

[25] "Anglo Leasing List of Shame" (October 13, 2006), available on the killcoruption.blogspot.com website; and "Kenya: IDPs Tops 2009 List of Shame," available on the allafrica.com website.

[26] Ayittey, *Indigenous African Institutions*, 23–28.

[27] Ibid., 29.

[28] Magesa, *African Religion*, 272.

[29] Ibid., 272–73.

[30] Ibid., 245.

[31] Ibid., 282.

[32] Ibid., 283.

[33] Ibid.

[34] Ibid.

[35] See the Africa Faith and Justice Network, *The African Synod: Documents, Reflections and Perspectives* (Maryknoll, NY: Orbis Books, 1996), 128–29.

[36] Ibid., 129.

[37] "Le dessein de Dieu pour le salut de l'Afrique est à l'origine de l'implantation de l'Eglise sur le continent Africain. Mais l'Eglise instituée par le Christ étant missionaire par nature, il s'en suit que l'Eglise en Afrique doit elle-même jouer un rôle actif au service de ce plan de Dieu" (Cheza, *Le Synode africain*, 288).

[38] Kä Mana, *Christ d'Afrique, Enjeux éthiques de la foi africaine en Jésus Christ* (Paris: Karthala, 1994), 20.

[39] Ambassador Bethuel Kiplagat's credibility is in question, apparently due to his ambiguous roles in the government of the former president Daniel Arap Moi.

[40] Amartya Sen, *Development as Freedom* (Oxford: Oxford University Press, 1999).

Epilogue

A Balancing Act

Facing the Challenge of Implementing the Directions of the Second African Synod

PETER J. HENRIOT

- Certainly the church should be more actively involved in politics if it is to promote the reconciliation, justice and peace that Africa needs so badly.

- Surely the church's contribution to reconciliation, justice, and peace in Africa is primarily to build up the spiritual life of the people.

These two contrasting views of the mission of the church relating to the theme of the second African Synod were evident in the preparation of this significant ecclesial event. They were also voiced during the actual sessions of the synod and have been heard in the discussions surrounding the implementation of the synod's *Message to the People of God of the Second Special Assembly for Africa of the Synod of Bishops* and the recommendations found in the synod's *Final List of 57 Propositions*.[1]

How politically engaged should the church be? How strong a spiritual emphasis should mark the church's social engagement? Answers to these and similar questions will have a profound effect on the direction that the post-synodal church in Africa takes in facing the many sociopolitical, economic, and cultural issues of the coming decades. The challenge will be to find some clear guidelines to apply, even in significantly different situations, if the church is to make any significant contribution to the future of Africa's development.

Faith and Justice

This is a challenge I personally have felt over the many years of my engagement in what we Jesuits call the social apostolate. This challenge has arisen in the pursuit of the Jesuit mission of "serving the faith and promoting justice" since the 1970s. However, it certainly is a challenge more widely experienced than simply in Jesuit circles. Indeed, I would argue that it is central to the life of the church since Vatican II's programmatic articulation of mission found in *Gaudium et Spes* in 1965: "The joys and hopes, the griefs and the anxieties of women and men of this age, especially those who are poor or in any way afflicted, these are the joys and hopes, the griefs and anxieties of the followers of Christ" (no. 1). This statement formulates a permanent challenge to the church's self-understanding as a community in mission.

A Balancing Act

Pope Benedict XVI responded to the challenge of the church's authentic mission at the conclusion of the African Synod in his brief remarks during a luncheon he hosted for the synod participants following the final session on October 24, 2009. He touched directly on the dilemma facing those of us who want to see reconciliation, justice, and peace as central to the church's mission in the days ahead. According to the pope, the task of implementing the synod entails two dangers.

The first danger is that the theme—reconciliation, justice, and peace—certainly implies a strong political dimension, even if it is obvious that reconciliation, justice, and peace are not possible without a profound purification of the heart; without a renewal of thought, a *metanoia*; without a newness that must come precisely from the encounter with God. But even if this spiritual dimension is profound and fundamental, the political dimension is also very real, because without political realizations, these new things of the Spirit are not commonly realized. Thus, the temptation could have been to politicize the theme, to speak less of pastoral work and more about politics, with a competence that is not ours.

The other danger was—precisely in order to flee from the first temptation—that of retreating into a purely spiritual world, into an abstract and beautiful but unrealistic world. But the discourse of a pastor must be realistic; it must deal with reality, but do so from the perspective of God and God's Word. This mediation involves, on one hand, being truly connected with reality and attentive to speaking of what is and, on the other hand, not to fall into technically political solutions; that means indicating a concrete but faith-inspired approach to reality. This was the great issue of the synod and, I think, thanks be to God, we successfully resolved it.[2]

What Benedict is arguing is that effective implementation of the synod will require a *balancing act* that is not new but is now ever more urgent. The challenge is to avoid over-politicization and under-spiritualization, on the one hand, and over-spiritualization and under-politicization, on the other hand. Indeed, a very great challenge!

The Zambian Experience

Let me reflect on how I have personally experienced the practical side of this challenge in working in a "faith and justice" center in Zambia. This experience exemplifies not only the difficulty of the challenge of maintaining this balance, but also the value of facing it realistically, as the pope counsels.

Since independence in 1964 Zambia has moved from being a one-party state to a multi-party democracy. It has also undergone profound socioeconomic changes. Rich in resources (including minerals, land, tourist sites), 65 percent of its population lives below the poverty line. Zambia possesses great potential but also faces great problems.

Even before the country's independence the Catholic bishops of Zambia played a very public role in speaking to the government of the day about meeting its responsibilities to serve the people of the nation. In a long series of pastoral letters (often ecumenically signed), in public statements and private meetings, and through strong support for their national and local justice and peace commissions, the bishops have been active promoters of reconciliation, justice, and peace.[3]

The Zambian Conference of Bishops and its pastoral, development, and justice offices have been outspoken on issues of economic development and the needs of the poor, governance and the curse of corruption, and elections and constitutional reform. Their activities have surely been "political" but not "partisan." They have engaged with real-life situations but have not endorsed any particular political party.

Over-politicalization?

Examples abound of the bishops' engagement in activities judged to be patently political by some critics. At the time of the 1991 transition from a one-party state to a multi-party democracy, the bishops were seen as "midwives" to a truly historical moment through their encouragement of the political process and their education of citizens about the values of democracy. During the Structural Adjustment Programme of the 1990s, when Zambia was pressured by the World Bank and the International Monetary Fund to move into a more free-market economy, the bishops spoke out about the need to pay attention to the effects of liberalization on the poor. And throughout the heated debates in very recent years over a new republican constitution, the bishops' voices have been heard on issues such as human rights and the death penalty.

This involvement of the bishops has brought them some praise but also criticism—the latter especially from government officials who have not appreciated the challenges raised by the bishops. At times, such disapproval has been voiced with a call for outspoken bishops or priests to "come out from behind the altar and engage in political fights!" For many, it might at times have looked as if the church was becoming more political than pastoral.

Considered more objectively, what has distinguished the bishops from a purely "political" stance has been their heavy reliance on the church's social teaching. This body of social wisdom—found primarily in the scriptures and articulated in statements from popes, councils, synods, and bishops, and developed through theological reflection—is what has grounded the bishops' engagement in sociopolitical issues. It has provided the foundation for what Pope Benedict has called "a profound purification of the heart . . . a renewal of thought, a 'metanoia' (conversion) . . . a newness that must come precisely from the encounter with God."

For example, in a pastoral letter discussing the economic problems facing Zambia that cause immense hardships for the majority poor in the country, the bishops speak passionately about the suffering of the people and engage critically in analyzing the failures of the government to respond effectively. However, the bishops readily admit that "it is neither the role nor the expertise of the Church to offer detailed programmes to meet our economic crisis." Notwithstanding, they do feel capable of offering a few specific recommendations "that arise from our position as pastoral leaders and from our perspective of social justice and concern for the poor."[4]

Similarly, in a pastoral letter released at the start of a constitutional review process in 2003,[5] the bishops reminded readers that it was very fitting and proper for them to offer guidance on such an important topic as the constitution. They recalled that the Catholic bishops of Northern Rhodesia (Zambia prior to independence) had in 1958 made very explicit "the right and duty to teach and guide Christians not alone in purely religious matters but also in social, economic and political affairs in so far as they are connected with the moral order." And they reminded the people that Pope John Paul II in 1991 had praised democracy as a system of government befitting human dignity (*Centesimus Annus*, no. 46).

The point of the foregoing is not to emphasize the need to cite documents of Catholic social teaching to bolster the bishops' arguments but to establish the legitimacy and efficacy of identifying the spiritual dimension and moral foundation of the church's stance in political debates. Failure to do this exposes the church's dialogue with political affairs to the risk of being simply another social voice, the cry of a nongovernmental organization pushing what might be perceived as simply a secular position.

Over-spiritualization?

Had Pope Benedict stopped at this point, his instruction would have been quite one sided. For as much as there is danger in an *over-politicization* of church intervention in political affairs, there is also a danger of an *over-spiritualization*. The pope recognized this as a second danger to face if the church is to effectively implement the synod's call for it to be at the service of reconciliation, justice, and peace.

Having listened to three weeks of discussions and debates, and followed the arguments leading to the synod's decisions and recommendations, Pope Benedict surely was aware of the wider picture involved in the pastoral-political scene. Hence, he could readily caution against "retreating into a purely spiritual world, into an abstract and beautiful but unrealistic world." Such a retreat would be marked by expressions of pious nonentities about political matters and self-serving critiques by some church bodies of the more politically grounded expressions of social concern coming from the Catholic Church.

Unfortunately, Zambia has not been spared the danger of such a retreat, as evidenced by some other churches who readily supply pious justifications for questionable government policies and programs. There have been multiple voices supportive of the government's displeasure with the Catholic Church's commentary on political affairs. These voices come not only from political agents, but also from some church groups that claim that the mission of the church is primarily spiritual and as such it should not be engaged in worldly affairs such as economic policies or constitutional debate.

Critiques of the church's sociopolitical involvement have even gone so far as to claim endorsement from a very narrow reading of Roman 13:1–3. Paul's call to submit to civil authority has been expanded to mean that challenging elected officials is not an acceptable practice for Christians. Authorities are always to be respected, since they have been put in place by God's appointment. Certainly, according to this interpretation, good Christians don't get involved in political issues or challenge the actions of state rulers.

This biased interpretation of Romans 13:1–3 can of course be tested by a *context* analysis of the specific situation that Paul was addressing. But even more telling is a *content* analysis that points beyond verses 1–3 to verse 4, which reminds us that authorities are in place to serve the good of those over whom they have authority. Without that service, they have no authority. Surely, then, it is the church's legitimate role to challenge those who claim authority but do not serve. However one chooses to interpret this role, it is clearly political action on the part of the church.

It is encouraging that even in the face of some very sharp and unfair criticism the Catholic Church in Zambia has continued to speak out for social justice and to share special concern for the poor. In its plans for implementation of the African Synod, the Bishops' Conference has scheduled workshops across all dioceses to share the message of the synod. The bishops issued a pastoral statement soon after the conclusion of the synod to call for "a conversion of hearts and living out of the Gospel values of reconciliation, justice and peace." This represents a concrete application of what Pope Benedict calls for when he urges that "the discourse of a pastor must be realistic; it must deal with reality, but from the perspective of God and his Word."

Pastoral and Political

At a continental level, another concrete example of how the church in Africa is grappling with the two dangers (over-politicization and over-spiritualization) in promoting reconciliation, justice, and peace can be found in a very significant consultation that occurred in May 2010. This was a gathering of over 135 pastoral agents from all over Africa, including fifty bishops, to plan for the implementation of the outcomes of the African Synod. Significantly, this consultation occurred even before the publication of the anticipated Apostolic Exhortation of Pope Benedict XVI.

As a participant in this consultation, I felt that both its discussions and outcomes were strongly influenced by the keynote address delivered by Cardinal Peter Turkson, president of the Pontifical Council for Justice and Peace. Cardinal Turkson, a Ghanaian, served as one of the co-presidents of the second African Synod.

He emphasized the "inseparable" link between the first African Synod (1994) and the second African Synod. The former developed the specific *identity* of the church as family of God, and the latter focused on the *mission* of this church-family.

> For it is in its theological content and character as family of God that the church-family becomes an image of and a foreshadowing of the kingdom of God on earth and in history, animating the African society and the world with values of the kingdom of God, namely, reconciliation, justice, truth and peace.[6]

Linking the family of God *identity* with the reconciliation, justice, and peace *mission* provides the key to overcoming the two dangers that Pope Benedict spoke of and that have formed the framework for this reflection. Precisely, this link strengthens the bond between the pastoral and the political. Ultimately, there is no authentic pastoral identity without a political mission. The recognition of this pivotal relationship generated vigorous discussions at the consultation and influenced the final declaration, entitled, "A New Pentecost for Africa."[7] This declaration emerged from lively debates and constructive conversations among the participants. Its language echoed the synod's *Message to the People of God* and the synod's *Final List of 57 Propositions,* refined by the pastoral and political experiences of the members of the consultation.

The declaration acknowledges the need for "a change of attitude and priorities: the Church is not addressing the needs of modern society [in Africa] adequately and should reach out more to marginalised groups, especially women, young people, people living with disabilities and the poorest of the poor." "Reconciliation, justice and peace must be high on the agendas of all dioceses; Justice and Peace Commissions are mandatory, not optional." "The Church must engage in political issues to bring real change, but should avoid being partisan."

According to the opening paragraph of the *Message to the People of God* of the second African Synod, this historic gathering in Rome was a "providential opportunity to celebrate the blessings of the Lord on our continent, to assess our stewardship as Pastors of God's flock, and to seek fresh inspiration and encouragement for the tasks and challenges that lie ahead" (no. 1). That *fresh inspiration and encouragement* of the synod is evident in the efforts of the Zambian church to be at service to reconciliation, justice, and peace. Being faithful to its pastoral identity (with a spiritual foundation), it can be courageous in its political mission (in a nonpartisan fashion).

There is much to build on for the future in Zambia, in Africa, and in the wider world, within such a church!

Notes

¹ For a fuller discussion of the process and content of the second African Synod, see Peter J. Henriot, "Justice, Peace, Reconciliation, and Forgiveness: Theological and Conceptual Underpinnings and Linkages," in *AMECEA Synod Delegates Workshop: Shaping the Prophetic Voice of the Region* (Nairobi: AMECEA, 2009), 37–49; and idem, "The Second African Synod: Challenge and Help for Our Future Church," *Hekima Review* 41 (December 2009): 8–18.

² Holy See Press Office, African Synod, *Bulletin* no. 34 (October 25, 2009).

³ For Zambian documents cited in this essay and for historical background, see Joe Komakoma, ed., *The Social Teaching to the Catholic Bishops and Other Christian Leaders in Zambia: Major Pastoral Letters and Statements, 1953–2001* (Ndola, Zambia: Mission Press, 2003).

⁴ "Hear the Cry of the Poor: A Pastoral Letter on the Current Suffering of the People of Zambia" (July 1993). Available on the afcast.org.zw website.

⁵ "Let My People Go: A Pastoral Letter form the Catholic Bishops of Zambia on the 2003 Constitutional Review Process" (November 2003).

⁶ Cardinal Peter Turkson, "The Second Synod of Bishops for Africa—A New Pentecost for the Church in Africa," Maputo, Mozambique, May 24, 2010.

⁷ Caritas Africa and SECAM, "Mumemo Declaration: A New Pentecost for Africa" (May 26, 2010). Mumemo is the site of the large conference center on the outskirts of Maputo where the consultation was held.

Contributors

Anne Arabome is a Catholic woman religious and member of the Sisters of Social Service of Los Angeles, California. She holds a doctor of ministry degree in spirituality from the Catholic Theological Union (Chicago, Illinois). Originally from Nigeria, she now resides in the United States. Her research interests include ethical and theological issues that shape the spiritual and devotional lives of African women in the Diaspora.

Paul Béré* is a Jesuit priest from Burkina Faso. He teaches the Old Testament and biblical languages (Greek and Hebrew) at the Institut de Théologie de la Compagnie de Jésus, Abidjan, Ivory Coast, and other academic institutions. His current interests are exegesis of the Hebrew Bible (OT) and texts in "cultures of the word."

Michael Czerny* is an English Canadian Jesuit who holds a doctorate from the University of Chicago. He was the founding director of the Jesuit Centre for Social Faith and Justice, Toronto (1979–89) and, for two years in El Salvador, vice-rector of the University of Central America and director of its Human Rights Institute. He was social justice secretary at the Jesuit Headquarters in Rome (1992–2002) and founding director of the African Jesuit AIDS Network (2002–10).

Anthony Egan is a South African Jesuit who is member of the Jesuit Institute, Johannesburg, South Africa. He holds a PhD in politics from Witwatersrand University and a licentiate in moral theology from the Weston Jesuit School of Theology, Cambridge, Massachusetts. He also teaches part time at St. Augustine College of South Africa.

Yvon Christian Elenga holds a doctorate in theology from the Weston Jesuit School of Theology, Cambridge, Massachusetts. He teaches systematic theology at the Institut de Théologie de la Compagnie de Jésus, Abidjan, Ivory Coast, and was a visiting professor of systematic theology at Saint Joseph's University, Philadelphia, Pennsylvania, in 2008–9. He is also a lecturer at the Centre de Recherche et d'Action pour la Paix in Abidjan.

Joseph G. Healey is an American Maryknoll missionary priest who teaches a course entitled "Small Christian Communities (SCCs) as a New Model of Church in Africa Today" at Hekima College and Tangaza College (Catholic University of Eastern Africa) in Nairobi, Kenya. He animates SCCs in

---

*Synod participants

245

Eastern Africa. He co-edited *Small Christian Communities Today: Capturing the New Moment* (Orbis Books and Paulines Publications Africa) and is an adviser to the Small Christian Communities Global Collaborative Website (www.smallchristiancommunities.org).

Peter J. Henriot* is a member of Zambia-Malawi Province of the Society of Jesus. He came to Zambia in 1989 after working with the Center of Concern in Washington DC for seventeen years. As a staff member with the Jesuit Centre for Theological Reflection in Lusaka, he has engaged in research, education, and advocacy for social justice issues, using the perspective of Catholic social teaching.

Peter Kanyandago is a priest of the Archdiocese of Mbarara in Uganda and is currently the director of the School of Postgraduate Studies at Uganda Martyrs University, where he is a professor of ethics and development studies. He holds a PhD in canon law from the University of Louvain. His research focuses on the interface between theology and anthropology.

David Kaulem is regional coordinator for Eastern and Southern Africa of the African Forum for Catholic Social Teachings (AFCAST) and a lecturer at Arrupe College School of Philosophy and the Humanities, Harare, Zimbabwe. He was chair of the Department of Religious Studies, Classics, and Philosophy at the University of Zimbabwe. He has been an international visiting fellow at the Woodstock Theological Center, Georgetown University (USA), and the Centre for Sustainable International Development, the University of Aberdeen (UK).

Peter Knox completed undergraduate studies in chemistry before joining the Society of Jesus in 1983. He has studied, taught, and conducted pastoral ministry in South Africa, Canada, and England. A member of the Jesuit Institute–South Africa, he also teaches systematic theology at St. John Vianney Seminary in Pretoria and St. Augustine College in Johannesburg. From an early age, he has been concerned about the preservation of Africa's rich cultural, faunal, and floral heritage.

Laurenti Magesa is a priest of the diocese of Musoma in Tanzania. Since 1986 he has lectured in different institutions in Africa and overseas. He is author of several books, the most recent being *African Religion in the Dialogue Debate* (2010). His research interest is in African culture and religion. At present, he lectures in African theology at Hekima College Jesuit School of Theology in Nairobi, Kenya.

Festo Mkenda is a Tanzanian Jesuit priest. He holds a D.Phil. in history and has interest in contextualized theology and spirituality. He has published articles in these areas and translated material into Kiswahili, including *The Spiritual Exercises of St Ignatius of Loyola*. He recently worked at St. Joseph the Worker Parish in Nairobi, Kenya, and is currently carrying out postdoctoral research at Campion Hall, the University of Oxford.

Gabriel Mmassi is the rector of Hekima College, where he lectures in systematic theology. He holds a doctorate in theology from the Jesuit School of Theology, Santa Clara University, California. He has also lectured at the Institut de Théologie de la Compagnie de Jésus in Abidjan, Ivory Coast, and he is a visiting lecturer at St. Augustine College of South Africa. His area of specialization is the theology of Vatican II.

Paterne-Auxence Mombé is a Jesuit from the Central African Republic. Author of *Rays of Hope: Managing HIV/AIDS in Africa* and founding director of the Centre Espérance Loyola, a Jesuit holistic program to fight AIDS in Lomé, Togo, he is now director of the African Jesuit AIDS Network (AJAN).

Odomaro Mubangizi, a Ugandan Jesuit priest, is a lecturer at Arrupe College, Harare, Zimbabwe. His research and academic interests cover issues in globalization, democracy, civil society and NGOs, social ethics, and international relations, areas in which he has published articles, presented papers, and completed doctoral studies.

Paulinus I. Odozor,* a Spiritan priest, earned his STD from Regis College, Toronto, and his ThD from the University of Toronto. He is an associate professor of moral theology and the theology of world church at the University of Notre Dame (USA). Recent publications include "An African Moral Theology of Inculturation," *Theological Studies* (2008) and "Truly Africa and Wealthy! What Africa Can Learn from Catholic Social Teaching about Sustainable Economic Prosperity," in *The True Wealth of Nations*, edited by Daniel Finn (Oxford, 2010).

Teresa Okure* is a professor of New Testament and gender hermeneutics at the Catholic Institute of West Africa, Port Harcourt, Nigeria. She has authored books and articles in refereed journals and lectured on five continents. Currently, she is the foundational president of the Catholic Biblical Association of Nigeria (CABAN) and co-editor of the new Commentary Series, Texts@Contexts, published by Fortress. She attended the second African Synod as an *adiutrix*.

Elias Omondi Opongo is a Jesuit priest from Kenya and a peace practitioner. He is currently a doctoral researcher at the Department of Peace Studies, the University of Bradford, UK. He is a former director of Jesuit Hakimani Center, Nairobi, Kenya, and immediate former director of justice and peace programs for Jesuits of Africa and Madagascar. He has taught conflict resolution courses at universities in Africa and the United States and published several articles and three books.

Nathanaël Yaovi Soédé, a priest of the Diocese of Lokossa (Benin), was professor of Christian Ethics at the Catholic University of West Africa/Unit of Abidjan (Ivory Coast) from 1990 to 2009. He is currently executive director of the Association of African Theologians and visiting professor at

ITCJ and CFMA in Abidjan. His research focuses on African Christian ethics and issues in African Christian theology.

Ngozi Frances Uti is a religious of the Congregation of the Handmaids of the Holy Child Jesus. Until recently, she was director of the Centre for Women Studies and Intervention, Abuja, Nigeria, which advocates the empowerment of women and girls and the elimination of cultural practices against them. She has been involved in advocacy on gender-based violence issues in church and society. She is presently the provincial superior of the South-Eastern Province of her congregation.

Index